"About Your Financial Murd...

A non-fiction journey inside the professional financial looting of your retirement savings…and your society.

Financial professions have learned how to fly above and around criminal laws, in the same way that a pilot can dodge storms if they can get above, or go around.

"Whiskey Tango Foxtrot you are cleared out of control."

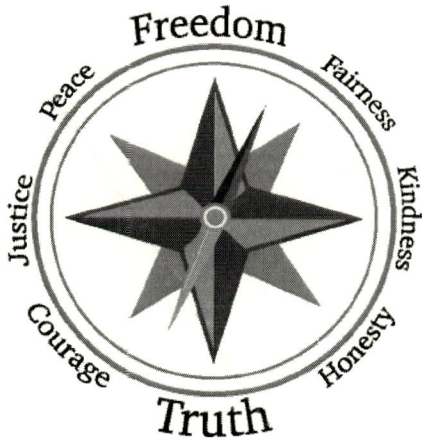

Introduction

This book shines light into a financial world where organized professionals operate above rules and laws. It looks at how they collaborate in ways which harm the financial health of society.

It goes as far as to suggest, with some examples, that professional, systemic, well orchestrated financial schemes can at times drain North American society, by as much or more than the cost of all typical criminal acts in the land…combined.

This book makes the argument that many of the public institutions and professions that we rely upon financially, have been taken-over, or taken-in, to systems that perfected bending the promise of 'serving' the public into financially 'farming' the public.

Aided by legal and regulatory agents which have been become systems of apologists, defenders, and 'insulators', often serving to protect the multi-billion dollar harvest…and not the public.

I believe that at certain times in history, "the truth which must not be spoken"…must truly be spoken.

When the world slips into a lawless, 'self'-regulated financial game infused with a 'winner takes all' mentality, it becomes a national pandemic. It becomes like a cancer within our society.

The resulting unfairness causes grave financial, moral, and mental injury to millions of North Americans.

===========

North American society is not going insane.
It is in pain…
Herein are some hidden causes of that pain.

===========

Personal pain is the other reason to write this book. Writing it out will help to heal my own moral injuries, and perhaps save someone from having to make my mistakes. I write to try and get better, instead of getting bitter, and to turn traumatic stress and psychological abuse into fuel for the journey.

As a financial industry whistleblower (truth teller), my injury came from the 'death by a thousand cuts', that corporate, legal or bureaucratic entities often inflict upon those who speak out to protect the public. Speak out rather than stay 'silent' and participate in the abuse of others. The injuries are real, the pain is real. This is the journey

EXECUTIVE SUMMARY

Your financial 'professional' most often does not hold the license or the legal registration for the role they use to sell themselves to investors. They are often hiding this most essential item of information.

This is contrary to Securities Acts, rules, laws, and honest business practices. Unfortunately it is a common investment industry practice…to deceive in order to sell. The difference is increased profits for an investment Broker/Dealer, while investors retirement savings can be secretly cut in half.

By adding salesperson costs of just 2% to your investment account, the future value of your account can be cut by half, over a 35-year investment horizon. Each investment dealer knows this and each broker/dealer knows how to do this without even disturbing your slumber. This book is a wake-up call.

Government securities regulators are willing to look the other way at this, and other systemic deceptions. I believe the reason is related to the many built in 'double binds', beginning with who picks or pays the regulators.

Criminal prosecutions for systemic financial fraud are statistically zero, and yet I believe that systemic financial crimes do more harm to North Americans than **all other crimes in the country…combined**. This book is about crime that is organized well enough to be kept almost perfectly hidden from the public.

You will not be informed by the media or the investment industry about hidden, systemic frauds. Dealers do not wish to lose the 'skim' of half your life future investment value, and the media does not wish to lose billions in advertising dollars from banks and broker dealers.

Because systemic fraud consists of 'hidden' ways of picking investors' pockets, most people have no idea they are being cheated. Most do not even wish to know. I find that trying to tell people they are being deceived by their 'advisor' is more difficult than it was for the salesperson to dupe them. Many investors shy away from news that they are being cheated for reasons such as "Cognitive Dissonance". More on this disorder later in the book.

If you wish to learn the difference between fraud and theft, and understand how the financial industry can freely come away with half your future retirement income in their pockets, this book is for you.

"I think that those giving financial advice who don't have a fiduciary duty to their clients should have to explicitly state that fact in writing. How many people would invest with anyone who had the disclaimer "We have no legal requirement to operate in your best interest"?

Fraud vs. Theft

You are likely a victim without knowing.

The fraud victim is the smiling face on the left, because financial abuse is so cleverly concealed within the industry that victims never even know they are abuse victims.

Victims of theft, know that something has been taken from them and they are sad. Victims of fraud, on the other hand, often have no idea that they have been defrauded, certainly when it is done to them by the very best fraud artists or by the system…so they are happy.

Dedication and Gratitude

To my understanding family and wonderful wife, who have allowed me to explore this rabbit hole. It has cost them dearly to have to witness my Quixotic quest. Without their understanding I would not have made it out.

To the many who have come before me and tried their best to stand up and warn the public about financial abuse by financial professionals. I stand on the shoulders of giants.

To your children and grandchildren. Here's hoping that they can grow up in a safer, free and fair world.

To Kent Shirley, an investment industry whistleblower, silenced after taking his life in 2004, after being subjected to the bullying and beating tactics of financial and legal gangs. His voice was thus never heard. It was his suicide in 2004 which caused a turning point for me.

To my courageous friend Joe Killoran, who stood so tall for victims of systemic abuse, that he was sentenced to spend time in a Calgary jail, by a system that 'required' his silence.

===========

"ABOUT YOUR FINANCIAL MURDER…"

Copyright 2017 Larry Elford

Feel free to reproduce <u>portions</u> of this book which might be of benefit to the public interest, to a maximum of <u>one chapter</u>, with proper recognition of the original source.

Please do not copy, duplicate or reproduce the book in its entirety.

Publisher, Visual Investigations

Printed in the USA

Yellow V27 Mar/2018

Project 21477169,

"ABOUT YOUR FINANCIAL MURDER…"

ISBN: 978-1-387-23865-1

May I might beg your forgiveness, before we begin…

Seth Godin (THE ICARUS DECEPTION) says we need to dig deeper and invest in long-term connection, through our art. We must be genuine. We must get real with ourselves before we can expect anyone to really take us seriously. We must withdraw ourselves from the popularity contest and stand up for what we believe in. Create art and conversation that is meaningful, not polished and perfect.

I ask for your understanding that this book is a labour of love, and not firstly a commercial pursuit. A work of passion, perhaps obsession, and not one of compliance. It may not be perfectly polished, edited and vetted, but I hope to give you something of even greater value in exchange.

It is a look at something that few publishers might touch. It shares "truths which must not be spoken…" abuses by powerful people and organizations.

Like most forms of abuse in history, there is a time when the abuses are secret and protected by fear of the powerful abusers. Then there comes a time when they are exposed. Finally, long after they are exposed, they may become a safe topic of discourse.

Financial abuse of millions of people, by trusted professionals, aided by politicians, lawyers, regulators, and other handmaids, is not a topic for open public discourse…yet.

I hope you will forgive me for the many shortcomings you will no-doubt find in this book, the annoying links for e-readers, the broken web-links which are 'edited out' by regulators just as soon as found, and so on.

The rarest element in the world today is someone who is willing to tell the truth, in a world increasingly run on lies.

Here is my truth. I hope others can build upon it to protect themselves.

Thank you.

Larry Elford

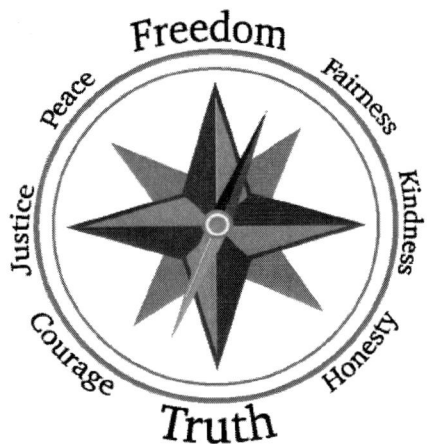

Freedom requires fairness.

Fairness requires kindness.

Kindness involves honesty.

Honesty involves truth.

Truth requires courage.

Courage enables justice.

Justice allows peace.

Peace allows freedom.

Those are some of the values I remind myself to work towards. In a world where right and wrong can be confused and shifted almost daily, it is imperative that we find and identify principles to try to live by.

-- Larry Elford 2018

Thanks to these heroes, who have shown me the way and set a positive example to learn from, and to live by:

Stan Buell	Mac and Reyko Nishiyama
Ken Kivenko	Derrick Gayowski
Robert Kyle	Mark Mason, "Subtle Art of Not..
Dr. Al Rosen	Prof Dan Ariely
Hugh and Diane Urquhart	Maria Konnikova
Debra McFadden	Dr. George Lakoff
Andrew Teasdale	Maria Konnikova
Dave and Joyce Elford	Jon Rappoport
Travis Elford	Russell Mokhiber
Penny Elford	Micah Hauptman
Nikki Demers	Barbara Roper
Casey Morris	Dan Solin
Bill Wilson	Professor Bill Black
Dr. Robert Smith	Barry Ritholz
Sharon Fredrick	Russ and Pam Marten
Marvin Livingston	Joe Killoran

And so many unnamed others who selflessly gave me love and support, when I deserved neither.

To 100 million-plus investors in Canada and the U.S., who have been deceived by the most powerful predators known to modern man, bankers, investment dealers, and their many handmaidens.

For retail investors who have not yet figured out that **they** are the product which is being "managed" professionally, while being told that it is their money that is being managed...professionally.

I worked on the inside for twenty years, and try as I might, I could not change things for the better. There was too much money involved, and too great was the rapacious addiction to 'more'.

I have learned that those with an uncontrolled financial addiction, and who work in a 'lawless' environment of self regulation, are able to do more economic harm to individuals and to society, than is being done by every other traditional criminal activity in the land....combined.

Come along and let me tell you a story or two...

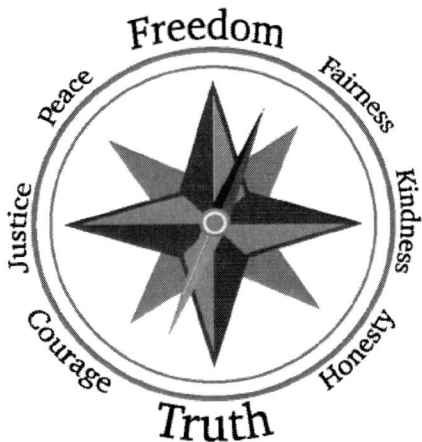

Table of Contents

Ch 1. HERD MENTALITY, MORAL INJURY 1
Ch 2. WHO IS @RecoveredBroker? 7
Ch 3. THE FAKE-ADVISOR VOWEL MOVEMENT 26
Ch 4. "RULES ARE ONLY FOR FOOLS" 58
Ch 5. FOUR OUT OF FIVE ADVISORS RECOMMEND… 69
Ch 6. $25 BILLION MUTUAL FUND HAIRCUT 77
Ch 7. THREE KINDS OF "ADVICE GIVER" 81
Ch 8. KYC AN INVESTOR SETUP? 89
Ch 9. EXEMPTIONS TO THE LAW 98
Ch 10. CAPTURING THE POLICE 118
Ch 11. "LAUNDERING CRIME" 127
Ch 12. AS PROTECTED AS IF YOU ARE IN AN LA RIOT… 142
Ch 13. SEE NO EVIL 150
Ch 14. THE UNIQUE VIOLENCE OF FINANCIAL CRIME 155
Ch 15. THE CO$T OF FINANCIAL TRICKERY 161
Ch 16. HIGH STATUS CRIME WORKS JUST FINE 175
Ch 17. CRASHING SOCIETY 187
Ch 18. CRASHING A HELICOPTER 193
Ch 19. LITIGATION: THE ART OF STORYTELLING* 202
Ch 20. MORAL INJURY, CRASHING A LIFE 212
Ch 21. SPOTTING THE SUBCLINICAL PSYCHOPATH 246
Ch 22. MEDIA AS HANDMAIDENS 256
Ch 23. SOLUTIONS and FINANCIAL SELF-DEFENSE 263
Ch 24. CLASSIC CARS AND PROCESSED FOOD 292
Ch 25. THE INDUSTRY OF ACCOUNTABILITY 304

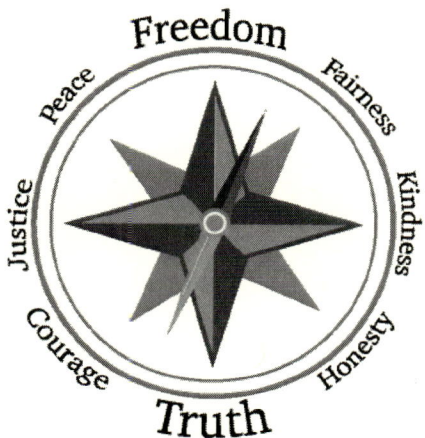

CHAPTER ONE

HERD MENTALITY, MORAL INJURY

"Shucks, we was just having us a little fun..."

What are the differences in principle, between being silent witness to a financial assault, sexual assault or any other kind of assault?

I see few differences in principle. I see similarities. I was there. For years. I have now seen a million assaults of the vulnerable, by the powerful. Picture an entire industry of Harvey Weinstein and Bill Cosby types, all incentivized to do harm, but financial harm and not sexual harm. Encouraged. Allowed. Rewarded. Silenced.

When the boys stood around the pool table in a 3 minute scene from THE ACCUSED, while actress Jodie Foster played the part of an assault victim, I was not there. I was not one of that gang.

When I found myself around the boardroom table where ethical laws and principles were violated to deceive and violate investment clients, I knew I was not one of that gang. But I was there. What an interesting double bind to find myself in.

Forgive me if I am still trying to find clarity, to understand the big picture. Thank you for allowing me this chance to think it out, by writing it out.

============

Film: The Accused (1988)
Director: Jonathan Kaplan
Stars: Kelly McGillis, Jodie Foster, Bernie Coulson

Loosely inspired by a real crime, "The Accused" is a courtroom drama. The crime? Rape. Jodie Foster's character is gang-raped by several drunk men at a bar one night. Adding to the trauma, multiple patrons watch the event but fail to act.

Not only are viewers forced to watch, but they are forced to watch others watching, while not doing anything. It's a reminder of the dangers of passively absorbing violence. Of being a bystander while others are being harmed.

I worked inside the offices, and the boardrooms of major investment dealers over a twenty year span. What I saw in boardroom sales meetings, felt at times like being forced to watch the 3 minute rape scene in The Accused. Except it was not physical assault, but financial assault that was on the table. It took me almost ten years to learn the industry well enough, to find clarity in what was going on beneath the surface in my industry.

Yes, I was forced to watch so-called financial professionals assault their clients. I thought I was an investment advisor, since the company labeled me as such in 1988, but did not learn until 2013 that there is no such term (advisor) found in law (in Securities Acts in USA or Canada). So many deceptions. A lie now repeated a million times over, so firms can more easily earn the trust, and gather the assets of investors.

Financial assault is far easier, and continues in secrecy today, as I write this in 2017. The assault by highly entitled, high status businessmen is very much a 'herd mentality' act, and it is well protected by large herds.

It is easier, because of the human ability to link self-interests to others-interests, joining financial players to regulatory players, regulatory to police, to prosecutors, to judicial, and so on. Even at the highest political offices in the land I watch as highly positioned, politicians choose silence, to remain in the herd, rather than step outside and speak what their internal voices might be saying. The risk of losing the comfort of the herd, the protection of the herd, is so strong as to hold people's moral courage back. It is also held back by the 'double bind' that says, "be a team player" (meaning keep your mouth shut), "or else".

Duke Professor of Psychology and Behavioral Economics at Duke University, Dan Ariely has done mind-expanding work that ties directly into how persons or systems of authority can be captured and corrupted like child's play. See his recent book/film titled (Dis)Honesty, The Truth About Lies, for a new world-view around simple statements like the following:

"a shared interest in silence."
"fit in, or be left on the other side of the wall."

How ironic if the watchdogs and caretakers in a land can become 'blind' to truth, by simple human self-protective instincts, while the so-called 'blind' system of justice, can have its sight restored when faced with high wealth, upper status citizens.

===========

WHY POLICE DISMISS 1 IN 5 SEXUAL ASSAULT CLAIMS AS BASELESS

In a 20-month investigation into how police handle sexual assault allegations, The Globe and Mail gathered data from more than 870 police forces. The findings expose deep flaws at every step of the process

The Globe found that police in 115 communities dismiss at least one-third of sex-assault complaints as unfounded.
BY ROBYN DOOLITTLE LONDON, ONT.
PUBLISHED FRIDAY, FEBRUARY 3, 2017

"Suddenly, there was a flash. Ava looked over and saw four or five men pointing cellphone cameras in her direction. She became frantic. The man on top of her ran away. He left his wallet behind. She was left naked and curled on the ground, her back and hair covered in dirt. Two women who heard her sobbing found Ava shortly after.

It was Oct. 16, 2010, more than five years before an eerily similar attack at Stanford University would make international headlines. Ava's story, however, never made the news. Her case did not go to court. Her assailant was never arrested, never charged.

In fact, the London Ontario Police Service detective concluded that what happened to Ava that night was not a crime.

There are many ways to shut a case without laying a charge. Not enough evidence? There's a closure code for that. Complainant doesn't want to proceed with charges? There's a code for that, too.

On Nov. 13, 2010, the detective closed Ava's file as "unfounded," another formal police classification that rendered her allegations baseless.

It meant a crime was neither attempted, nor occurred. It did not immediately brand Ava a liar, necessarily. But it meant she was not raped.

Financial assaults, when done by high-status abusers, are often be deemed to be 'not crimes' worthy of police interest. Ironically, as I edit these words, the biggest news story today is high status sexual abusers who get away with criminal acts, for decades, simply due to the 'untouchability' of the high status. I ask you to try to imagine what kinds of abuses happen in the financial industry? What is it doing to our society?

(Update late 2017, Hollywood sexual abusers are miraculously outed in numbers. How fast the tide can change.)

Why do I care? Because _any_ story of abuse and assault, rings an alarm somewhere in my brain. Probably in the brain stem, in or near the amygdala. Abuse has too many similarities to the kinds of 'abuses of power', of status, that were my career and thus my life. You see, when I was named a financial 'advisor', for the biggest bank in the country, I immersed myself in the career with a great deal of respect for my role, and for the trust that my investment clients placed in me.

I was not at all prepared for what I discovered beneath the surface of the industry, how 80% of participants were making higher amounts of money, by taking advantage of the trust of the vulnerable and the trusting. I just did not go to work with the biggest bank in the land, and among the top-ten in the U.S., with the expectation that I would be asked to punch my clients in the face...financially.

Each bank-owned investment dealer in Canada, had a secret that was not allowed to be shared with a single investment broker or customer. The secret was that despite using the title "advisor', virtually 100% of those in my position, were actually registered with the Securities Commissions in a category called "Salesperson". ('Salesperson' in Canada, 'Broker' in USA)

This secret was easy for investment Broker/Dealers to keep since no employees did their own license or registration paperwork, nor did any employees (that I knew of) ever hold a copy of their license. All was taken care of by the bank/broker/dealer. Brokers just forward marched, following orders, driven by incentives.

Why did I not shut up and go along. Why not stay rich and become richer? Because my conscience would not allow it, without having to consume enough alcohol to blot out my mind to the abuses that I was being pushed to participate in, or be silent on.

Imagine turning to an addiction (alcohol), to treat a moral injury brought upon by corporate managers who themselves had dual addictions, (or double binds).

Financial rape, cheating or shortchanging of people to whom I have promised trust is not my gig.

It was either speak out and risk losing all, or remain silent and lose all that matters. Another double bind. I chose to speak.

===========

This book hopes to bring to light another invisible form of abuse. A rampant form of abuse, which is covered-up almost completely in Canada. It is financial abuse by financial professionals. Something that I have now become an expert in.

An interesting situation exists in systemic or other financial assaults, when highest status corporations are the perpetrators. Our systems of justice seem to find it easiest for justice to flow on a 'downward' path, and rarely can justice be easily applied in an upward direction toward great power. Why is that?

Author and environmental protector Derrick Jensen speaks of similar invisible 'gravitational' forces with regard to violence, power or accountability. Apparently these things can be perpetrated down from any position of power without trouble, however if accountability is directed upward towards persons of higher status, it is immediately faced with dramatic, often violent consequences.

This leads me to wonder at times if we have systems of justice, or systems of power or status, in disguise?

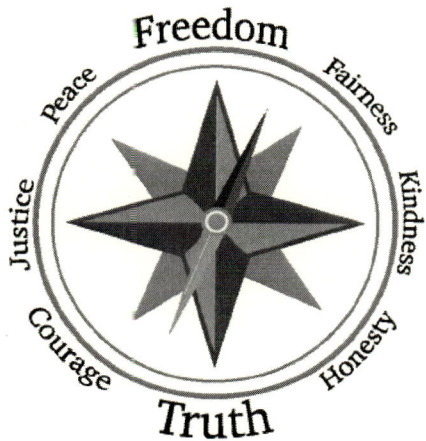

CHAPTER TWO

WHO IS @RecoveredBroker?

It was in the late '80's that I bet my future on my faith in the ethics at Canada's largest bank. It was the last decade of the twentieth century and banks still held some of the reputation they had in my father's day—the time before computers, the Internet, and instant communications, and perhaps most importantly, financial deregulation.

Back in my father's day a bank could not get away with robbing an entire society with the click of a mouse. Today the whole world can be taken advantage of…it's just that simple…and systemic.

In my defense, at well under 30 years old I was too young to know any better. It is only as I write this in 2017 that it has become obvious to the world that financial Corporations will do whatever necessary to make those working within insanely richer. The Corporation becomes the un-prosecutable 'shield' which allows unimaginable acts to be done. (Read Prof Harry Glasbeek's work on Corporations as the "invisible friend" to crime. "I did not do it...my invisible friend, (the corporation) did")

Someone said that the saddest day in a man's life is the day that he learns how to make money without having to do any work. The financial industry has learned this too well for the good of any society.

However corporations cannot in themselves be sad, so the sadness instead trickles down onto employees, who are abused and silenced, then to customers who are farmed financially. Twenty years into my journey I learned of the term "moral injury". At the outset I had no idea what lengths trusted corporations would go to in order to make money without doing any work. This is a gift to them from an almost complete position of market (and regulatory) dominance.

===========

The following was written with the help of a former newspaper editor who conducted interviews with myself and others in 2004 to document the bizarre situation I found myself in. It thus serves as a fitting introduction and backdrop to my journey.

Written Tuesday, March 09, 2004

A terse memorandum on RBC Investments letterhead left little room to wiggle.

The stern directive, thought Larry Elford, a 16-year veteran financial advisor with RBC Investments, was his employer's way of cocking the corporate pistol and aiming at a 16-year career spent in pursuit of his clients' best interests, a mission from which he had yet to waver, but one which was becoming increasingly perilous to his future job security.

The three paragraphs threatening him with potential termination were penned not for any breach of ethics or legalities. Quite the contrary; Elford was being court marshaled, as he had been a scant two years earlier, for championing the rights of investors, a value on which his employer, apparently, placed less weight than on its own pecuniary interests and that of its other advisors.

In his regular investment column in the Lethbridge, Alta., Sunday Herald of May 19, 2002, in the middle of a lengthy piece on guaranteed investment funds, Elford, a regular contributor to the newspaper for a decade and recipient of congratulatory memos from RBC's head office for his writings, penned this offending paragraph:

"If you shop around, you should not have to pay a front-end or back-end fee to buy them and your only expense will be the annual management fee that every mutual fund charges to operate."

A fairly innocuous statement and a piece of advice, felt Elford, investors have a right to know. But not one, apparently, that the Royal Bank wants widely circulated because it triggered, 10 days later, this grammatically fractured reprimand:

"By having this article published without obtaining prior approval… you have contravened IDA (Investment Dealers Association) regulations as well as (the) firm's policies… Should any re-occurrence be brought to our attention or other breach of conduct, it will be grounds for further disciplinary measures that may result in the termination of your employment."

What RBC's Lethbridge office manager, failed to charge in his threatening memo was that Elford had written anything inaccurate or untrue. Neither was the newspaper cautioned about printing misinformation.

Instead, the memo mentioned Elford's failure to obtain RBC's pre-publication blessing. Not that doing so seemed all that important, considering Elford had been published regularly for years with RBC's apparent carte blanche approval.

The matter, of course, had nothing to do with obtaining approval and everything to do with the fact Elford had stood high waving a flag at investors —some of whom, supposedly, have trusted their savings to RBC - alerting them to look for funds which charged them no fees front and back.

"It's been made clear to me I was chastised for mentioning clients can purchase funds without paying commissions," says Elford today. *"It threatened other advisors sales revenue."*

Elford admits his first reprimand surprised him for the sheer fact he believed he was following RBC's written code of ethics which exhorts financial advisors to go soar above the letter of all *"legislative and regulatory requirements"* to insure the *"highest ethical principles are integral components of every business transaction and relationship."*

It's a code Elford believes in himself, especially when it lights the bonfire of *"integrity and fair dealing"* so that *"every transaction or activity that we are involved in will stand the test of complete and open public scrutiny,"* as RBC penmanship would put it. Too often, however, he feels as if his employer is more content keeping the public gaze away from ethics which are quietly hung in a rear closet when RBC financial advisors gird themselves in the quest for higher profits.

'RBC is constantly raising the bar on ethics, but there is a big difference between talking the talk and walking the walk," he says. "When I got the first reprimand, I didn't believe in this day and age you could be chastised for trying to do what is best for clients. On a second occasion, I realized it was true. You can be punished if you are a few ethical steps ahead of your firm's top producers.

"For them to go on record opposing what I had done is extremely shortsighted. It changed everything I believed in."

There were quiet, almost whispered accolades from fellow investors both inside and outside the RBC perimeter. But even the praise carried ominous warnings. "We agree with what you've done," they said. "We just hope you keep your job." But some workmates campaigned within RBC to have Elford censured or dismissed.

"It has made it extremely difficult to go to work," he says. "It was making other advisors look bad." (At the time RBC commissions were in excess of $70 million from the DSC (deferred sales charges) that earned RBC and salespeople a quick (and silent) 5% on each sale)

And that, it appears, is more important to RBC hierarchy than customer satisfaction. Elford took his concerns up the corporate ladder to Edmonton and then through the strata that is head office in Toronto. His courage was lauded, but he was again ordered to refrain from any more such nonsense.

"At all management levels I got the same answer: 'what you're doing is great, but keep your mouth shut.' The higher I took it, the more I sensed they were trying to hurt me. I was pounding my head against a wall."

The memo has put Elford in the dicey position of knowing that the next column could be his last, Charter of Rights and Freedoms notwithstanding. Either he can drop his column, tiptoe around such breaches of RBC policy as putting client interest first, or publish and be damned.

"I've been walking with a rock in my shoe for two years," he says now. I had to decide whether to leave the firm or get someone in the company to listen to me. I went straight to the top and got more harassment and intimidation for my efforts."

Elford believes the only time the Royal Bank changes its tone is when its laundry is washed in public. The glare of publicity pays for another round of ethics tutorials from a self-righteous head office before everyone heads back to business as usual.

"My dad didn't teach me to go to work for people and take advantage of them," says Elford. "It's been a long two years, but if I have to hide the truth and toe the line and lie to Mr. and Mrs. Public when they've put their faith in me, I'd sooner go and pump gas." (My first job, and the one I recall fondly was pumping gas at age 15)

And so a veteran advisor who has always placed his clients before his own profits is faced with some agonizing decisions. He can take his battle to a court of law or to the court of public opinion. Either forum he chooses likely means his career with RBC is over.

Conflict of interest is a shifting perception in many professions, from journalism to medicine to politics. It is often measured on an open-ended scale and open to the vagaries of public interest. Doctors who accept free trips from drug companies have recently been under heightened scrutiny by a public which wants to know it is being prescribed the best prescriptions possible, not ones which will earn their prescriber a week in the Bahamas.

Larry Elford was fairly new to the investment business when he began to question why members of his profession were given lavish rewards for selling particular mutual funds when, in fact, those funds may not have been the best buys for their clients. Wasn't the practice, he wondered, a conflict of interest? It was often, he says, a question of whether a broker should sell the best mutual fund possible or head to the beach on someone else's American Express card. When Bud Jorgenson, a Globe and Mail business journalist began to openly question the practice, Elford was encouraged; someone had stepped up to blow the whistle. He finds it difficult today to admit his naiveté when he thought his company would share his elation.

"We talked about it in the boardroom. I said I thought Jorgenson was right. My views were extremely frowned upon by management. I was looked at as if I had three eyes. There were guys there who were being given yearly trips to the Indy 500."

It was the end of Elford's virginity. "It was the first instance I had run into of the keep-your-mouth-shut philosophy. I realized then there were other motivating factors beyond client benefit. I realized there was a code of silence – almost mafia-like, which, when broken, gets you fired. I was 27 years old."

At first blush, the all-encompassing RBC code of no media contact was enforced. But Jorgenson kept writing his articles and the Globe kept publishing them. Slowly things began to change.

"It was the first experience I had with the power of the media," says Elford, still slightly in awe. "It actually changed the policy of a very powerful company into following its code of ethics instead of just talking about it."

Elford's comfort level with RBC took another whack when he was criticized by management for his stand on mutual fund deferred sales charges, or DSCs. He considers the practice insidious because it lulls investors – his clients – into a false sense of security by making them believe they are free and clear of investment costs.

Basically, clients are told when they plunk down their money they won't be hit with front-end loads (fees paid at the time of purchase). Instead, every penny will be invested and put to work for them immediately. They leave with a peaceful, easy feeling, safe in the belief their investment advisor has gone to bat for them to secure them the best deal available.

What they are often not told is they face the potential of heavy penalties should they pull out of the chosen fund before the term expires. Their money is invested for a set number of years, and should they decide to move their cash they will be charged a penalty based on every year they fall short of this time frame. Thus the elation they felt when diving into a fund can be tarnished should they climb out early.

That in itself might not worry an ethical broker. After all, there are similar penalties assessed on bank loans, vehicle leases and similar purchases. But in most cases, those penalties are clearly explained before signatures are applied. The customer knows what lies down the road. That is not often true in the case of mutual funds.

Increasing Elford's unease – which has patently deteriorated into disgust – is the penchant many agents have for pushing clients to jump from fund to fund without knowledge of the penalties they are accruing.

"Markets change quickly and yesterday's hot funds are replaced by the next great thing to come along," he explains. "Seven years is too long a time to be trapped in any one fund. Clients were getting hurt with redemption charges. They couldn't switch funds without this burden.

"There is always something better coming along two or three years later; clients pay a huge penalty to take advantage of it."

Much of the industry started to recognize the problem in the late 1990s. Elford, in attempting to stay on the leading edge of his industry, began advising clients against DSCs, a decision which cost him and RBC money, but ultimately proved to be in his customers' best interests.

"Our business is one of earning client trust. We lead you to believe we are there for you. Instead, you won't know until years later – or not at all – if an agent was abusing that trust. It's one of the great mysteries of the business how we can represent ourselves as your servants, then sell you funds which give us the highest compensation." (71% of RBC fund holdings then were in the DSC sales option)

Underpinning the problem is the voracious competition involved in the industry. There are no salaried agents; no one earns a guaranteed wage from their employer. Instead, they live and die by their hustle and guile.

The DSC practice alone might not have been enough to pull Elford over to the "dark side," but yet another line was drawn in the game of "don't know-don't tell" he felt compelled to cross. When agents are rewarded by their clients' naiveté or lack of investing sophistication, they are ripe for abuse. And that, he says, has become an industry mantra. Agents are financially rewarded every time a client has to pay a DSC. The more often they switch funds, the more an agent makes. Thus it is in the agent's – not the client's – best interest to convince the customer to switch as often as possible, rolling up deferred charges like a gleaner in a fall rye field.

"Agents who are in a get-rich-quick mode can trigger a five-per-cent fee to the client for getting a client to move (the DSC) and earn another five per cent when they purchase a new fund," says Elford. "Some do it over and over." (Those are the ones who earned the coveted, but fake, 'Vice President' moniker for top commissions generated.)

Curiously, in a business which prides itself on high ethical behavior, so much remains hidden from the customer. It's become a contradiction with which Elford has long been uneasy.

"As I say, this is supposed to be a relationship of trust. My role is to earn yours so that you'll go through fire and brimstone with me. I have the ability to take that trust and either do what's in your best interest, or do what's best for me.
"The client is considered to be an asset looking to get milked by some 'advisors.' That's a dangerous thing."

Ah, but that "milking" can be done in numerous ways by less scrupulous advisors who want not merely to put their hand in one pocket, but two. The practice of "double dipping" isn't confined to the investment business, but it has certainly been refined there. It has become so bloated and so blatant, the mystery isn't how or when it's done, but why consumers still stand for this fiscal sleight-of-hand.

Again, says Elford, one must look south to determine the industry standard he'd prefer to follow. The U.S. banned the practice of double dipping some time ago. In Canada, it continues unabashedly unabated and, in fact, has been honed to an art form.

"It is a huge revenue generator and helps any agent up the ladder of success where each rung is a measure not of how an agent has contributed to the financial well-being of clients but of how often and lucratively clients have contributed to the financial well-being of RBC."

The backslapping which accompanies the release of each "ladder" is, says Elford, more akin to a sales convention than an investment corporation.

"It has become known as the 'Ladder of Litigation' because often the highest revenue generated was not done so in the most legal fashion."

So widespread is double dipping, and so accepted as a fact of doing business, it is boasted about in corporate hallways. Elford recalls an instance in 1999 in which an agent, with mutual funds of $37 million, used double dipping to hit the client on both ends of a transaction. Elford took the matter to RBC's compliance department hoping for an admonition and, perhaps, an eventual edict from management to cease and desist.

"They blew it off. Instead, I was chastised for speaking up. There was no 'enforced' rule against double dipping in Canada. You're basically on your own. Even the compliance department looked the other way."

Clients, therefore, are not advised of the practice, nor do they ask. It's a bit like telling off-color jokes in church. Instead, many older clients are still cognizant of the old days when fees were iron clad and high. When they're offered a reduction in the front-end fee, they believe they're getting a deal.

Elford's frustrations are only exacerbated when he attends educational seminars in the U.S. where tighter regulations squeeze dirty secrets such as double dipping until they pop like a pimple, hopefully before the public notices. Upon his return home, he again faces the same shoddy practices.

"You learn things down there we haven't even addressed yet and you try to put them to work here to be on the leading edge, only to find yourself out of step and getting into trouble for speaking up. We shouldn't be allowed to represent ourselves as our clients' faithful advisors and at the same time not be able to do what's in their best interests."

What, and have to accept a rung down on the Ladder of Success? So profit driven is the industry, clients bear a frighteningly close resemblance to warehoused seniors who, as long as the money doesn't run out, are seen merely as assets rather than patients.

"Agents who make $100,000 a year are considered losers by management," says Elford. "They're at the low rung on the ladder of success."

Ethics can be so tedious to some organizations. They spend mints of money developing high ethical standards and even more on advertising to publicly brag about their sense of honesty, yet when they are faced with their own set of rules, they chafe under the weight.

RBC has an online ethics test which its financial advisors are expected to take. In fact, anyone with access to the Web site can take – and easily pass – the test. Why? Because the software alerts you to wrong answers and gives you the answer to resubmit. Anyone who can't record 100 per cent on this exam probably can't use the phone, either.

Elford has taken his issues to the highest levels of the Royal Bank only to be harassed and intimidated to where he no longer feels part of the RBC family. His "Tough Love" approach to the parent firm for whom he has toiled graciously all these years has not made a dent in the corporate facade.

"The only way the company has changed in the past is if the issue is publicized in the media. Once a matter is in the public domain, the company snaps to attention. I'm sure that's common in other large firms."

He has also taken his concerns to regulatory agencies who astoundingly have told him they can only deal with consumer complaints, not with those initiated within the industry.

And he's not alone in his beliefs, he's only alone in standing up for what he believes.

"He's not supposed to have an opinion on behalf of RBC," says a close workmate and confidante who requests anonymity. "When he sent out a flyer explaining to clients about front-end and back-end fees, other brokers went on the rampage because it made them look bad."

She admits when the fees were exposed five years ago, there wasn't much of an outcry from the public, partly because the level of understanding is not particularly high.

"People don't understand they pay fees," she says. "The publicity only served to antagonize others in the firm. Larry felt if he was doing these great things, he should be allowed to tell people."

Brokers who do charge the extra fees are not crooks, she says, as long as they're up front about it with their clients.

"If everything is on the table, that's OK." But then you should be able to defend charging them.

"All of this has become a personal issue for Larry," says his colleague. "He's not wrong in what he's doing, yet he has been reprimanded for it. This company is not looking for people with their own opinions."

Elford's colleague is also considering a move elsewhere.

"It would be preferable to me if something would happen which would allow me to stay; if we could deal with our clients as we like," she says. "But there's always been an open door elsewhere. It's hard to imagine staying after all of this."

Perhaps if he hadn't spent almost two decades selling its wares and singing its praises, and perhaps if his own moral code wasn't so hot-wired to the truth, Larry Elford could have found an easier gambit against the Royal Bank than king pawn to knight three. But in what had rapidly become a chess match of life, Elford hung in and hung on, knowing RBC was determined to checkmate him if it could.

Fall turned to winter and, while he pondered his next move, RBC minions were gearing up for a showdown. Approval for his newspaper column was less than hearty and sanctions for his advertisements and newsletters to clients were denied. His e-mails disappeared into the ether without being answered, phone calls went unreturned.

"Larry Elford? We don't know him," seemed to be the stock answer when his name came up. Wording for an important new concept for index-linked bonds, ammunition against the stingiest bear market since 1929, was a victim of corporate foot-dragging, garnering neither approval nor refusal and placing Elford and his associates in limbo.

"We were in a Catch-22 in the middle of the worst market environment in 75 years," he says. "And on top of that, I appeared to have been singled out for retribution."

The Herald column, through which RBC had enjoyed free advertising for several years, was being edited by Toronto until, like a toothpaste tube, it was squeezed until there was nothing left in it to interest readers, unless they wanted to read of the bank's high moral tenor.

Working in an office which resembled a DMZ, handcuffed by an employer seemingly determined to break his spirit and worrying daily about protecting clients' money in the midst of an economic calamity, Elford knew his own gears were running dry and, if the situation didn't change, were in danger of seizing.

"You can't leave the office after a day of that and come home as a loving husband and understanding father," he says. "I knew I had been slipping. I had been living in an angry, bitter and depressed sort of way for a number of years.

"I didn't used to be an angry person. I thought it was just middle age that had jumped up and slapped me one day. You know, you're wearing out and stuff happens."

But Elford is convinced now that the swings in his temperament and the erosion of his ability to handle the rigours of home and office were not so much related to aging as they were to his growing anxiety with his employer's attempts to muzzle his complaints about RBC's lack of candour and apparent moral double standard.

"I could always handle clients, co-workers and markets," he says. "It wasn't until this code of silence thing that it got out of hand. After eight hours a day, day after day, it had compounded to where I had had enough."

"I was worn out, beat up."

And yet he walked the tightropes of his existence, balancing the need to earn a living with the fear of dismissal, balancing his relationship with trusted clients with an employer bent on his destruction, balancing a work atmosphere that was sucking the light from his day with his responsibilities as a family man. This was the three-ring circus of Elford's life as 2002 drew to a close.

He and the RBC employees who worked for him began plotting their course to leave the bank's employ and find solace and substance elsewhere. Like prisoners, they met clandestinely, careful of what they said and to whom, less they give RBC a cause to fill in their escape tunnel.

Elford and his associates went to work for ScotiaMcLeod in a separate locale, armed with desks, phones and computers in an otherwise empty office. They had been warned RBC was unlikely to accept their leaving benignly and would be watching for any opportunity to shut them down.

Prudently and with some degree of paranoia, Elford was careful to make sure every minuscule IDA regulation was followed, even as RBC employees cruised the street outside each day taking photographs in hope of catching some evidence of missile buildup.

Some insiders later told Elford it was the roughest they'd ever seen RBC play. His clients were told he and his team had left "in the middle of the night" and left no forwarding address.

"They tried to plant seeds of doubt with our customers."

However, says Elford, the innuendo spread by RBC merely served to convince many clients to stick with him and his team.

"They helped us immensely," he says. "We couldn't have asked for worse competitors."

His new employer was pleased to have reaped a harvest of experience and expertise at a time when the finance industry most needs it. Proven professionals switching allegiances to competitors happens in other areas, but in the investment world the ramifications can be explosive. In fact, there were moments of terror.

Phone calls were made from RBC in Lethbridge to head office in Toronto alerting Royal Bank hierarchy of the defection.

Top-floor RBC boffins then dropped a dime to their counterparts at ScotiaMcLeod to (falsely) warn them about an Elford plot to publicly humiliate RBC at a client meeting. The Royal threatened to subpoena everyone at the public meeting, basically ScotiaMcLeod customers.

Anxious calls were then made back to ScotiaMcLeod in Lethbridge to ascertain if this was, in fact, true. It wasn't, but deep breaths were required for ScotiaMcLeod to stay the course with its new employees.

He had been at ScotiaMcLeod for 20 days and was as close as he had ever been at RBC to being fired.

"We were under very close scrutiny," says Elford. "RBC did what it could to poison our relationship and keep about $100 million in assets. We were warned RBC, upon losing half its office and millions in revenue, would not take it lying down."

"We were told later by RBC employees they had never seen this level of vindictiveness."

The harassment didn't stop at street-side spying. Almost daily, a courier brought yet another threatening letter from an RBC lawyer in Toronto advising Elford his future would best be served in another line of work or, even better, another city. The company also wanted him and his cohorts to hand over their personal computers. He knew he could be in for a lengthy court battle in a legal war he knew he would lose by attrition.

Gallows humour pervaded the office in an attempt to keep the harassment in context through "Paranoid Thought Of The Day." But in reality, there was little to laugh about.

Elford is fond of a quote by James Baldwin: "The price one pays for pursuing any profession is an intimate knowledge of its ugly side." How one reacts to the discovery that their chosen field has a darker element to it depends on whether their own moral code meshes with, condones or accepts it with quiet desperation. For Elford, acceptance was the very most he could stomach and even that, after a time, became impossible.

Elford's pride in his ethical treatment of clients provided the bulwark of his career. His intransigent refusal to lower those standards to better reflect the changing philosophy of RBC was non-negotiable. The months of struggling to maintain those ethics with clients on one hand while warding off incursions by RBC to force him to change was a daily sword fight no amount of swashbuckling derring-do could ultimately win.

For Elford, the highest price by far was not watching as a few unethical advisors or managers at RBC ran up the bill to clients by double dipping or overcharging commissions. It came long after this started, when he finally realized he had stopped being a husband to his wife, or a father to his children, due to the stress of trying to survive and thrive in an environment where ethics were treated as nothing more than words on paper. (In the end something had to give, and Elford was forced to leave the business, or stay and leave his health.)

Author Yann Martel writes: "People move because of the wear and tear of anxiety. Because of the gnawing feeling that no matter how hard they work, their efforts will yield nothing, that what they build up in one year will be torn down in one day by others. Because of the impression that the future is blocked up, that nothing will change, that happiness and prosperity are possible only somewhere else."**

Yet, Elford still maintains he is fortunate for the opportunity fate has handed him. He knows fighting RBC is a difficult and ultimately dangerous war. He's already picked up a few hits, some of which he'll carry with him a long time. But he believes the risk is worth the opportunity to prove the mettle of his ideals and to hope for improvement in the industry he has chosen to spend his efforts.

(End of Peter Scott 2004 documenting Elford's situation)

===========

Royal Bank of Canada to repay clients $21-million as part of excess fee settlement.

Jun 27, 2017 - RBC is the latest in a string of large financial institutions to enter a no-contest settlement with regulators after self-reporting the issue of excess fees on funds, along with a plan to reimburse clients. In a no-contest settlement, which in RBC's case will include a further $925,000 "voluntary payment" to the OSC, …
http://business.financialpost.com/news/fp-street/royal-bank-of-canada-to-repay-clients-21-million-as-part-of-excess-fee-settlement-with-osc

===========

My Financial Industry Education:

- Certified Financial Planner designation
- Certified Investment Manager designation
- Recognition as a Fellow of the Canadian Securities Institute (FCSI)
- FSCI is the highest honor awarded by the Canadian Securities Institute
- Associate Portfolio Manager designation

For two decades, I was employed in the retail investment sales divisions of various Canadian investment dealers. In this capacity I was responsible for thousands of investment clients and managed relationships with over $100 Million in client assets. I was licensed/registered in the category of "salesperson" until September, 2009, when this salesperson category of registration was replaced in Canada with the category called a "dealing representative". This salesperson category is in 2017 still officially called "Dealing representative" by the Canadian Securities Administrators, with the "salesperson" term added in brackets by the CSA to more clearly explain the term.

I have provided testimony to four (4) separate Canadian legislatures, through Federal or Provincial legislative committees, listed below.

Such legislative or Parliamentary committees are asked to propose or to review legislation before it becomes law in Canada or after it is law if there are concerns about its effectiveness.

Ontario Standing Committee on Finance and Economic Affairs –
August 19, 2004 - "Ontario Securities Commission Review"

Federal Standing Committee on Finance, 39th Parliament, 2nd Session, Number 35, April 10, 2008 "Asset-Backed Commercial Paper in Canada"

Federal Standing Committee on Justice and Human Rights,
"Minimum Sentences for White Collar Crime"
40th Parliament, 2nd Second Session, Number 053, 2009

Federal Standing Committee on Finance (FINA) 42nd Parliament, 1st Session

Meeting No. 99 Wednesday, June 7, 2017, "Consumer Protection and Oversight in Relation to Schedule I Banks"

Room 253-D, Centre Block

===========

Financial industry experience:

Midland Doherty Investments	1984 to 1986
RBC Dominion Securities	1986 to 2002
Scotia McLeod	2002 to 2004

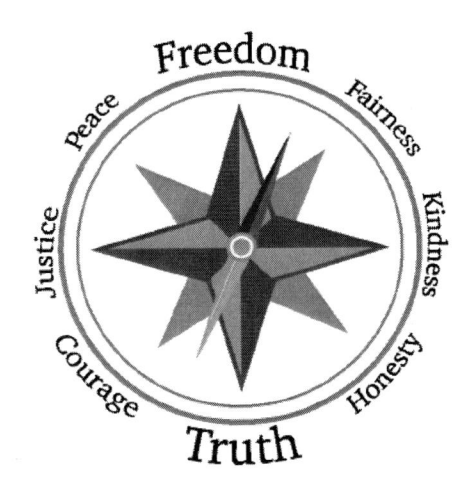

CHAPTER THREE

THE FAKE-ADVISOR VOWEL MOVEMENT

"Mrs Jones, of course you can trust me, I am not only your advisor, but I am also a docter..." (All vowel 'movements' intended)

"...financial advis<u>or</u> is generic term that usually refers to a broker by contrast, investment advis<u>er</u> is a legal term."
http://www.finra.org/investors/investment-advisers (2017)

The Consumer Federation of America published revelations in 2017 about an "advisor" misrepresentation game, in which hundreds of thousands of commission investment-brokers, promise something entirely different to the public, when seeking client's money, than what they represent to the courts when defending their actions.

Is Your Financial Advisor Misleading You?

WHAT THEY TELL THE INVESTOR

You have meaningful goals. Our **Financial Advisors** can help you reach them... We understand our clients' aspirations, and **we're as devoted to their goals as they are.**

- Morgan Stanley Website

WHAT THEY TELL THE JUDGE

Broker-dealers sell investment products **(not advice).**

- Morgan Stanley's Trade Association

(Just imagine what mixed, messed up messages they tell employees...)

Review of 25 Major Brokerage Firms & Insurance Companies Find All Posing as Fiduciaries, Misleading Consumers

Consumer Federation of America Underscores Need for Rule Requiring Salespeople to Act Like the Trusted Financial Advisors They Claim to Be; Deceptive Trade Practices Highlighted

January 18, 2017 Press Release
Washington, D.C. — Twenty-five top U.S. brokerage firms and insurance companies present their employees as trusted financial advisors putting client interests first even as their lobbyists argue in court that they are nothing more than commission-driven salespeople, according to a major new report from the Consumer Federation of America (CFA) and Americans for Financial Reform (AFR). The report also dissects how brokerage firms and insurance companies are systematically misleading unwary consumers.

From http://consumerfed.org/press_release/review-25-major-brokerage-firms-insurance-companies-find-posing-fiduciaries-misleading-consumers/

https://consumerfed.org/reports/financial-advisor-or-investment-salesperson-brokers-and-insurers-want-to-have-it-both-ways/

I will insert two other images in this chapter, which follow along the lines of the image above, where the Consumer Federation of America (CFA) and Americans for Financial Reform (AFR) work to reveal the hypocrisy of professional financial abusers of America.

===========

I first ran across Norah Cosgrove in 2000, when I worked at RBC.

She was mentioned in a news article after losing a $10,000 case in small claims court. RBC brought in one of the top lawyers in Canada to beat her with the claim that RBC did not owe this 80 something year old widow a fiduciary duty. RBC were claiming in court that the 80 year old was on her own, and that RBC did at no time owe her the duty of a fiduciary financial professional. It shocked me when I saw all of RBC's marketing efforts to assure or imply to each client that they were to expect that kind of duty.

A few years prior, RBC had come to myself, and a thousand other brokers on their staff, announcing that we were to change our business titles to "Advisor".

Why would they then argue in court that they did not owe an 'adviser duty of care' to an elderly widow? What was I missing? I didn't learn the mechanics of this marketing 'illusion' by RBC until 2013. It is <u>that good</u> of an illusion.

I was a professional, an insider in the industry and at one time among the top 5% of all RBC salespersons in Canada. I certainly felt I owed my clients this duty of care. It is in every industry training manual that I still possess.

A fiduciary duty is the highest principled legal duty, owed to people who are being given advice from a true professional. It should also be a requirement in law even when someone is <u>faking</u>, or <u>'pretending'</u> to be that professional. But something breaks down in between those two. I discovered that investment dealers 'rely' upon this breakdown, in order to make the con-game succeed.

Investors trust and rely on professional financial advice, accepting that it is to be treated as if it were advice from a doctor or a lawyer. It is the polar opposite of a "buyer beware" relationship (like the private sale of a used car) and it is backed by a few hundred years of legal tradition and understanding.

However, the financial industry has succeeded in artfully 'blending' those roles, in a clever shell-game, so that no consumer can tell which relationship is which, or which type of 'advice giver' they have. Regulators are paid billions by the investment industry, and in return hide license category meanings from the public and join in the shell-game because, well, that double bind again.

The 'bait and switch' upon millions of North American investors is to promise (the bait) absolute trust and integrity…..and then to deliver (the switch) commission salespersons without the requisite duty for trust and integrity.

"Advisor?, Adviser? Clients will never be the wiser." (National sales manager at a bank owned investment dealer)

As a financial professional working with RBC and having inside knowledge of the promises of client-first behavior and all transactions having to be in the clients' best interests, I found it shocking that RBC would take a contrary approach, and to do it in court. I found myself working for a firm that punched clients in the face…financially.

When Norah called out the #1 bank owned investment dealer, whose ethical codes and promises state they can be trusted, on the products they sold her, I could not believe their first line of defense was you shouldn't have trusted us. ("At no time did we owe you a fiduciary duty…." were their actual words)

At this stage of my career my tolerance for investment industry lies and/or client deception was wearing thin. I found myself close to the end of my rope with what looked to me more like client-harvesting, than the promised client-servicing. Baiting vulnerable and elderly

Canadians with a lure of absolute and professional trust, and then delivering them a salesperson with a 'buyer beware' duty of care.

Then, when caught or called upon the carpet, they lawyer-up with the ill gotten money, and beat the client on technicalities and legal fabrications which did not come close to what was promised or implied by the firm.

In my mind, I was a professional in this industry and I felt both invested in, and responsible for the reputation of my industry and firm. You could say I was naive. You *could* say I was as stunned as a kitten fresh out of the dryer.

Most of my colleagues found it simply easier to 'shoot, shut up, and shovel in the money'...because of the corporate double-bind that says, "do what we tell you to do...or else." Since my mental framework requires me to do the <u>exact opposite</u> of anything I am <u>told</u> to do, I had to try the "else".

I called Norah Cosgrove in Ontario. She was a very kind lady, but as she was in her late 80s or early 90s at that time and she referred me to her daughter who was her source of family help and support.

My reason for calling was to apologize and to tell her how sorry I was for her poor experience with the industry. I was growing increasingly concerned that what I had thought of as a good profession was turning out to be a fee-farming racket.

Brokers were incentivized and rewarded for gathering the greatest amounts of fees and commissions from customers. I did not sign up for this—to hurt my customers while making RBC richer (richer by cheating?). Nor did RBC policies say that doing financial harm to clients was fair game. In fact, it was a daily operating practice. I found myself caught between the two narratives in the firm, first the story told to customers, and second, the internal story told to the sales staff.

(Update: in 2017 RBC would admit to numerous investment practices which gouged investment clients, and would pay a $20 million penalty. The harm to mutual fund investors on sales charges alone amounted to $70 million...in 1996, from RBC's own records. Thus they <u>made money</u> (profited) on the voluntary regulator settlement.)

Patricia Cosgrove told me of her mother giving her investment account to a close family friend who happened to work at RBC.

Her account was originally in blue chip investments, with dividends and zero fees to operate the account aside from a purchase or a sale, which need never happen in a 80 year old's buy and hold account. This is perhaps the best type of investing I have ever seen (see Ch. 24), but not the best for RBC's daily revenues. Shortly after, her mother was urged to switch these long-term investments to Sovereign funds, the RBC house-brand fund at the time.

These house-brand funds had 2.5% in annual management fees, with RBC receiving a good portion of that action. Moving clients from little to no-fees, on a buy and hold account, to 2.5% fees could add tens or hundreds of millions to a firm's bottom line. Thus it was thought by many that moving clients' money from blue chip to fee based investments was in the better interests of investment dealers, than clients.

To give you the briefest financial snapshot to see how that looks to a salesperson let's take an example. At a given time I helped roughly 200-300 clients with total combined assets of $100 million to $150 million. They held a variety of investments based upon my best knowledge and their best nterests. Most of those investments did not carry an annual cost or fee to the investor.

The firm then came up with a series of house-brand products, which carried an annual fee of 2 5% and they sold it to their salesforce...hard. Their (management's) internal sales-pitch was that if I switched all my clients investments into the house-brand products, I (and the dealer) would have an immediate revenue stream of 2.5% on $100 million. An annual income would flow into the firm of $2.5 million dollars, assured to the firm on day one of each year, as opposed to myself and the firm having to "make a trade" in a single client's account to earn revenue.

Fee based products were the greatest invention in the world...for brokers and dealers (those who are not legally required to owe investors a fiduciary duty).

It allowed every non-fiduciary salesperson and investment dealer to increase their revenues by many times...

Around that time the Ontario Securities Commission did a report called the Fair Dealing Model, and in the section titled "Compensation Biases" they noted that by switching client assets into house brand funds the investment firm could realize gains of between twelve to twenty six times in revenues. Now that is exciting to any investment salesperson and every sales manager. It was also bad, as it tended to cause investment dealers and salespersons to go a little crazy with the sales-spin they gave customers in order to get this easy money. It is especially easy when a friend of the family is posing as a trusted professional, and making the suggestion to an elderly widow. Back to Norah Cosgrove...

===========

What was truly disturbing, however, was that rather than apologize and "make the client whole again" as used to be common practice in the industry when errors were spotted, RBC decided to take another approach. The lawyer up and deny wrongdoing approach. This is perhaps the greatest change that I witnessed after banks became the owners of Canadian investment dealers. They suddenly became above the rules of fairness...with the banks as owners they were in a whole different class of air space).

To defend their actions RBC hired one of Canada's top lawyers to attend a $10,000 small claims court action, and to argue that "at no time did RBC owe a fiduciary duty" (a duty of professional loyalty) to this client.

That went against nearly everything I had been led to believe—all advertising promises, industry conduct and practices manuals, and so on. It was like RBC was saying one thing when it came to luring customers, and then doing something entirely different when it came to serving them. Martin Luther King Jr. said that "there comes a time when silence becomes betrayal." I was at a crossroads.

In their statement of defense things started to jump out at me (see Cosgrove v RBCDS at http://investorvoice.ca/Cases/Investor/Cosgrove/Cosgrove_index.htm):

1. They list in paragraph four that the RBC salesperson was an advisor, when the correct license and registration category at that time for RBC salespersons was 'salesperson' in Canada, ('broker' in the U.S). This is an illegal concealment of the true license or registration held, a misrepresentation to the public, and a misrepresentation to the court. But this is RBC, and who is going to challenge the #1 bank on the truth?

2. As it was described to me, when one of Canada's highest rated lawyers appears in a small claims court, the small claims judge is humbled by their presence. I have since found out that the legal game (internally) is one of upward respect, to a point of reverence. In today's courts, pecking order, politics, and so on, sometimes appears to carry as much weight as facts. They certainly seem able to alter facts in cases I have seen. Personalities before principles, was something I would come to accept as 'normal' when it came to how courts sometimes dealt with Canada's most powerful banks.

3. The RBC 'advisor' was listed as being a vice president of RBC. It has since become known that 'Vice President' is a made-up title which does not refer to an executive position in the firm. It should be read like "million dollar round table producer", in the life insurance sales game. It is described by Justice Senecal in the court case of Markarian (another elderly victim) verses CIBC, as a "phony marketing title, meant to lower the distrust of the customer…" Read the shocking case at investorvoice.ca

4. In paragraph seven, RBC states that Nora Cosgrove is not "vulnerable" despite being in her late 80s and widowed. This is debatable, but notable to see how big banks behave

against the customer when things become problematic. Banks now seem to turn mean, rather than giving clients half a chance. It is almost as if they have learned that they are no longer being held to account for our laws, if only they hire the "right" lawyers...

5. In paragraph ten, RBC makes it appear as if investment in RBC house brand funds (with many times more fee income to RBC) was the client's idea ... which is simply an out of real-world assumption. It is inconceivable to imagine an 80 year old widow, making the discovery of these new RBC owned fund products on her own.

6. It was paragraph sixteen that truly opened my eyes. RBC states: "At no time were the defendants acting in a fiduciary capacity, or in the alternative at no time did the defendants breach any fiduciary obligations owed to the plaintiff." I am no lawyer, but it seemed they were saying we did nothing wrong, and if it turns out we did do something wrong, then we did nothing wrong. This is why I felt I had to call and apologize to this lady, for the actions, the double-speak, and the double-dealing of my company. I was personally ashamed and embarrassed to be part of an elder abusing game.

To make a long story shorter, Mrs. Cosgrove and her daughter discovered after the fact that they had been lured into the house branded fund by sales-patter from the RBC salesperson. The investment performance was poor and the fees made it worse. They took it upon themselves to right an injustice, and RBC took it upon itself to not right that wrong. Norah got beat out of a $10,000 claim and RBC kept the fat fees.

I knew then it was time to start re-evaluating my involvement with such a company. I did not sign up to harm my clients, the vulnerable, or the elderly, just to help a bank make another billion dollars or make myself richer. That was not the job that I was offered at all.

Go ahead and read the case, while you are thinking about your life savings in the hands of any financial corporation. RBC was once the most highly regarded out there, so a rare glimpse into what they do to their customers behind the scenes might be your best investment lesson. And it is free. One of the hoped for results of this book is that you become better able to spot the predator at the table in any financial relationship. (read Warren Buffet about that) My wish is for you to absorb everything you can, so you can protect everything you have.

The case is online at InvestorVoice.ca   Cosgrove v RBCDS
http://investorvoice.ca/Cases/Investor/Cosgrove/Cosgrove_RBCDS_SOD.PDF

And while you perhaps visit InvestorVoice.ca, check out the case "Markarian v CIBC", I assure you it is worth 2 years of university education when it comes to your financial literacy. It is a true story of what a giant bank will do to the elderly…

===========

Is Your Financial Advisor Misleading You?

WHAT THEY TELL THE INVESTOR

Contact a NAIFA member for **advice you can trust**. NAIFA members adhere to a code of ethics that is about honesty and integrity. They're committed to working with you and **guiding you with a financial plan** that will lead you to a secure future and a retirement you'll enjoy.

- National Association of Insurance and Financial Advisors, **"Advisors You Can Trust"**

WHAT THEY TELL THE JUDGE

Ordinary sales conversations where both parties understand that they are acting at arms' length … are **not** in a fiduciary relationship of trust or confidence

- National Association of Insurance and Financial Advisors

Then there is this contradiction in stories…

Imagine being in a business where deceiving the customer in order to earn their trust is an unwritten requirement…and often the standard industry practice.

Imagine the phrase "you can trust me, I am an advisor," can contain two lies in eight words.

In the United States, the number of 'brokers' (commission sales brokers) is over 600,000, according to FINRA (Financial Industry Regulatory Authority). FINRA sales brokers manage 109 Million investment accounts for my American neighbors. I have observed that most of them also do this while promising they are "advisors".

The 'bait and switch' trick is to become licensed as a commission sales broker, but pretend to investors to be a licensed fiduciary professional, which requires an "adviser' registration under the law. Most imposters can be spotted using the word "advisor' to dodge the legal requirements of 'adviser'. A mere 'vowel movement' is all that is needed to dupe millions into a dangerous and often false granting of trust.

THE ADVISOR NAME GAME

Anyone in investment management or investment sales wants to call themselves the financial equivalent of "a Doctor"

Why? Respect, inferred credibility, objectivity, professionalism, instant respect, and nearly instant trust.

The problem is that in the investment game, nobody gets in the door without starting out in a selling capacity...well almost nobody. Virtually any entry level investment job is; "go out and bring in as much money as you can for us to manage and earn commissions/fees..." It is called asset gathering. Almost everyone has to start there. There is no free ticket into the big leagues of money management.

The most common sales-trick is to morph the commission sales role into one that sounds like you are the equivalent of a doctor...hence the use of the word "advisor"

It is a 'bait and switch' whereby consumers 'believe' they are promised the services of a professional financial advice giver, someone who is on the same side of the table as the customer, and advises ONLY in the interests of the customer.

While the truth most often is that <u>the customer</u> is <u>the 'product'</u>. The dealer and its salespersons are 'counter-parties' to most investors, and the false advisor can 'milk' fees and commissions while pretending to be a trusted partner, adviser and service provider. The self protection racket called self-regulation allows this to happen today to millions of investors.

The high earning 'advisors' are not those who manage <u>money</u> the best, but those who manage <u>clients</u> best....Those who 'gather' your assets into their firm. Are <u>you</u> being managed professionally, or is your money being managed professionally? 99% of investors never know the difference. How would they? (answer is in Chapter 8)

Here is what Warren Buffet had to say about his short stint in the broker-sales game back in the 1950's:

"I had to explain to people who didn't know enough about whether they should take Aspirin or Anacin", and people would do anything the "guy in the white coat"...the stock broker...told them to do.

"The stockbroker got paid based on turnover instead of advice. In other words, "getting paid based on how many pills he sells. He's getting paid more for some pills than others. You wouldn't go to a doctor whose pay was totally contingent on how many pills you took."

But that's how the business of being a stockbroker worked at the time. Today these same commission jockeys are called "advisors" and POOF! Smoke Bomb distraction!

He'd recommend a stock like GEICO to his friends and family, And tell him that the best thing to do was to hold it for 20 years. That meant that he didn't get any more commissions from them.

"You can't make a living that way. The system pits your interest against your clients".

The previous in italics is an excerpt from the book The SNOWBALL, Warren Buffet and the Business of Life, by Alice Schroeder. Published by Bantam
Purchased here: https://www.amazon.ca/Snowball-Warren-Buffett-Business-Life/dp/0553384619

============

Further Financial Advisor Trickery:

Former American Banker editor in chief Neil Weinberg writes about the 'advisor' bait and switch scam that affects 99% of investors in North America. The following is an excerpt from his article, "Where Wrongdoing Still Thrives on Wall Street" (October 18, 2013):

Financial Advisor Chicanery: Imagine a two-tiered health care system in which some doctors were legally obligated to do what's right for their patients and others, like snake oil salesmen of yore, could recommend whatever treatments made them the most money, as long as they didn't kill patients outright. Now imagine that the shysters did all they could to blend in with the real doctors. That's effectively the type of system we have today among the people Americans count on to tell them how to invest their life's savings. Registered investment advisors must, by law, put clients' interests first. Many thousands of other "advisors" at places like Morgan Stanley, Merrill Lynch and smaller shops are held to a much lower "suitability" standard. In essence, even though these people often refer to themselves as "financial advisors" or by some other comfort-inducing title, they're really glorified salesmen. Some do a great job serving their clients. Others don't. It's up them. Under the law, as long as they avoid putting an 85 year-old widow into an exotic derivative with a 20 year lockup, they're bulletproof. Few clients know this fiduciary-suitability gap exists. The suitability crowd has worked tirelessly to keep the standard low and the distinctions murky. The cost to the public is incalculable but huge.

http://www.americanbanker.com/bankthink/where-wrongdoing-still-thrives-on-wall-street-1062940-1.html

============

A recent $15.00 haircut was given to me by a young lady who required about 3000 hours of salon academy training and work experience, to become a licensed hairstylist. In contrast, the average bank or investment seller can hire you and have you licensed to sell products in 30 days, if you are a candidate who can bring money and fees into the firm.

===========

From the U.S.:
www.nasaa.org
Registration or Licensing Status of Financial Professionals

"Financial professional titles and licenses are not the same. A financial professional may use various titles whether or not he or she is registered or licensed with a regulatory authority. Financial professionals who are registered as broker-dealers or investment advisers (*note the e in advisers*) have obtained registrations and licenses granted by federal or state regulatory authorities. Working with a financial professional who is registered with or licensed by federal or state authorities affords you certain legal protections."

===========

I became such a bother to the Alberta Securities Commission, (ASC), that by 2016 they felt obligated to release a snippet of consumer protective truth to the public. In this ASC blog they reveal that the salesperson registration (called a 'Dealing Representative' in Canada since 2009) is to be trusted about the same as one might a salesperson at an auto dealership. (the 'dealing representative' has to represent the interests of the dealer, they just don't have to tell you…)

===========

The following is from The Alberta Securities Commission publication, "What's in a name? Does the title of your investment professional matter?"

7/7/2016 Category: Investor education; Investment scams

Persons who are registered under the Securities Act (Alberta) as Dealing Representatives (for example) are generally licensed to sell you products sold by the investment firm they work for, and are obligated to provide you with advice on the suitability of those products for your circumstances.

In that sense, it's not unlike purchasing a car from a dealership. If you walk into a Volvo dealership, and explain your needs (four-door, certain horsepower) the person working there will suggest the most suitable Volvo for your needs. While they might have a small selection of other makes and models in their inventory, they are not required to know about, or recommend, any make or model that is not in their inventory that might meet your needs as well, or better. This is true no matter what job title they use, be that "personal banking associate," "investment representative," "investment specialist" or any other title.

http://www.albertasecurities.com/investor/investor-resources/you-ascd-blog/Lists/Posts/Post.aspx?ID=63

It was like pulling teeth for over a decade to get the ASC to quietly whisper this consumer warning. (10 years at $30 million dollars per year equals about $300 million in salaries, paid to just this one regulator…for 10 years of silence on the public interest) There are over ten thousand paid regulators in North America. (FINRA, SIFMA, SEC, CSA, NASAA, IIROC etc) You would think that one of them would have shared this 'bait and switch' with the public.

Some will post something on their web sites, in an effort to cover themselves…but none so far will proactively work to inform the public.

I have read many stories of dentists and other medical professionals caught in the crime of impersonating a professional without a license. The usually involve a criminal charge. I keep asking myself why a fake Dentist gets a jail term, while a fake advisor gets…another condo?

Have you ever stopped to think how many investment 'advisors' do not actually hold the advisor license? It is statistically 100%, with no exceptions, in Canada, and I am coming to learn that similar sleight of hand may be used to help up to 600,000 (FINRA regulated brokers in the U.S.) also pretend to be something many are not registered as.

How does this happen you ask? Well, remember that part about the industry paying 100% of regulators' salaries? There is more. A slow evolution has taken place in the financial industry over the past thirty years.

Thirty years ago the investment industry consisted of stockbrokers who transacted trades for clients The broker business wasn't as much about advice or financial planning as it was about earning a commission from making a trade. At my level (retail brokerage) it was 100% transaction based.

The evolution that took place while my career was growing allowed me to witness an almost complete demise of stock jockeys (stockbrokers) and the emergence of investment 'advisors,' financial planners, or other so-called professional advice providers.

'Advice' (or "advisor") became a marketing disguise for salespeople to cloak themselves in, to cause customers to more easily surrender their trust. The public is kept in the dark as to what is an advisor vs an adviser, and any business newspaper will help keep that deception hidden, in return for the financial advertising revenues.

Transaction commissions meant the industry could only eat what they killed that day. (they had to make a sale, to make a living) Annual advisory fees, on the other hand, get into the realm of having "$35 billion in fee accounts earning money for RBC every day ..."

Fee programs are like putting your money on a plan—like a cellphone plan or a membership to the local gym—except for one tiny thing: the power of compound interest means that a cost of just 2% (for fees or lesser performing investments, or both), when compounded over 35 years, cuts your future retirement capital in HALF. Banks know compound interest better than anyone, and they know how easy it is to get that 2% 'skim' from their customers.

Warren Buffett is one of the richest people in the world who has a net worth of approx. $75 billion. He is arguably the most famous and successful investor in history. If he had paid a 2% "advisory fee" on his investments like most retail investors he would be worth closer to $25 billion today. Fees kill.

Some investment salespeople today can be forgiven for not knowing what they should call themselves. In the 20 years I worked in the industry I never got a look at my license, never held it in my hands, and never had one on my wall. When I visit investment dealers offices today I look at what is on the walls, and there are still virtually no examples of the license the salesperson holds.

They display courses, diplomas, and city business licenses. But the true financial selling or broker license to this day appears not a good enough marketing tool to display. So they tout a fabricated title that does not exist in law, nor are they duty bound to honor for the customer. After all, advisor is a 'title' and not a legal registration category. <u>Gotcha!</u>

===========

I saw the rules, regulations, the inside marketing, and the capture of each regulatory body to allow the industry to get away with this. If anyone in the industry thought of speaking out on behalf of the public, they were silenced and bullied, under threat of job loss.

"Anyone who talks to the press is fired", were words from my manager's mouth more than a few times. That and the mention of being "team players" often. I learned that to be a "team player" meant being willing to "shut up" and look the other way at harm or cheating of clients, so long as it made more money for the firm.

The investment dealer who gave me my license in 1984 knew my license category was 'salesperson.' So in truth, my bank-owned investment dealer was deceiving both its employees and customers when it claimed I was an investment advisor.

I forged ahead in the belief that I was a honest-to-goodness investment 'advisor' (as it implied) with an honest duty of care for my clients, often even a fiduciary duty as suggested in the training materials and in our Conduct and Practices Course books.

Who knew that the joke was on me? My investment dealer knew all along that my license and those of the other 120,000+ brokers in Canada was, until it was changed in September 2009, "salesperson." Nothing whatsoever had changed except the 'marketing' spin that the public was given. By 2017, all 13 Securities Commissions have almost totally 'erased' the old "salesperson" registration category, in a wonderful revision of history. In a few years, it will be as if the bait and switch fraud will never have existed. POOF! Smoke Bomb!

The industry will have succeeded in turning 600,000 commission sales brokers, plus who knows how many fund sellers, and life insurance sellers in the US, and 120,000+ commission sales agents in Canada, into full blown "professionals". No one will even know of the switch…Presto! Change-o!

===========

The word <u>'suitable', as it relates to investment product requirements</u> is as subjective, therefore useless and potentially harmful to investors today as the word 'drinkable.' Fiduciary, on the other hand, is quite clear <u>and</u> protected in law.

From The United States Institute for Fiduciary Standards:

"Fiduciary duties exist to mitigate the information asymmetry (also known as the "knowledge gap") between expert providers of socially important services – such as law, finance and medicine – and the non-expert, consumers of these services. This knowledge gap is neutralized by requiring experts to be fiduciaries.

Fiduciaries are bound by an undivided loyalty to clients, to put clients' interests first, ahead of their own interests. Here is the legal and practical basis for investors to rely on the advice of experts, and enter relationships of trust and confidence. Fiduciary law, then, is the foundation on which investor trust is based."
http://www.thefiduciaryinstitute.org/wp-content/uploads/2013/09/InstituteSixCoreFiduciaryDuties.pdf

===========

An interesting side benefit of dealing with a legally registered 'adviser' is that usually the investment management fees start out in the neighborhood of 1% to 1 1/4%, go DOWN from there, and there are no commission sales-people who may be motivated to increase those fees in ways that can harm the customer.

===========

What your investment 'advisor' needs from you.

While I was working as an investment salesperson my sales manager informed me $400,000 was the "break even" point for the firm. According to him, the costs of desk, phone, computer, training, back office, etc. were such that any broker bringing in less than $400,000 in commissions or fees was losing money for the firm.

TD recently raised the commission/fee production requirement for its lowest payout grid to $400,000, effectively telling anyone who does not produce this amount in fees or commissions from their book of clients to "achieve or leave."
Evelyn Juan / October 29, 2013, Advisor.ca, "TD REMODELS ADVISOR PAY PLAN"

TD sales employees who do not produce about $2000 per day in fees or commissions for TD are thus paid out at the lowest commission level (called a commission grid) of 20%, while their bigger producing salespeople keep up to 50% of each dollar they generate. This system of incentives is not about what is best for the client, and mostly punishes those who place client interests first.

If the person claiming to be your advisor needs to produce half a million dollars to keep from being fired ("achieve or leave"), and if they have, say, 200 clients, they would need to produce $2500 in commissions or fees each year from each client. The easiest way to do this is not to charge clients 1% fees, and then proceed to find them the very best investment products/solutions in the world, but to charge the client as much as humanely possible without getting arrested, and clients end up paying 2% to 5% for company-brand products. In nine out of ten cases that I observe today the investor is being 'farmed' in this manner by investment salespersons.

===========

Commission quotas—just like the monthly sales quotas at some car dealerships—are a daily management topic. They were the <u>number one topic</u> in the inner workings of the investment industry. To earn a living, and be left relatively un-harassed by management, one needed to generate $500,000 to $1,000,000 in commissions. Sales managers at brokerage firms are there to maximize fees brought into the firm.

To do this with 250 clients (a reasonable size to manage) means pulling $2000 to $4000 in fees or commissions, at a minimum, from each client's account.

This all occurs in tens of millions of investment accounts each day, in North America. It is why your banks are richer than you think. They can cheat by misrepresenting their agents to you as something you should trust with your life... and life savings. Then they 'self' regulate so they can get away with this misrepresentation, and face no consequences.

They do this by deception (similar to the VW Emissions deception) to fool and mislead clients into giving away their trust.

Each broker, each day, with each telephone call intended to make a sale, struggles with this moral dilemma. Do I place the interests of the client first, or the interests of myself, my commissions, and ultimately my dealer first? The good brokers can handle this ethical challenge well, the poor ones cannot. The industry actually prefers the poorer ones, ethically speaking. The industry is far better than most brokers are at designing incentive plans to feather their own nests before the nests of their customers.

My manager used to tell me how the firm wanted them to encourage the brokers to buy a bigger house and more expensive cars.

Anything to put the sales agent into a deeper level of debt...and thus sales desperation.

Remember that only a legal fiduciary is 'required by law' to help you manage your money without any double-bind ethical choices on their backs. Only a "fiduciary" adviser cannot legally act as a counter-party to your financial interests.

In recent times I am also starting to see the former sacrosanct term of "Portfolio Manager", be diluted, 'borrowed', exempted, and so on, so that persons who are registered as broker/salesperson can add prestige to their position, and lower the levels of suspicion of their sales targets.

Even the best salespeople out there, even the professionals, are pressured all the time to sell less than stellar investments. Sometimes junk. At some less credible firms it is often junk. Most of the time it takes a very experienced (and morally courageous) broker to be able to tell in advance what is junk and what is quality, so they do not steer clients wrong. Brokers are under daily management pressure to "achieve or leave".

Imagine lunch hour at your local brokerage office, with the road show from a new investment issue, or a mutual fund company, sponsoring lunch for the brokers. They will buy pizza or sandwiches any day we let them in, for the same reason pharmaceutical sales reps buy pizza for medical doctors—to get in their faces and pitch products.

The very first question out of some brokers' mouths is, "What is the commission?" (Translation: "What is in it for me?")

The junkier the investment, the higher the commission needed to catch salespeople's interest. The higher the commission, the higher the sales. No, it does not make sense...but it does make money.

True advice givers always want to know exactly what is in it for the client. When I was in the industry it was a real contrast to see brokers who were on the "get rich quick" plan (for themselves) versus the "get rich slowly" plan, with clients interests coming first. That was the smarter, longer term plan for the 10% or 20% of brokers out there with integrity.

I would not need to share this information with you if the industry could be trusted to police itself. Sadly, the "we police ourselves" thing has worked out perfectly—for the investment industry, not for the public's interest.

Standard of Conduct for Investment Advisers and Broker-Dealers. http://consumerfed.org/wp-content/uploads/2017/09/cfa-letter-to-sec-on-standard-of-conduct-rfi.pdf

Which is it, Mr. Brown?

WHAT FSI'S BROWN SAYS PUBLICLY	WHAT FSI TOLD THE COURT
"[R]etirement savers need **access to advice** to plan for a dignified retirement — and **that's what our adviser members provide.**" - Dale Brown, President and CEO Financial Services Institute	This is "a short-term relationship **whose essence [is] sales** rather than significant investment advice provided on a regular basis and through an established relationship." - Financial Services Institute

There are two (2) people in the US, who in my view, do more to benefit the American public than some thousands who work in regulatory agencies in North America. One is Barbara Roper of the Consumers Federation of America and the other is Micah Hauptman. Forgive me for the others whom I am less familiar with, and might overlook as I write this. However these two are literally doing more honest benefit to America than thousands of industry regulators combined. They do this because they are not caught in a double bind which requires them to act against the public.

(The Consumer Federation of America should not be confused with the other honorable CFA entity known as Chartered Financial Analysts)

48

CFA (analysts) Institute is a global association of investment professionals that traces its lineage back to the establishment of the Financial Analysts Federation (FAF) in 1947.

Leadership of the FAF established an independent organization — the Institute of Chartered Financial Analysts (ICFA) — to administer the CFA credentialing program in 1959

It is worth mention that the CFA is the highest quality educational standard for financial professionals. Highest education, highest ethical reputation in my experience. I am not a CFA, so my suggestion here is not in service of self.

===========

AGENCY DUTIES OF INVESTMENT SELLERS AS COMPARED TO REAL ESTATE SELLERS

My local real estate agent explained to me the undivided loyalty a real estate agent owes a customer:

Responsibilities of the Agent

1. Undivided Loyalty
   The agent must act solely in your best interests, must always put your interests above their own and above the interests of other parties (from the Real Estate Industry)."

I will stop there, since this first requirement sums up nearly all that is missing in the investment industry codes of conduct. Nearly every investment firm will say these words in their marketing material, but unless you have several hundred thousand dollars, and ten years of your life to take them to court, you may not actually receive those promises. Regulators will then generally not bite the hand that feeds them...by helping you.

===========

"Dual agency" is an area of conflict that every real estate professional must disclose. Each real estate transaction that I am aware of must come with disclosure of who is representing whom, and which team they are playing for. The investment industry is exempt from having to disclose when they are playing 'against' their clients.

> I recently (2017) ran across internal documents from a Canadian bank-owned investment dealer, which stated that the 'registration category of the registered representative would be made available to the investor, upon written request". Imagine having things so well rigged, that a bank that deals with millions and millions of Canadians can hide the registration of its sales force, so clients are not warned or properly informed. Now imagine that every bank/dealer does this…Duty to warn, or deception class action?

Banks and investment dealers can act as heavily-armored (lawyered) 'antagonists' to their investment clients and it will all "stay within the family" so to speak. I am referring to the non-fiduciary industry when I describe this.

When you think about it, nearly every initial public offering (IPO) (newly minted shares or securities) sold by your broker/dealer is the result of the dealer playing both sides of the deal. When the dealer is both underwriter (sponsor, or sponsoring dealer,) and then purporting to give "advice" to the public (to buy their new product) at the same time.

You would not allow your lawyer to represent both parties in a divorce, especially if the lawyer were on a commission. That is a bit like what happens when you have the non-fiduciary 'advisor.' The advisor is a dealer "rep" of the firm, while telling you that they are also your representative. They cannot act for both without being an undisclosed dual-agent…which they do every day to millions of people.

When added to the faking of a professional pedigree, implying a professional standard similar to doctors or lawyers, the retail investor has virtually no chance for fairness.

Or, as in many examples in the United States, brokers are commonly found to hold TWO separate license and registration categories. One being a 'broker' with the duty of care that provides and another as an SEC or State Registered fiduciary "Adviser" as found in the law. (Securities Act 1935, Securities Act 1940 USA)

One result of this is they have 'two hats' to wear, or to 'choose' to wear, while these hats are invisible to the customer or client. With someone selling financial products, for a commission or annual fee, who could stake a claim in both those camps, without the client knowing when, how and what professional 'hat' they are wearing…is a rather curious, and dangerous combination.

I note that lately this "two hat" financial person has been spotted more frequently in Canada, now that the scam is out, about faked "advisor" titles. Some are borrowing a "Portfolio Manager" title (who will ever check?), some making up the rules as they go along, and some dealers obtain 'exemption' from our laws, which are touched upon in an upcoming chapter.

The industry changes faster than any government or regulator is paid to keep track of. Second, we have long been able to self-regulate, which gives the ability to make things up as we go along. Third, government or industry regulators are picked or paid, by industry, making them (at the top) mere handmaids to the financial industry. My most informed contacts call industry-paid regulators a simple and effective "protection racket", which insulates the industry from being held accountable to rules and laws. I agree. It did take decades for me to see its perfect design though. I had to learn to think like a criminal, and then there is was, plain as day.

This (self regulation) leads to simply 'making up' whatever titles marketing folks think will garner the most business, using whichever title will gain trust fastest from potential customers. Regulators appear to be paid more than required, to faithfully remain '20 years behind the times'… so they are always '20 years behind the crimes.'

===========

I hope you have found one of the 10 or 20 percent of broker-salespersons out there who believe in placing the best interests of the client ahead of their own. My experience is that even when you find the very best, keep in mind that behind that unique individual, lurks a bank or investment dealer who is unwilling to put the interests of the customer first, regardless of their marketing promises.

Letting the industry get away with promoting its product-sellers as some kind of trusted professional is fraud. It causes consumers to be fooled into a false sense of security, believing their 'advisor' may in fact have to act in the customer's best interests. This is simply not true, and rigging public opinion in this manner allows extra billions of dollars to be skimmed and pocketed from trusting and vulnerable clients each year.

Update 2017: I now learn that, there are two different working relationships that a consumer can have with a real estate professional in my area: the consumer can be a client, in which case the real estate professional is acting as their "agent," or the consumer can be a customer, and forgo agency representation. The world is changing everywhere.

===========

The investment industry spends billions on purchasing regulators, purchasing media, advertorials etc., to insure that the customers of an investment 'advisor' will never learn whether they are a buyer beware 'customer', or the 'client' of a professional financial person.

In conclusion:

- Your investment 'advisor' can act as a financial 'counter-party' giving you advice which harms you while benefitting himself and his dealer. (this thanks to the 'suitability' standard of every US broker and Canadian dealer rep)

Fraud, misrepresentation, and false pretenses may be used to harm you.

- Your investment 'advisor' does not have to be a licensed or registered "Adviser" with the proper authority. (the confusion of this "vowel movement" is worth a Trillion dollars, and is quite intentional)

- Your 'advisor's' conflicts and incentives mean that harming your interests allows improved profit to the industry. (Chapter 10)

- The law will not be applied to help, if you are harmed in these or other systemic ways.

- The law may even be 'exempted' so your investment firm can more easily profit, by doing additional financial harm to you.

- Self-regulation allows persons paid by the investment industry to act as if they are paid to protect the public, which is often not the case.

- Investors, and our shared society, loses hundreds of billions of dollars every year, while the strongest financial institutions in the world unjustly gain those billions.

- This book concerns itself with intentional misrepresentation of millions of North American investors, so that greater wealth can be 'extracted' from them whilst they are given improper and deceptive information.

- I think that the Class Action suits that could result from this kind of systemic deception will far exceed those of the VW Emissions deceptions, and could also exceed some of the major tobacco industry suits…when financial abusers are finally fair game.

- The industry gets to play countless deception games, and at not time and by no authority in the land, are they held to a responsible duty to warn the public.

===========

One percent (in fees) is a fair going rate for the world's top professional money managers today. Try and keep your investment fees, like your milk, at 1% fat or less. The best investors pay zero. Ask Warren Buffet.

===========

Don't take my word for any of this:
Further select reading on the topic of THE FAKE-ADVISOR VOWEL MOVEMENT

"Brokerage firms now engage in advertising that is clearly calculated to leave the false impression with investors that stockbrokers take the same fiduciary care as a doctor or a lawyer," claims the report, which was co-authored by Christine Lazaro, director of the St. John's School of Law securities arbitration clinic.

"But, while brokerage firms advertise as though they are trusted guardians of their clients' best interests, they arbitrate any resulting disputes as though they are used car salesmen," wrote the attorneys.

Their report claimed that Merrill Lynch, Fidelity Investments, Ameriprise, Wells Fargo, Morgan Stanley, Allstate Financial, UBS, Berthel Fisher, and Charles Schwab all advertise "in a fashion that is designed to lull investors into the belief that they are being offered the services of a fiduciary."

https://piaba.org/in-the-media/witness-says-brokers-try-pass-themselves-fiduciaries-nick-thornton

===========

This report by the Consumer Federation of America points quite clearly to the "head fake", of promising safe investment 'advice' to 100 million American investors, whilst backing up that pretense with 'tough luck, you lose', or if any customers figure out the scam.
http://consumerfed.org/wp-content/uploads/2017/01/1-18-17-Advisor-or-Salesperson_Report.pdf

===========

The Honorable Justice Jean-Pierre Senécal, J.S.C. uses the word "fraud" 155 times in his judgement against CIBC, in the fascinating "Markarian versus CIBC".

Here are just a few of the Judge's comments:

(B) DEFENDANT'S FAULTS

¶ 262   But there is more here. This is a case where the defendant (CIBC) can be held liable because of its own faults. It itself committed faults in the performance of its duties and the fulfilment of its responsibilities, including false representations about the quality of its representative and, above all, the lack of protection for clients, as well as a serious failure to provide supervision and control.

(C) MISLEADING TITLES

¶ 263   The defendant attributed to Migirdic (CIBC broker) fake titles, i.e. "vice-president" and "vice-president and director," in addition to letting him use the title "specialist in retirement investments." Those titles were false representations that misled the plaintiffs, hid reality from them, disinformed them, comforted them in their confidence in Migirdic (CIBC broker), reduced their distrust, and contributed to Migirdic (CIBC broker)'s fraud. The defendant committed a fault in terms of its obligation to inform and advise, in addition to misleading the plaintiffs.

¶ 264   In principle, a vice-president is a person in a management position in a firm. The vice-president is immediately below the president and reports to the president. The vice-president acts in the absence of the president. It is a prestigious title in a firm, a title held by few individuals. The English word "director," the incorrect origin of the word used here in French, designates either the member of a board of directors of a firm or the head of a department or office. That is also a prestigious title, at least when it is attributed in a prestigious firm.

¶ 265   In the defendant's operations, these titles also have that meaning, but not that meaning alone! They are given as well to any representative (also called an "investment advisor" or previously a "financial consultant") who reaches a certain level of commissions in a given year, in short, who "sells" a lot and brings in a lot of commissions. A person is awarded the title essentially in "recognition" of work and as a marketing tool, as the president of CIBC Wood Gundy, Tom Monahan, acknowledged. However, to have the title of "vice-president" or "vice-president and director" adds no new responsibility or any management role. What is more, it testifies to neither greater competence nor more reliability.

¶ 266   In the defendant's operations, the titles are, in fact attributed to many people. In 1995, there were 206 vice-presidents and 44 vice-presidents and directors out of 556 representatives. In 1997, there were 217 vice-presidents and 109 vice-presidents and directors out of 612 representatives. In 1999, there were 197 vice-presidents and 101 vice-presidents and directors out of 725 representatives, the proportions were about the same in 2000. That year, about 300 of the 700 representatives had a title!

¶ 267   The problem is that clients do not know that these titles are simply marketing tools, i.e. a means to convince them that they have an excellent representative, and recognition for the volume of commissions. Clients therefore believe they have a "very special" and "eminently acknowledged" representative when the representative has the title of "vice-president" or "vice-president and director." That was what Mr. Markarian (the elderly victim) in fact believed, as he testified. Richard Papazian, another witness (and also a victim) thought the same thing. So the titles create a false feeling of trust, comfort and prestige, the role of which is not trivial in the commission of fraud.

¶ 268   The plaintiffs were the victims of these false representations by the defendant in their regard.

¶ 269   Migirdic (CIBC broker) received the title of vice-president in 1986, then vice-president and director in the early 1990s. He retained the titles until he left, because of the enormous volume of commissions he generated. In fact, the titles increased Mr. Markarian's trust in Migirdic (CIBC broker) and prompted him to guard against him and his actions even less. The defendant committed a fault in acting to ensure that.

The entire case can be found at this link:
http://investorvoice.ca/Cases/Investor/Markarian/Markarian_v_CIBCWorldMarketsInc.htm

===========

Said to me from a financial victim:

"Larry, another way of expressing the repugnancy of the deception is as follows.

We were lead to believe that we were opening up a relationship with a person representing an investment dealer who was going to be sitting on our side of the table, giving us the best "advice" to protect our capital, as we were already in our retirement years.

Instead we were suckered into opening up a relationship with an investment dealer and the Representative who were actually sitting on the other side of the table, whose job was to relieve us of the maximum amount of commissions regardless of the ensuing financial damage to our assets.

Especially, in our case, they used fraudulent misrepresentation that regulators are not interested in pursuing."

Peter Whitehouse, author of the above few paragraphs spent almost a decade making hundreds upon hundreds of written contacts to Canadian protective bodies, securities commissions etc. To my knowledge he found no Canadian organization or person who was willing or able to protect the public, or even to enforce the law. Watching him write those letters for a decade was a bit like the old stories of doing battle with the Chinese Army. They have enough 'foot soldiers' to keep an abused investor running in complete circles forever, without ever getting a result.

Chapter Take-aways

The false investment advisor can financially 'punch' you in the face.

It could be a very gentle punch, it could be a blow to the back of the head, and it could even be explained away as an accident… so sorry, but over a lifetime of investing, the injuries compound, just like interest compounds.

The registered fiduciary Adviser <u>cannot</u> legally do harm to his or her clients. Full stop.

The repeated blows of the non-fiduciary advice giver can cut your retirement savings by half of what it should have been, if you had learned about the fiduciary duty.

And yet...

My friend Derek correctly points out to me that this is your 'best case scenario', with the non-fiduciary…to be cut in half. He says that this is the harm if the false advisor 'only' hits you for 2%.

If they happen to do more self-dealing than average, your entire account could be destroyed. How will you ever know that it was not the fault of "the markets"? How do you know whether you have a fiduciary or not?

I have yet to meet a retail nvestor who knows this, and it is your greatest learning opportunity…to learn perhaps the broadest financial scam in the world.

CHAPTER FOUR

"RULES ARE ONLY FOR FOOLS"
(said the sales manager to me during a discussion about ethics)

"The Best Investment Since 1926? Apple"
According to Jeff Sommer, writing in the New York Times September 22, 2017, "...Apple has pulled ahead of Exxon Mobil, with total net wealth creation of somewhere in the vicinity of $1 trillion. Counting dividends."

The iPhone helped to catapult Apple into its position as the world's most valuable publicly traded company. But now Apple has another and, arguably, more exalted stock market distinction.

In the history of the markets since 1926, Apple has generated more profit for investors than any other American company.

Apple has generated more wealth for shareholders than any other of the top 50 companies, which account for 40 percent of stock market wealth.

https://www.nytimes.com/2017/09/22/business/apple-investment.html?smid=nytcore-ipad-share&smprod=nytcore-ipad

Alexander Scotland Clark began his career at the age of 18 in Scotland, United Kingdom, with Pye Records, arguably UK's second largest record company, competing with EMI (the record company for the "Fab 4" a.k.a The Beatles). Alex and his wife immigrated to Canada in 1966 with three children, ages 6 months, 1.5 years, and 2.5 years.

Fresh off the boat, the tough young lad from a Scottish coal town joined Capitol Records, the North American arm of his old competitor, EMI. In 1966 the Beatles released "Yesterday and Today", famously known as the "Butcher Cover" album on which were sadistically parodying limbs of a bleeding baby. Alex was given a carton of 25 albums, carefully wrapped, packaged, and sealed. At the age of 22, his job was to hit the road and promote the group throughout the four Maritime Provinces.

The album was subsequently withdrawn due to the distasteful cover content. His boss told him to collect them all, do not give them out, get rid of them, and don't bother incurring return shipping costs.

Today the Butcher Cover sells for $15,000 to $20,000.00 each. But that is not the real loss in this story.

The real loss comes when we fast forward about four decades and Alex steps into retirement. Along the way, he watched with a professional interest as a company called Apple created something called an iPod. On this gadget a person could store hundreds or even thousands of favorite songs.

By this time Alex was a multi-decade veteran of the record industry and sensed perhaps more than anyone what that would mean in sales for Apple. He took his record company pension plan and invested ALL of it in Apple shares. At the time (2004) they were worth something like $30.75 per share, and after a two-for-one stock split in February 2005, his original cost per Apple share was $15.38.

He went about life, enjoying and planning carefully every move of his retirement. He had given his best for more than four decades and he and his wife had earned a rest. He had worked with folks like Rod Stewart, Phil Collins, Neil Young, ABBA, ZZ Top, Cher, and many more. He has shown me photos of himself working with each of them, and emails of those he still keeps in touch with. Life was good.

Alex entered into serious retirement planning with people claiming to be investment advisors at TD Bank. TD gave Alex a plan to follow, including, among other things, financial advice which included how to avoid paying the maximum in taxes.

His TD plan included information on how, if a person gives up their Canadian citizenship, as a non-resident of Canada they could then withdraw money in their pension plan at a tax rate of 25%, as opposed to the 40% or more many wealthy Canadians pay.

Since Alex was from Scotland and had family there, he thought that he might be able to save a portion of his wealth, by returning, investing, and living there with family, which included his Mother, who was then 86 years old.

With a written guide from his TD 'advisors', he set out to do just that. By this time the value of Apple shares were closer to $44 each, and by 2014 they reached $651.26.

Again, life was good. He visited home and traveled Europe, confident his wealth was in good hands. He even started making plans and investments overseas in preparation for his new life.

Then, it all went awry…

Carefully following the advice of his TD experts Alex attempted to make his first withdrawal. He had followed TD Bank's advice every step of the way. What could go wrong?

The first thing that went wrong was that Alex's TD 'advisor' had mistakenly checked an incorrect box when setting up his locked-in retirement account, choosing the box indicating Alex's pension plan was "federally ruled" as opposed to "provincially ruled" under Pension Legislation. This changed everything. I had the same experience with my own pension, so I understood Alex when he described the experience.

At the precise moment that Alex needed his funds, TD Bank closed the door on his money due to a paperwork error.

Over the next couple of years Alex had to move back to Canada and was forced to sleep on the couches of helpful friends and relatives, while he tried over and over to obtain answers from TD. What had happened with his money? Why was it not available to him as instructed by TD?

It turns out (Alex had to learn all this himself) that the check-box (federal or provincial) that his non-licensed 'advisor' had arbitrarily selected upon opening the account, made enough of a difference that withdrawing cash out was either allowed by the rules, or not. TD had created his plan, moved Alex's pension into it, and TD had also made a tremendous paperwork error in executing the plan.

Now that this was clearly understood, it should have been simple to fix. TD only needed to "make the client whole," just as all banks used to do in response to a mistake…back in my father's day. (My fathers' day was pre-2000)

But these are no longer my father's times, and today's banks do not follow the courtesies of just two decades ago. Instead they clam up, lawyer up, and take down the little guy, rather than admit wrongdoing. It is simply easier to use client's money to beat them in court, than set a bad precedent by "making them whole".

So, in the fighting spirit of his heritage on the streets of Scotland, Alex was left with no other choice but to take TD to task.

Months progressed into years. After spending most of his available money on lawyers to no avail, Alex fired his legal team and finally got

TD to trial on his own. In the courtroom, after years of denial, TD finally admitted to making a "temporary administrative error" on the classification of his locked-in pension account.

Did TD then make the client whole? With the aid of a judge? Not a chance.

The banks of today have some of the most rapacious lawyers in the land on retainer. Thus, with clients' money in hand, they can easily afford to beat the client a second time, (or more) using the legal system which they know all too well.

Alex has spent the last best years of his life in pursuit of justice, and of what he rightfully earned over a lifetime of work. He has lost a kidney to cancer in the process and has still stayed on his feet in the ring with TD. Having suffered so badly at the hands of TD's mistake, he can no longer afford lawyers' bills, so he does his own legal work. I get the impression he is getting as badly abused by the courts as well, who often look down their noses at 'self-represented' litigants.

For Alex, legal spin games that would make the Tasmanian Devil ill, Latin jargon to keep the public in the dark, (like priests did in the Dark Ages) word games and apologetic tones toward those with the best lawyers, and blaming tones for those with no lawyer occur repeatedly. Mind you, he is not the easiest man to talk to, since his opinions are firm, and he does not tolerate being pushed around.

Even when the courts found that TD had made the error in filling out Alex's pension form, the judge went well out of his way to gloss over the mistake, brushing it aside as if it did not matter. He already had his chosen 'winner" and no amount of facts was going to get in the way...

The mistake was the root cause of everything that followed and prevented Alex from access to his retirement money when it was needed. It changed his life forever, ended his retirement lifestyle, and forced his wife to take work to help make ends meet. When I first met her, she was working in a dry cleaning store, taking in orders and doing sewing and mending. She carried herself like a true lady, despite being forced back to work in her 70's.

Alex contacted me after seeing some of my writing on investoradvocates.ca, and we had a conversation or two. He was fresh from being beaten and drummed out of a court which seemed unwelcoming to members of the public who don't have lawyers, and he was defeated. Momentarily.

As he described his story to me I asked him casually who his TD adviser had been. I typed the name into the broker search function at the Canadian Securities Administrators (CSA), now also found at http://aretheyregistered.ca, and after a few seconds asked, "Alex, what would you say if I told you your 'adviser' at TD is not now, nor ever was, licensed or registered in the category of adviser?"

His response, in Scottish brawler style, was to indicate this was totally wrong. (cognitive dissonance....<u>every</u> investor does it...to this day I have yet to meet ONE investor who is willing to initially believe that they have been so easily scammed...by the biggest banks in the land)

(Experiential blindness will not allow any person (none I have met to date) with a "trusted financial advisor", to see, when shown, that their advice giver holds no registered advisor or adviser registration...once shown, the pain of learning they have been duped (cognitive dissonance) causes them to then dismiss it rather than admit the having been conned) See also a great resource for those interested is New York Times best selling author Maria Konnikova's book, "The Confidence Game: Why We Fall for It...Every Time"

He <u>assured</u> me that he had checked everything at TD, and there was no doubt in his mind his adviser was an adviser. Knowing what I knew then, and realizing he had been deceived like most every investor in Canada, completely oblivious to the fraud, I simply repeated my question, a bit more slowly this time for emphasis: "Alex, please...What would you say to me... if I told you that your 'advisor' at TD... is not now...nor ever was, licensed or registered in the category of an adviser...?"

===========

The conversation ended without having convinced Alex what I had said was true. Indeed, no one in Canada in 2013 and 2014 would believe intentional deception and misrepresentation could be standard practice by the country's most trusted financial institutions? Alex was one of the smarter and better informed people in Canada, so he was not about to believe that he had been duped.

Mark Twain once said "it is easier to fool people than to convince them they have been fooled." This is so true when we do not wish to be thought of as having been duped. Most of us will do anything to not have to deal with that painful cognitive dissonance.

Alex called me up again, weeks after our conversation, having had some time to think. He asked me to tell him again what I had told him about his TD 'advisor' and to walk him through the search page on his computer. He sat in Okotoks, Alberta where he lives, and looked up the CSA registration search page as I told him where to look and what to search for. Search for "ARE THEY REGISTERED" or "CHECK FIRST" in Canada to find the registration. In the U.S. go to http://brokercheck.finra.org

We both clicked away, putting in the name of his broker. The results showed that his TD 'advisor' was licensed neither as an advisor, nor as an adviser (the actual term used in the law), but in the category of what is termed a "dealing representative." A "salesperson" is the way that category is further described by the Canadian Securities Administrators (CSA).

Sad to say, the CSA has since altered this search page (2016), making it much more difficult to find the true registration category of each so called "advisor," and making it nearly impossible for the public to find out what each category of license means. What the license means is the more important part, and this is the part they hide best from the public. Protection of the public is the regulators top mandate, but in truth (based on who pays them...) it should probably read "industry protection from the public". Update 2018, the CSA has "quietly" removed the "salesperson" description.

After Alex learned his TD Advisor was not even licensed in the category in which the bank promotes its people—and that in reality they are salespersons, not as fully qualified as promised or implied—he went back to his drawing board. Much discussion ensued, a meeting or two, and some extensive research. The result was that Alex filed what to my knowledge is the first ever legal suit alleging fraud against a major Canadian bank. I believe he has a case, as I know what the misrepresentation is, but I also know he is up against a legal system which could possibly be putting 'personalities before principles'. The legal system seems to already have chosen their preferred dance partner, in what might be the largest systemic public deception since the tobacco industry.

Good luck to Alex, his case is nearly the 'Rosa Parks' equivalent of the common man standing up against all odds, to try and obtain fairness. If we are to ever live in prosperity and peace, in a world where the strong are not allowed to abuse those who are weaker, we better get our acts together in areas of fairness, honesty and good faith. Alex Clark is fighting for the right not to be lied to, and then financially abused, and abused again for complaining about being abused. We should all be interested in the good fight when the battle he is fighting applies to nearly every retail investor in North America.

His statement of claim, filed in Calgary court, is linked here:

http://www.investoradvocates.ca/viewtopic.php?f=1&t=6&p=3848&hilit=clark&sid=a5b74fa6474fe94ac911aeeb91660ffe#p3848

Update 2017: Alex has now filed his case (by himself, without legal help) in the Supreme Court of Canada. It is the hero's battle that he fights. The journey that could make life easier for millions of Canadians and Americans when a man like this takes a stand.

He is still trying to hold TD to task for posing it's bank dealing representatives as trusted financial advisors, and hiding their true registration/duty of care from TD investors. I wish him all the luck in the world, he is going to need it. What he is going up against is equivalent to fighting the Catholic Church....in the 16th Century.

Update May 1, 2017:

Bounced from Supreme Court in May, back to Alberta Court, then likely back to Supreme Court, in what might be the extreme endurance test to eliminate 99.999% of the public access to justice?

Alex is the epitome of the little guy doing battle, solo, against one of the largest corporations in the land. He also has to do it through the most inconvenient process of justice imaginable, for the little guy.

He has persevered through lack of money, through loss of a kidney, through cancer which he battles, and he keeps going.

TD has given him the ultimate gift, which is the "achilles heel" of giant corporations everywhere…they simply left him with NO other options. The bully tactics of giants is so similar in all cases that I have seen, that they see no need to even **consider** other options, besides complete legal annihilation of any investment victims who complain.

Mr. Clark is thus left to consider privately filed criminal charges (laying an information before the court), which any citizen has right to do, if his efforts within the civil justice system amount to nothing. He is "all in", fully invested in a fight which is a grave mistake for a giant corporation to make. Who would be foolish enough to risk the reputation of a billion dollar corporation, one built upon no 'products' other than mere trust, against something as inconsequential as a man holding the truth…

Once again, the search page to see how your broker is legally registered is found here:
www.aretheyregistered.ca
and in the USA see BrokerCheck. If they have two different registrations, remember that they often can lure you with the professional (SEC) "Adviser" pitch, and then deal your cards using their (salesperson) "broker" hat. How will you know?

To make things more difficult for consumers to understand, the meaning of each registration category at the CSA is kept out of easy-sight here: http://www.securities-administrators.ca/uploadedFiles/General/pdfs/UnderstandingRegistration_EN.pdf

The 1/4 billion in salaries paid to just four (out of 13) Canadian Securities commissions encourages them to be 'team players', and let the public remain under the impression that their advisor is registered, while keeping hidden from view the category of their registration…and the important meaning of that category.

===========

To find the meaning of each Canadian Securities Administrators (CSA) registration category, a Canadian investor generally only need look at two categories on the above page:

1. **Dealing Representative** means they represent the "Dealer," not the customer, and are considered by the CSA to be a salesperson. (this is equivalent to a 'broker' in the U.S.) In Canada a person can go from cutting hair in a salon, to being this faked investment "advisor" in as little as 30 days.

   (update 2018, I now find that all securities commissions in Canada have further ethically cleansed" their definitions of what a dealing rep is by removing the clarifying term of "salesperson" that previously was added to the "dealing representative" category)

2. **Advising Representative** means they have a higher level duty of care to protect the client; a level of professional duty akin to what a doctor must provide. A sole loyalty. Advising representatives are purist money managers, and that role—vastly different from the role of a salesperson—can be better understood here: www.portfoliomanagement.org (this the equivalent to an SEC registered Fiduciary 'Adviser' in the U.S.). This role takes years and years to achieve.

As mentioned previously, the "Dealing representative license or registration category was formerly called "Salesperson" in the rules and regs, until September 2009, when this license category was phased out…for clarity…

The difference between having a 'counter-party' (salesperson who can extract your wealth) and a 'fiduciary' (the adviser who must only work to enhance your wealth) is sufficient to cut your retirement easily by half, or more. In this short video, retired TD CEO Ed Clark lets it slip how they can often act as counter-party to their clients. If only they told clients that part, instead of hiding it behind their banks…er…..backs.

In the YouTube video linked below, Ex TD CEO Ed Clark, is being interviewed by AMERICAN BANKER MAGAZINE and is asked by the interviewer how we found ourselves in a 'culture of greed'. Mr Clark answers, "you must realize, that if you start a business model that says our clients are not really our clients, they are counter-parties that we can make money off of, then you should not be surprised if this creates a culture of greed…."

https://youtu.be/23xWWsGp6vU   At 1 min 20 sec mark of a 4 minute video titled "Retired TD Banker compared to Tony Robbins".

In the financial industry I slowly learned that there are only two rules that matter to management. Rule one is to never embarrass the firm, and rule two is to increase revenue. No written rules rank above these two, despite thousands of rules purporting to. Like any three dimensional game in life, the unwritten rules are often of far greater sanctity than those written down.

Who knew we could become a society where secret standards apply to investment dealers. It can become a game of "Winner Steal All," for those who follow their own set of rules or principles. It is my view of how some professionals use the system to enrich themselves while profiting at the expense of their clients.
WINNER STEAL ALL, Professional Investment Misconduct YouTube
https://youtu.be/EyAuod1QxhQ

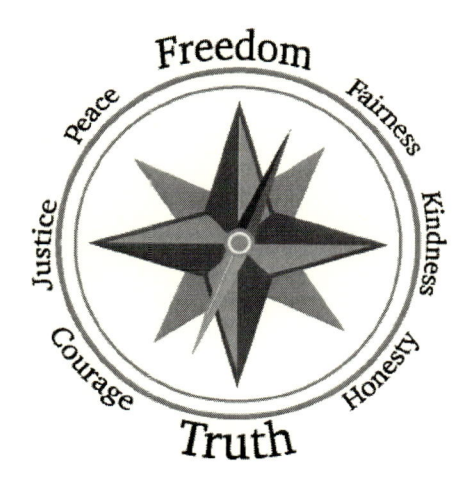

CHAPTER FIVE

FOUR OUT OF FIVE ADVISORS RECOMMEND...

...the product which produces the most benefit to themselves.
(which also happens to be the product which does most financial harm to the investor)

Suitability investment standard means "Good enough to foist upon an unsuspecting public" (the quality standard of the Dollar store product)

Fiduciary investment standard means "Only the best...for the client"   (the standard of some of the world's top products)

==========

I will never forget the raucous laughter that filled the RBC boardroom the day the sales manager told us about what one of the other salespersons had just done. A couple wanted to park their money for a short period of time, months only, to be used for a home purchase. This salesperson had placed the couple into a money market fund, paying something like 2.5%, which in itself was not a bad choice at the time.

However, he had placed them in the DSC (deferred sales charge 'option') version of the fund when he should have put them into one of several other less costly, even free choices.

It would have been best for his client to hold money for a few months at zero commission, since they would be earning practically nothing. It was just a safe parking spot for a short term.

But of course every salesperson was under daily pressure to "achieve or leave", by management, so he took a 5% commission for himself on the client's investment, and attached a back-end exit fee of 7% when they sold it. He was so desperate to make his commission requirements that he did not care, and this is what the laughter was about. The clients had no idea what he had done to them, and would not learn of their loss until months later.

Giving the client a 7% fund redemption penalty on a cash parking spot that might earn them 0.6% or less over a few months, was something to laugh about…for that manager, and the sales staff of the office.

The office was making fun of his desperation, like one might poke fun at the guy who drank too much and knocked over the office Christmas tree. Nobody seemed the least concerned for the client, who faced a 7% redemption cost on a money market fund.

The office manager's bonus depended upon those commissions, so his laughter was his only management action taken. That is how brokerage management supervision works in a sales game. By making sure each manager is paid based upon branch profitability the bank gets exactly the kind of sales behavior they seek. Fast forward to CBC Go Public stories March 29, 2017, where 3000 bank employees in Canada have stepped forward to state that many of them are being made ill, by the pressure from management to do financial harm to clients. Such is the mental double bind of "do what we say....or else."

YouTube video 3 min, CBC National News, with Peter Mansbridge March 29th, 2017.   Titled "Copy of CBC NATIONAL NEWS. FINANCIAL SALES TITLE TRICKERY MAR 29 2017 https://youtu.be/UAYHrCOgTLU   Or just Google "Larry Elford CBC"

TWO BROTHERS

Two former clients came to see me in 2012. They brought their mother's investment accounts and wanted my thoughts on them. What I saw was so bad I talked about it on my speaking bit for a book launch. The book was Thieves of Bay Street. I was honored to be included (not as a thief, thankfully, perhaps as a fool:). When it was my turn to speak at the Calgary book launch event, I wanted to illustrate what the 'Thieves of Bay Street' would do to your money, if you trust them with your money.

Here is the summary. I opened the investment statements and on page one I saw the first deceit. In bold letters it stated who the investment "advisor" was. Off to a bad start.

The second page revealed that this was a "fee based" account—wherein the firm collects money whether you do a transaction or not. It is a gift to brokers and investment dealers if they can place you into such an account, since they now effectively have a lifetime annuity from your money. It is like putting your investment holdings into a monthly fee plan—just to hold your holdings…get it? Strike two for the customer's interests…

The third page then brought up the actual investments this "advisor" had placed in the account. The funny thing is that every investment was in mutual funds. The sad thing is every mutual fund **also** charged its own annual fee to operate. Strike three, and the client is probably 'out' at this point. Out of luck for earning much of a return. Such is the result of a "suitability" loophole that 9 of 10 investment sellers utilize, more on that later.

The "advisor" had so far done nothing to manage the client's money, except to place it into an expensive type of account, with expensive products which generated the most fees for her and her dealer. Of course the "advisors" were not advisors, (not even advisers:) but 'client relationship managers'. Salespersons.

Today investment dealers are on a very hard push to place client assets in "fee based" programs. These fee based accounts are brilliant methods for investment dealers to replace commission-based accounts. With fee accounts they can make money from <u>every client</u>, on <u>every dollar</u> you have, <u>every day</u> of the year. Party on!

Further, when I examined the mutual funds in this bank customer's account, I found that each fund sold to them was a proprietary fund, or the house brand product. (Remember they can earn an extra twelve to twenty six times more money when they sell you the house-product)

https://docs.google.com/document/d/1Q5SXN3x88T9Qx45Jfe8wRi-4dESV4JtONJpm33csn7Y/edit

So the bank customer was now down by four sales tricks, and the firm was ahead by four. Dare we look any closer?

One more peek into the major investment holdings of the house-brand funds in this account showed that in some cases the majority of investments in the fund were investments in…you guessed it…another mutual fund.

Yes, another manager, another fee, upon a fee, upon a fee… You get the picture. Five potential opportunities to serve the salesperson and the dealer, at the expense of the trusting clients.

I stopped looking at this point and closed the file. Sadly, these types of practices are not unusual, they are in the unwritten advisor rule book on how to be richer at client expense.

These practices are indicative of bad apples, but of a bad industry barrel, as Stan Buell tells it. Stan is an engineer by trade, and was swindled out of his investment savings when he went to work overseas, leaving his bank "advisor" to manage his account.

This was long before Stan understood the investment industry. He has since established the Small Investor Protection Association of Canada (www.sipa.ca) and worked tirelessly for over two decades to raise awareness of systemic industry abuses. He is one of the gentlemen I look up to, and I stand upon his shoulders in efforts I make.

===========

And in the U.S.A.:

"…'Currently, broker-dealers who advise individuals must ensure only that investments are suitable for their clients. That means they can recommend "the least suitable of suitable investments" and still comply,' says Barbara Roper, director of investor protection for the Consumer Federation of America, an advocacy group…"
She is absolutely correct.

===========

In addition to the higher annual overhead costs mentioned in the University of Toronto, Rotman study (coming up in next Chapter), there are a few other tricks that need to be mentioned if you are to protect yourself from abuse.

One is the industry trend started in 1987, of something called deferred sales charges (DSC). These have been almost completely phased out at major investment firms today, but they can still be found among independent and smaller firms as a method to harvest clients for semi-hidden commissions.

These were invented by the Industrial Horizon funds as a means whereby salespeople could be paid a full 5% commission taking it out of a specially funded commission pool, not out of the client's money initially.

The special pool that paid 5% commissions was a savings pool that would be reimbursed by charging the clients up to 7% redemption charges if they were to redeem their funds within a certain time period. The pool was also supplemented by higher management fees applied on those funds sold with the DSC option.

The client was thus hit with a double negative, designed so that the broker/dealer earns 5% at the time of sale, without having to take it out of the customer's account, or often even informing the customer they were putting them at such a disadvantage. The deferred sales charge was an industry invention to 'mask' or 'hide' the up front commissions paid to the sales agent, so that many clients were led into it blindly. "Trust me, I am your advisor…"

I was in the offices, boardrooms, lunchrooms and sales meetings for 20 years. I witnessed most brokers obtaining a hidden deferred sales charge commission by not informing the client about the redemption penalty at all.

Some company sales forces used the deferred sales charge option on more than 90% of the funds sold. The other sales "advisors" usually had to go with the most expensive for the client, to gain the most commission for their managers… or else.

This had the effect of earning $70 million in deferred sales charge, commissions for RBC and its salespeople. RBC made, and still makes, the promise that the interests of their clients always come first. The words did not always match the deeds.

I tell anyone who asks, that if they see the letters DSC behind a mutual fund purchase it is a top indicator that they have a salesperson, not a professional 'advice giver." It is literally taking advantage of the vulnerability of the client, in order to increase the commission for the salesperson. When I was at RBC their top holdings data showed that fully 71% of mutual funds held by their clients for the entire country were sold using the DSC sales commission option.

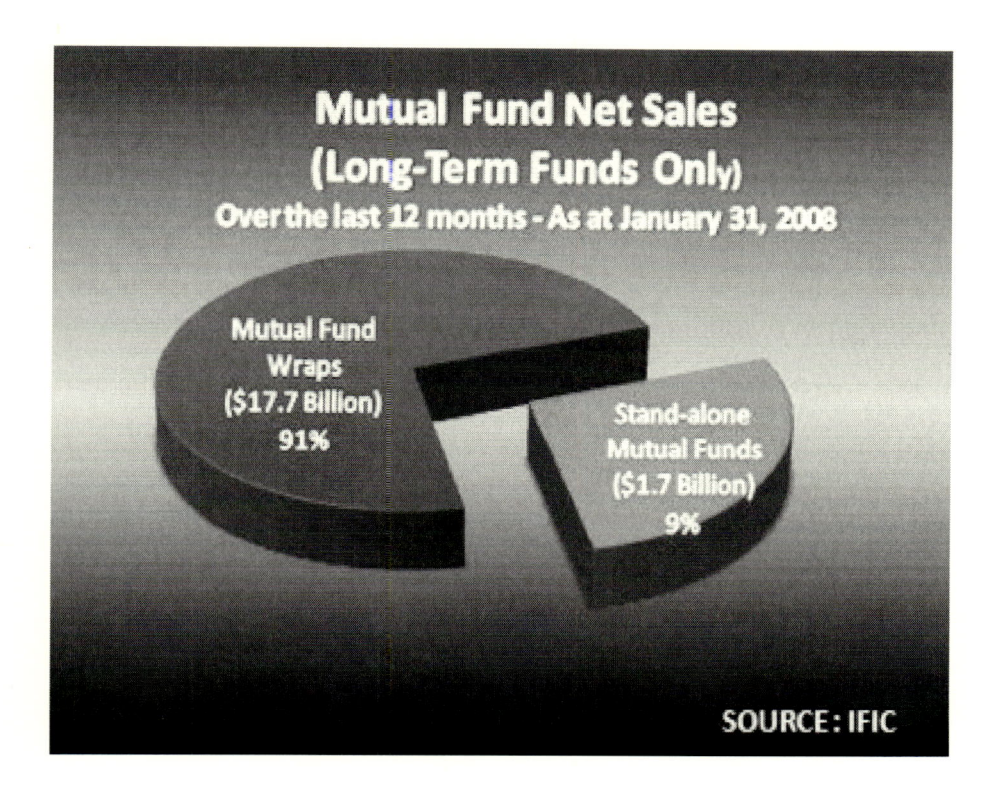

**Mutual Fund Net Sales
(Long-Term Funds Only)
Over the last 12 months - As at January 31, 2008**

- Mutual Fund Wraps ($17.7 Billion) 91%
- Stand-alone Mutual Funds ($1.7 Billion) 9%

SOURCE: IFIC

This indicates the opposite of the fair, honest and good faith requirements of the industry. Don't take my word for it, Google "Death of the Deferred Sales Charge", and see what the real world is saying.

The next trick was to then sell clients house-brand or proprietary funds. In fact, a fast talking 'vice president' salesperson might drag their clients back and forth between many such self dealing investments, one after the other, over a period of time, earning fees, upon, fees, upon commissions, upon hidden commissions.

As recently as the last ten years, up to 90% of the mutual funds sold have been in something called 'wrap accounts.' Most wrap accounts consist of mutual funds that consist of other mutual funds, or house-brand funds manufactured by the seller and marketed as their proprietary brand.

House-brand mutual funds could be thought of a bit like the house-brand cola-drink sold at a grocery or a drugstore chain. The house brand might be expected to be a bit cheaper, and also of lesser quality than the major brand cola. The difference is that companies have used the position-of-trust earned with their clients to market their house brand products at even higher premiums than the world's best performing, longest running mutual funds.

It is simply a matter of being able to position (or market) your commission sales force, in a way that causes the public to mistakenly assume that they are dealing with professional fiduciary-duty money managers…even when they are not.

Summary of sales tricks so far:
1. Double dipping, a form of extra-billing (adding "advisory" fees on top of commissions already paid).
2. Fees layered on top of other fees. See presentation at http://youtu.be/diEjitz-4So to view several ways an 'advisor' can cut a customer's retirement by half or more in an attempt to increase their own revenues.
3. Selling the highest-compensating choice of investment product. (Deferred sales charge funds just one example)
4. Selling the highest profit margin product. (According to the Investment Funds Institute of Canada, over 90% of mutual funds sold in 2007 were WRAP funds.)
5. WRAP funds include "funds made up of other funds" (and fees on top of other fees) as well as proprietary funds (house-brand funds) which increase profit margins to the seller up to 26 times (according to the OSC Fair Dealing Model Appendix F, page 10, titled "Compensation Bias's").
6. Fee based accounts add 2% and cut clients long term future in half.
7. Fee based accounts sold by non-fiduciaries are often choc-filled with investment products which also contain…their own fees.
8. The only fee based arrangement any professional investor should accept is one with a fiduciary…a legal fiduciary, not a 'self'-titled fiduciary. This fee should be approximately 1%, all in.

===========

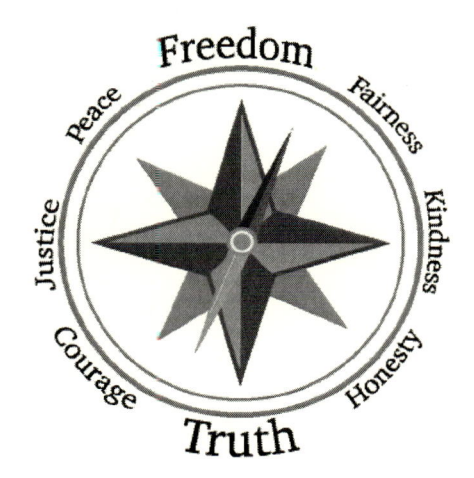

CHAPTER SIX

$25 BILLION MUTUAL FUND HAIRCUT

I have a brother who spent a lifetime in aviation, from beginning as a student pilot to work in the remote northern Canadian Bush. He ended up flying the worlds' richest families in the Middle East.

I asked him about using the analogy of "uncontrolled airspace", to describe how there seem to be little or no rules at the upper "elevations" in financial circles. He agreed with my understanding of the concept.

He recalled flights through the dark frozen North of Canada's arctic, where at some point the radio would crackle to life and an air traffic controller would inform him "Sierra X-Ray Tango, cleared out of control".

This story came to him immediately like it happened yesterday and he laughed at the terminology, "cleared out of control" is aviation short-speak for "you are now no longer in our control zone and are in uncontrolled airspace"…"good luck"… "you are on your own".

We talked (he is also an informed investment observer) about how the financial industry seemed also to have uncharted 'territories' and high elevations where truly there are no rules. It is as if "anything goes" in those zones.

These upper elevations, where regulators, police or other authorities dare not venture are the easiest place for investment players to create schemes that are off the radar.

He then pointed out that history is full of examples where explorers have ventured into un-mapped, uncharted, and unexplored territory, and in those examples, the lawful limits of what those explorers could do were nonexistent.

So it seems with billionaire financial players. "Cleared out of control…"

The crashes that often come from such activities can affect entire societies, and yet still cannot even be investigated…who is there to investigate what happens in a zone of unexplored lawlessness?

"Cleared out of control"

No rules. Anything goes…for Wall Street, as for pirates and explorers way back when-ago.

===========

Indeed, the $7 trillion U.S. mutual fund industry has become "the world's largest skimming operation," said Senator Peter G. Fitzgerald

(R-Ill.), chairman of the Senate Subcommittee quoted in RR Magazine on Financial Management in the 1990's. Two to three decades later it still works.

===========

Keith Ambachtsheer, University of Toronto Rotman School of Management, is a world-class expert who studies pensions. One of his publications is titled "The $25 Billion Haircut." It looks at the amount of over-charging and resulting underperformance of retail investors when compared to institutional investors in Canada. i.e. Just how much do retail investors get skimmed or gouged as compared to institutional investors? Even when they group together into institutional-sized pools of mutual funds, they are still harvested like a retail investor.

Institutional investors and large pension funds are usually investing at a wholesale cost level as little as 25 or 50 basis points (0.25% to 0.50% annual fees) to manage money professionally, whereas the average retail investor in Canada is lured into a retail sales-process where management fees can run in the 2 1/2% range, depending on the product, in addition to commissions of up to 5%. By professional standards, this is called 'harvesting', or 'farming' the client for fees.

The result, according to Ambachtsheer, is that $25 billion each year is cut from retail investors—ranging from the average mom-and-pop, to dentists and nearly everyone else's retirement account. ($25 Billion was HALF the government measured cost of all crime in the land)

That was back in 2007. Today it could approach double this amount, which would put the skim on par with the cost of each and every measured crime in the land combined. From one financial product sold badly.

I have to appreciate the professional manner in which Keith Ambachtsheer arrived at the $25 billion haircut number. I am nowhere near as thorough a researcher as Mr. Ambachtsheer, but his numbers coincide almost perfectly with what I have witnessed from my years in the financial selling industry, although I calculated mine from an entirely different perspective and data points.

The 3.8% skim that this study shows, if compounded over a 35-year horizon, would cause an average Canadian retail investor to retire with just 30%, or <u>less than a third</u>, of the amount they could retire with had they not been financially abused or farmed by the advice industry.

Next to buying a house, what is the average Canadian household's largest single lifetime expense?

Three guesses.

- Food
- Raising a child to age 18
- Investment Fees

Here's a hint.
The actual dollar amount is...
$323,654

And the winner is: **Investment Fees.**

Shocked? It's true. According to Nest Wealth, typical fees paid over an investor's lifetime are $323,654. That's $80,000 more than the cost of raising a child to age 18.*

It gets worse. According to Morningstar, Canada ranks last out of 25 countries when it comes to investment fees and expenses. Canadians pay twice as much – or more – compared to U.S. investors.**

CARP is leading the fight against outrageous investment costs.

Learn More at: carp.ca/StopFeeGouging

* NestWealth.com/InvestmentFees
** Morningstar Global Fund Investor Experience Report (2015)

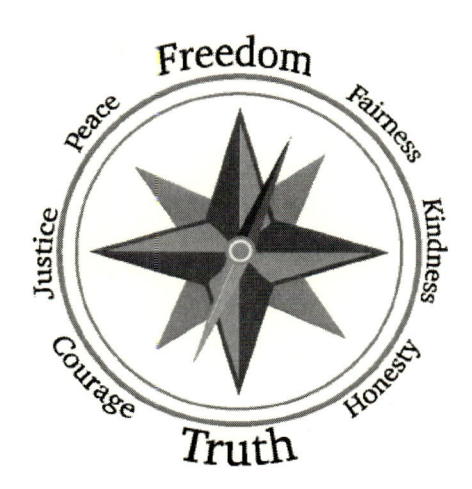

CHAPTER SEVEN

THREE KINDS OF "ADVICE GIVER"

1. The kind where your "advice giver" is invested in your success, as fundamental to her own. You both win.

2. The middle kind where your "advice giver" is going to use his knowledge to skim, or to unjustly profit from your lack of knowledge. This is like getting a bad financial haircut.

3. The kind where the "advice giver" is looking for a sucker and you are the sucker. You could get completely scalped.

Do you know which kind your "advice giver" (broker, advisor, adviser, wealth manager, planner, etc., etc) is? There are very specific legal registration categories involved. Which category is your advice giver in?

82

How do you <u>know</u> this for a legal certainty?

SO WHAT IS A LICENSED ADVIS<u>ER</u>? (vs an advis<u>or</u>)

"Although the terms sound similar, investment advis<u>ers</u> are not the same as financial advis<u>ors</u> and should not be confused. The term financial advis<u>or</u> is a generic term that usually refers to a broker (or, to use the technical term, a registered representative). By contrast, the term investment advi<u>ser</u> is a legal term that refers to an individual or company that is registered as such with either the Securities and Exchange Commission or a state securities regulator. "

Investment Advisers

Although most people would use an "o," we purposely spell adviser with an "e" when we talk about investment advisers. That's because the laws that govern this type of investment professional spell the title this way.

Many investment advisers are also brokers—but these two types of investment professional aren't the same. So as you choose among different professionals, here's what you need to know about **investment advisers**.

> **What they are:** An investment adviser is an individual or company who is paid for providing advice about securities to their clients. Although the terms sound similar, investment advisers are not the same as financial advisors and should not be confused. The term financial advisor is a generic term that usually refers to a broker (or, to use the technical term, a registered representative). By contrast, the term investment adviser is a legal term that refers to an individual or company that is registered as such with either the Securities and Exchange Commission or a state securities regulator. Common names for investment advisers include asset managers, investment counselors, investment managers, portfolio managers, and wealth managers. Investment adviser representatives are individuals who work for and give advice on behalf of registered investment advisers.

"The industry 'vowel movement' allows a self-professed financial 'advi<u>sor</u>' to say, with a straight face, that financial advis<u>ers</u> are obligated by law to have their clients' best interest at heart, and at the same time sell products (as an 'advi<u>sor</u>') that line their own pockets at the expense of the client."

Dr. Jin Choi <u>https://www.moneygeek.ca/weblog/2014/06/05/your-financial-advisor-deceiving-you/</u>

The above is the #1 investment industry "shell game".

==========

The following are public comments made by a then eighty-three year old abused investor, denied justice by <u>all</u> regulators, speaking to an Ontario Legislative Committee: Aug 19, 2004

My name is Ernest Wotton. I am a lighting designer. I am a Fellow of four professional organizations. I have practiced in Canada, the USA and the UK. I have taught lighting design at leading schools of architecture in Canada and the USA. I am 83.

In July 1999 I wrote to the Hon. Dalton McGuinty, then leader of the Opposition saying, "Not so long ago when you retired you received your 50-year pin and a pension. Today you receive neither. Nobody expects to spend a working life with the same employer.

Instead, one changes frequently.

These frequent changes mean that you have to make your own arrangements for a pension. Like most people, you know little about financial matters. You put the money you have set aside for a pension into the hands of a Financial Advisor.

Suppose that your Financial Advisor does not invest in line with your instructions and you lose money. You may spend months in fruitless discussion with the advisor in an effort to obtain reimbursement.

My letter to Mr. McGuinty, written over five years ago, did not end there. I will return to it in my story. It begins when, in February 1995, my wife and I took a bundle of solid securities and cash to a Financial Advisor employed by a leading investment firm. We asked him to manage an account for us.

I know nothing about managing money, but I can read a graph. The mid-1990s were a boom time for investors, yet a downward slope appeared in the graph of our portfolio. Every monthly statement from the investment firm directed its clients to make contact with their Financial Advisor if they had any questions. Accordingly I wrote to our advisor that the downward trend in the value of our portfolio was a "cause for concern." He stated that our portfolio was healthy. He also confirmed specifically that a particular security I named was healthy.

Then three things happened. Our advisor left the firm. The particular security became junk. The investment firm wrote that as we had written to our Financial Advisor and not to a Manager, it "had no responsibility for our Financial Advisor's statement that the portfolio was healthy."

I will not try even to outline my efforts to obtain compensation. My correspondence occupies two binders, each 3.5 inches thick. Some of the replies from the investment firm were marked "sub judice." I got no reply when I asked what this implied.

I drew to the attention of the president that his firm's newsletter referred to "the superb returns enjoyed over the past few years" and asked why I had not shared in that bounty. The president wrote that "we remain committed to serving you with the best possible advice (and to) building strong relationships with our clients." But he omitted to send a check.

Meanwhile I scouted for other ways to obtain restitution. I have mentioned my letter to Mr. McGuinty. He referred me to the Ontario Securities Commission. As did the Ministry of Finance. The OSC referred me to the Investment Dealers Association. From the time I wrote to the OSC in line with the advice from Queen's Park until the IDA hearing into what it referred to as "the matter" three years and seven months had elapsed.

I learned that a number of other investors had also complained against our Financial Advisor.

At this point in my story my wife and I had been unable to get compensation for the enormous loss in our investment. And we were unable to take part in the arbitration process set up by IDA, since our complaint fell outside its terms of reference.

But the Ontario Ombudsman told me of the Ombudsman for Banking Services and Investors (OBSI). Richard Bright of OBSI interviewed me and my wife and subsequently submitted his report to an arbitrator. We were awarded about 60% of our loss. Mr. Bright's report identified a number of examples of investments obviously made without due diligence. Yet they had eluded the investment firm.

May I now summarize my conclusions arising from this sad recital of facts:
1. *An investment firm will not conduct a rigorous investigation into a complaint against its staff.*
2. *An investment firm will use its enormous clout - including the use of legal terms in everyday correspondence - to wear down an investor, particularly the vulnerable.*
3. *The Provincial Government has delegated to OSC its authority to "protect investors from unfair or improper practices" without ensuring that this authority is being exercised.*
4. *OSC has delegated to IDA its authority to investigate complaints against Financial Advisors without ensuring that those investigations are swiftly and competently carried out.*
5. *Neither OSC nor IDA has assumed responsibility for ensuring that investors are compensated for their losses from investments carried out without due diligence. Instead both OSC and IDA recommend that the investor take legal advice. OSC has stated that the average fee for legal advice is $37,500. This is far beyond anything that many investors, particularly elderly pensioners, can afford.*
6. *The March 2, 2003 review of the Securities Act of Ontario does not address the above issues.*

7. *No investor, particularly the vulnerable, should have to go through the trouble and worry I had to go through, and that extended over eight years, in order to obtain relief.*

In April 2002 OSC mounted an "Investor Education Conference." About 100 delegates took part representing 40 user groups. They broke into spontaneous applause only once - when a journalist member of a discussion panel stated that:

The system is very wrong when one has to go to court for restitution. There must be another way. Companies must hold their employees accountable. Clients come first.

Ernest Wotton, Toronto, Ontario

Statement read to committee reviewing The Securities Act, Main Legislative Building, Queen's Park, Toronto, Ontario

Nothing has changed in almost 15 years since. The regulators are looking more like a protection racket for financial abusers.

===========

Mr. Wotton was "farmed" by a false advisor. The farming began for Mr. Wotton in 1995, and continues for most investors to this day, 2018. It continues as the perfect organized financial crime, harvesting the retirement security of much of the North American continent.

When you engage the services of a licensed fiduciary investment adviser, (spelled "er" under law) you are getting:
    a) someone who is <u>not</u> acting in a commission sales capacity
    b) someone who will give you <u>in writing</u>, a fiduciary duty to protect and serve your interests
    c) someone who is licensed and trained in the role of money management and <u>not</u> 'selling' which is 'client management'
    d) someone who has no dealer marketing-incentives to harm your interests
    e) the ability to have true professional advice, at a cost usually closer to institutional or wholesale pricing (1% or lower)

A fiduciary has duties to his client. They include:
- Not to place oneself in a position of conflict of duties relating to the principal and the fiduciary's interests;
- Not to make a profit out of the principal's trust;
- Not act for one's own benefit or the benefit of third parties, without the consent of the principal.

Professional portfolio managers will get you away from commission middlemen who are themselves driven by hungry investment dealers. Many will manage your account for less than 1% to 1.5%. Sales commissions and fees are only limited by personal ethics, and for many that means anything they and the dealer can get away with.

===========

Further reading on the top c of "BROKERS AS FIDUCIARIES" can be found at the following link.   Reference University of Pittsburgh Law Review,

http://lawreview.law.pitt.edu/ojs/index.php/lawreview/article/download/142/142

Link to FINRA image shown on page 112 of this chapter
http://www.finra.org/investors/investment-advisers

A good site to find/learn about Fiduciary Investment managers in Canada.
http://www.portfoliomanagement.org/index.php

===========

WARNING! Recently, investment salespersons have begun to market themselves using the title of "portfolio manager" often while still holding the 'salesperson' or 'broker' registration. Through the use of loopholes and self-regulation, some are doing this even while being legally registered as 'dealing representatives'. Dealing representative is the category for commission sales persons in

Canada...even those who claim to be putting you into a fee-based account. <u>Especially</u> those putting you into a fee-based account...

In addition, I have spotted a few 'exemptions' to laws for investment dealers who wish to portray their commission sales persons as if they were portfolio managers. Consumers would be wise to specify two important things, in writing, to their investment service provider:

One protective solution is to specify that the dealer/broker provide a copy of their government approved license and registration category, and <u>NOT the title</u> which they use for marketing upon sales purposes. This offer (to provide this info if the client requests it in writing) was seen in client documents recently for a major Canadian bank. You would think that they would divulge this info without forcing clients to request it...and you would be correct. It is in the law...but the law is not followed.

Inform them (again, in writing) that you are <u>relying</u> upon them for fair, honest and professional investment advice that is <u>entirely in your interest</u> and in the interests of none other.

In other-words, inform them on no uncertain terms that you expect that your financial relationship with any "advice giver" is one of a fiduciary level of care, as it is understood in law. You expect this regardless of marketing jargon or 'name games' that might be practiced by the industry. Ask them to confirm this to you in writing, and to reply if they cannot confirm this standard of care to you in writing.

My money says that the majority of broker/dealers will not be able to offer you anything like this level of service, but at least you will know where you stand.

You will\then have no question whatsoever of the nature of the relationship if there should ever arise a concern or a dispute.

Thanks to Ken Kivenko of http://www.canadianfundwatch.com for his ongoing efforts to improve fairness for investment consumers and for prompting this little story

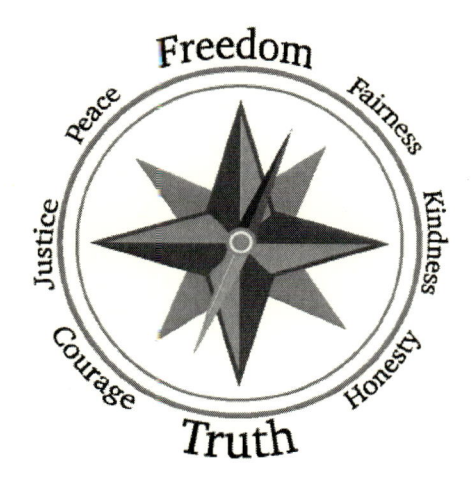

CHAPTER EIGHT

KYC AN INVESTOR SETUP?

How the "Know Your Client" document can trip the investor.

It took me until 2014 (I took my first securities industry course in 1980) to figure out this investor-trap. It (the trap) is that the confidential information you share with your newly hired investment "advisor" will likely be tainted from day one, and then subsequently used against you, if you ever figure out you have been financially violated.

Some years after you learn of the financial violation, this account opening trap will then be sprung, and Viola! Your hopes for justice will be gone. Investment dealers are decades ahead of their customers at the game, and many steps ahead at 'papering' things in their favor.

Dealers and their sales staff essentially know 'everything', and the average trusting client, by comparison knows nothing about investing. Otherwise customers would not be trusting them to advise them about their life savings. This is why a 'fiduciary' duty advice giver is essential. If you settle for any lower standard, then the dealer has a myriad of ways to abuse your interests for their greater gain.

KNOW YOUR CUSTOMER/CLIENT FORM   (KYC)

The Know Your Client/Customer (KYC) is called the 'holy grail' of documents, referred to as such by experts in court, and used extensively by the investment industry to defend and deflect consumer complaints against investment dealers.
<http://www.mfda.ca/regulation/bulletins14/Bulletin0611-C.pdf>

I have filled it out as a salesperson, and although it took me years to witness the flip side, I have also seen how cleverly it can be used against investors.

KYC completions are usually done by persons who truthfully are salespersons, (licensed as dealing representatives in Canada and – most commonly - brokers in the US). But at the moment of KYC completion, at the very beginning of a newly formed trust relationship, <u>the bank, dealer and salesperson have usually succeeded in misrepresenting themselves to the unsuspecting customer as licensed "professional" advice givers.</u> This is step one, in a well-planned deception.

This practice is designed to eliminate the caution that customers have for people who call themselves by any word which might imply 'salesperson'. Regulators collect billions to ignore this deception, making them essential handmaids to the deception.

Thus both parties (customer and salesperson) have a different understanding of the relationship from the outset. The only difference is the salesperson/advisor is aware of the misrepresentation and the customer is not. The investment dealer is always aware of the intentional deception. The regulators are paid (or picked) by investment dealers so…you know how it goes.

This usually leads to the customer following the advice of a salesperson the same way you or I would follow the advice of a doctor or other person whom we were led to believe was a professional. Asking a salesperson for financial advice is as wise as asking Burger King for culinary advice.

Once fooled, the customer can be 'coached' or 'guided' by the salesperson, and the KYC completed in the manner most beneficial to the dealer and salesperson. It also occurs to me that even the choice of which multiple choice answers are allowed on things such as risk, and experience, etc, may be designed to box the client's answers into easily defensible areas, dependent upon the ultimate product-selling designs of the firm.

If that were not true, the questions asked of clients would be about things that truly matter, like aspects of a fiduciary (or a sales) relationship, obligations of trust, agency duty etc. Courts use five or more 'elements' to determine if an agent is in a fiduciary relationship, and the non-fiduciary (sales) dealer will usually 'imply' these elements to a client, but will <u>never</u> put them in writing…without a vowel movement here and there.

Imagine signing a risk-disclosure form or consent form, for a medical procedure, and learning later that the person who guided you in the process was not (as was assured) a licensed doctor?

What if they had merely pushed you towards the most expensive or riskiest procedure for their own benefit? In the medical/dental professional this is treated as a criminal act, yet it is a daily standard practice with many non-fiduciary investment sellers.

Fast forward many years and I see a 90-year-old man, Harold Blanes of Kelowna in a court room, being bullied by investment firm lawyers.

The 90-year-old investment victim knows he has been taken advantage of, yet not how the "trick" worked. When abusers are so 'reputable' and polished, victims can take years, some decades, to understand what happened. Most never figure it out.

Compounding the problem is that at the upper 'elevations' of the legal industry, it seems as if the justice system can be bent to resemble a power system, or a 'status' system, perhaps more than a system of justice. Acts and actors get very strange, the further you fly above the hundred million dollar financial alititude.

What is evident, is that the 90-year-old victim is being abused a third time. First was the misrepresentation and abuse of his trust, second was abuse of his money, and third is the use of cunning lawyers to outwit the client out of justice. Each victim learns this the hard way, while banks and investment firms learned the slippery ways decades ago.

In too many cases the KYC is the fruit of a poisoned tree. It is another intentional deception cleverly perpetrated by a bad industry barrel. It is still relied upon in much of the financial industry's legal performances, despite it most often being completed under false pretenses.

Or as my friend Derek said to me while discussing this book, "the KYC form is like the legal waiver that everyone has to sign before bungee jumping". He went on to explain that it was designed more to protect the service provider than it was to assist the investor.

Unless one has stood in the same shoes I have, and seen the setup, the inside story, and the "gotcha" ending in a courtroom years later, one would never know how cleverly staged the KYC process actually is.

Anything you say to an advisor (even one who is faking it and not registered as such), can and will be used against you in a court of law by the dealer. The KYC is partially a salesperson-coached set-up. This salesperson set up has <u>never</u> been revealed in courtrooms, and the industry is pretty damn happy with that. Images of VW style Deception Class Actions must haunt them...

"Wish List":   (at risk of being a repeat, here is what would help protect most investors)

On the KYC, where questions and parameters require completion, I dream of the day when clients simply write the following: "I request and expect a <u>fiduciary relationship</u> with anyone giving me financial advice. I seek professional advice free of commission motivations, free of biased product and dealer conflicts of interests. I wish to pay 1% of the total of my assets to be in such a professional relationship."

<u>Consumer Alert!</u>
Some professional financial planning bodies promise that their members must adhere to fiduciary standards, while ignoring enforcement of those promises, and allowing members to be product sales-persons in disguise.

If clients were able to have a discussion, and fill out the forms in terms <u>they</u> understand, I believe the relationship with the investment dealer would be on a more professional footing.

Sadly, with the most-profitable financial services relationship, being one of deceiving clients about the relationship, most dealers will refuse to handle such a client demand, unless the client has sufficient investable assets to make the 1% number worth their while.

It might be well worth the rejection, simply to make yourself informed about the exact nature of the financial relationship you are in.

===========

<u>NFL Football Players better protected…</u>
Recently I had the opportunity to review the NFLPA Regulations and Code of Conduct Governing Registered Player Financial Advisors. These are a set of standards and requirements that financial vendors and advice givers must agree to adhere to, before being league approved as suitable persons to serve NFL players.

I expected to find large gaps when I first skimmed the terminology used, finding them using the word "advisor" liberally. Usually this means a lack of understanding of the key legal differences between a self titled "advisor" and a proper registered adviser.

I was pleasantly surprised to find, however they they had done a good job of covering the bases and designing the requirements to weed out many loopholes and traps that fake investment advisors use to separate investors from their trust.

One of the things that impressed me was a good requirement that the advice giver take serious steps to know, understand and <u>only</u> recommend investments which would be considered suitable, and they go further enough with the description, to protect the investor.

============

The following is an excerpt of the section that further clarifies suitability:

I. **Suitability of Investments and Risk Disclosure**

> A Registered Player Financial Advisor shall make a reasonable inquiry of the Player concerning his finances to determine whether the proposed investment recommendation or Financial Advice is suitable for the Player. That inquiry shall include, but not be limited to, consideration of the following:
>
> 1. The Player's assets and liquidity;
>
> 2. The Player's short and long-term liabilities;
>
> 3. The need for diversification in the Player's investments to protect against undue risk;
>
> 4. The Player's risk tolerance, investment objectives, and level of financial sophistication; and
>
> 5. Tax, estate, insurance, and retirement planning, where appropriate.
>
> The information obtained from the Player by the Registered Player Financial Advisor shall be updated as necessary. A Registered Player Financial Advisor shall not make any guarantees, either directly or by implication, regarding any investment, and shall communicate accurately its terms and potential risks.

This is a far sight different than the suitability standard that applies to the average North American retail investor. Any suitability requirement in place with regulators of today, is used as a loophole, a free get out of jail card for bad advice. The reason for that is that without the clarity and additional emphasis found in the NFL Advisor requirements, the average mom and pop investor is sold anything…just so long as the seller deems it to be suitable, and the seller can explain the poorest investments and the most expensive investments in the world, as still "suitable". It is a meaningless term intended to dupe investors… in court.

The players, in my view are protected just one small step clearer with the signed agreement in hand. Retail investors would have similar if the regulators were not industry picked and paid.

The second item that impressed me in the NFL doc was the section on fiduciary duty, shown here:

> III. Fiduciary Duty
>
> The Registered Player Financial Advisor acknowledges that it is a fiduciary with respect to each of its Player-clients and agrees to perform its duties as a Financial Advisor to such Player-client in good faith and with the care, skill, prudence, and diligence under the circumstances then prevailing that a prudent person acting in a like capacity and familiar with such matters would use in the conduct of an enterprise of a like character and with like aims and consistent with the Registered Player Financial Advisor's obligations and duties under applicable law, and consistent with the Registered Player Financial Advisor's existing practices and procedures, obligations, powers and duties under its written contract with the Player-client (required under Section Four (H) of the Regulations in the case of Registered Individual Player Financial Advisors).

The underlined portion (my underlining for emphasis) is of the utmost importance because it takes away the "he said/she said' nonsense that non-fiduciary sales types deal in. They often deal in pretending to be trusted like a fiduciary and then instead acting as a salesperson.

This agreement plus the 13 other mentions of the word fiduciary, in the agreement, leave less wiggle room for fake advisors…and if I have not made it clear yet, anyone who intentionally spells their title in a way contrary to how the Securities Act reads, is playing games.

Last, but not least the advice giver must be covered by fidelity bonding and professional liability insurance in an amount sufficient to protect against theft and fraud, and also against any errors, omissions, or other conduct by the Financial Advisor which causes financial damage to any Player. The minimum coverage amounts required are between $2 million and $10 million. I would prefer a bit better coverage here and more explanation of if the coverage is "per victim" or "total of all victims". If any one investor is covered up to $10 million, then simply keep your investments well under this, and if not, tell the 'advisor' to get better coverage.

On a note about errors and omissions insurance, I recall that when I worked with the big banks, they did not have any insurance (that I was aware of) for their sales brokers. Their immense size and influence with the regulators gave them a free pass around the requirement to insure themselves (or customers) against things like broker fraud. All others who sold investments had to be covered except the big banks. This meant two things. One was their profits were higher for not having to pay out this cost, and two was if they were ever caught in a fraud or an error, they found it easier to lawyer up and simply pound the investment victim into the ground…for a second savings in cost to the bank.

Regardless of who you are and who you deal with, suffice it to say that investors who wish to be protected from investment industry predatory tricks, will print out a copy of the NFL Players Association Financial Advisor Registration Program, rules and regulations, read it and ask any investment advice giver to give it a look.

If they can meet the essential elements that is great for your security, and if they cannot at least you know what you are dealing with.

Google this term or see the link below: NFL Players Association Financial Advisor Registration Program

https://nflpaweb.blob.core.windows.net/media/Default/NFLPA/FinancialAdvisors/Final%20Financial%20Advisors%20Regs%20October%2024.pdf

===========

Michael Kitces is one of the most followed financial planners in America and he nails an important issue with his discussion of two dimensions of risk tolerance…Simply put – risk tolerance and risk capacity should be measured separately. The NFL 'advisor' vetting process (back two pages on "suitability") touches upon this, and it is something that the average sales 'advisor' often blends, or bends to make a sale. Michael is worth following.

Adopting A Two-Dimensional Risk Tolerance Assessment Process - http://kitc.es/2jvdgdM

============

"When investment firm supervision consists of ensuring that their employees 'properly/appropriately' sell the firm's conflicted products, which are expressly designed to disadvantage the client, we are in a post irony world. "— Anonymous

============

P.S. Dear investment regulators, when might we expect an honest "know your salesperson' disclosure document?

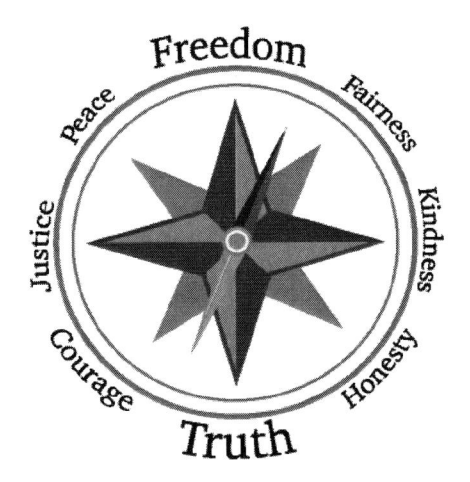

CHAPTER NINE

EXEMPTIONS TO THE LAW

"Move to Canada" ... they said.

"White collar crime is free" ... they said.

===========

My friend Joe had to explain to me what a **fifth column** is. It helped me to better understand the shocking concept that regulators and public protective agencies might have a vested interest and financial or employment incentives to allow harm to the public.

He told me of a group of people who undermine a larger group from within, usually in favor of an enemy group or nation. The activities of a fifth column can be overt or clandestine. Forces gathered in secret can mobilize openly to assist an external attack. This term is also extended to organized actions by military personnel. Clandestine fifth column activities can involve acts of sabotage, disinformation, or espionage executed within defense lines by secret sympathizers with an external force.

This concept applies frequently to inner acts of sabotage of the public interest, since most of the 'regulators' of utmost importance to the financial protection of the public, are chosen and/or funded by the investment industry.

This means that the investment protection game in Canada, and much of the game in the U.S. carries within it the inherent risk of a Fifth Column.

===========

Pop Quiz:

1. How much money could you make as an investor, if you could have semi-private, insider knowledge of billion dollar corporations who were granted permission to skirt the law?

2. How much money could you make as an investor if this kind of knowledge were not illegal to act upon, just made difficult for most investors to know of?

3. What if a company could 'eliminate' the need to make public the financial statements of companies they were acquiring?

4. What if a corporation could eliminate the need for the assets of the company to have independent and credible asset valuations, for purposes of financial reporting?

5. What if management could create those valuations numbers themselves?

6. How much money could you make if you were a publicly traded company, and learned that you could purchase a pass to be exempt from rules/laws?

"Dear Valeant Pharmaceutical, Welcome to Canada..."

===========

A timeline for a $100 billion dollar heist, gangster style:

June 21, 2010
Mississauga-based Biovail Corp. merges with **California-based Valeant**.

I now understand why a company like Valeant would move itself to Canada, rather than be based in the US. I believe it is because Canada has regulators who appear to be running a 'business within' the regulatory business.

I believe that a systemic side-business for regulators in Canada, is to sell-out the powers of 'discretion' they hold, to make faustian bargains in return for generous six figure salaries.

===========

On July 3, 2012, the Ontario Securities Commission granted VALEANT PHARMACEUTICALS permission to 'exempt themselves' from the lawful "requirement to include the financial statement disclosure..." The rest is legal gobbledygook, and can be found at the link below:

http://www.osc.gov.on.ca/en/SecuritiesLaw_ord_20120802_211_valeant.htm

If the link to the regulator exemption is removed (as is often the case) from the web, see the copy below on Google Drive. (Securities regulators in Canada seem to do continual 'revisions' to their public data, removing or redacting incriminating matters).

https://drive.google.com/file/d/0BzE_LMPDi9UOY0xiblkzWXYwd2M/view?usp=sharing

I know of a US hedge fund manager who lost $4 Billion on his investment in Valeant. He might be less likely to invest in Canada if he knew that Canadian regulators have a special side operation to sell 'hall passes' around our protective laws.

===========

July 24, 2015
Valeant (Stock symbol VRX) passes RBC to become **most valuable company** on TSX (Toronto Stock Exchange) at $250.00 per share (Cdn).

Valeant Pharmaceutical was one of the largest companies (by stock market capitalization (dollar size of all shares combined)). Both it and Royal Bank were in the neighborhood of $400 billion market valuation, but Valeant was slightly ahead.

===========

In **February 2016**, Valeant disclosed that it was under investigation by the U.S. Securities and Exchange Commission, and by the U.S. Attorney's Offices for the Southern District of New York.

The company has been criticized for pioneering the highly lucrative business model of acquiring pharmaceutical companies or their drugs, incorporating these drugs into Valeant's sales and supply chain and then raising the prices of these medications to levels contemporaneous with similar pharmaceutical products
https://en.wikipedia.org/wiki/Valeant_Pharmaceuticals

============

Valeant also pays extremely low taxes because it is officially based in Canada, although Mr. Pearson operates from New Jersey."
— New York Times **October 4, 2015**

https://en.wikipedia.org/wiki/Valeant_Pharmaceuticals

The rise and fall of Valeant Pharmaceuticals
Canadian drugmaker's fortunes fall amid fraud allegations, criminal investigations

CBC News **Mar 14, 2017** 2:10 PM ET
http://www.cbc.ca/news/business/valeant-pharmaceuticals-pershing-1.4023893

===========

March 2017, VRX falls to $14.77 per share, a market capitalization decline of tens of billions shaved from investors.

Imagine the profits to short sellers who knew about the exemption to the law that was obtained from Canadian regulators.

Now imagine why well organized financial looting is so profitable, so secretive and so entrenched in Canada.

There were well over 10,000 exemptions found in Canada in recent research.

===========

March 2017

Billionaire Bill Ackman Sells Disastrous Valeant Investment After Nearly $4 Billion Loss

CNBC first reported that Pershing Square sold its entire Valeant stake at levels of $11 per share. (US$ share pricing) Shares of Valeant Pharmaceuticals, once Ackman's biggest single position, have fallen by 96% since their highs in the summer of 2015 and now represent between 1.5% and 3% of Pershing Square's hedge funds.

https://www.forbes.com/sites/nathanvardi/2017/03/13/billionaire-bill-ackman-sells-disastrous-valeant-investment-after-nearly-4-billion-loss/#6e0f981374b2

===========

Excerpt from **April 8, 2017**
Lessons from Valeant

"Valeant was a highly accuisitive company, effectively a 'roll-up'. Such companies always carry more risks. Ackman has acknowledged past performance in acquisitions is not a durable asset. In the "Outsiders" presentation Ackman noted "Management has completed 100+ acquisitions and licenses, investing $19billion+ since 2008" ... "Acquisitions have been highly accretive" ... "Valeant management expects the majority of the company's future free cash flow will be allocated to its value-creating acquisition strategy"

I hope to have a conversation with Bill Ackman sometime, and make sure he is aware that investing in Canadian public companies carries the risk of mafia-like treatment of laws, rules and regulations.

===========

Valeant Pharmaceutical Backstory courtesy of Wikipedia

Valeant Pharmaceuticals International, Inc. is a multinational specialty pharmaceutical company based in Laval, Quebec, Canada. Valeant develops, manufactures and markets a broad range of pharmaceutical products primarily in the areas of dermatology, gastrointestinal disorders, eye health, neurology and branded generics. Valeant owns Bausch & Lomb, one of the largest manufacturers of contact lenses.

Valeant grew quickly with a series of mergers and acquisitions under the leadership of J. Michael Pearson and for a short period of time in 2015 was the most valuable company in Canada. Valeant was described as a platform company that grows by systematically acquiring other companies. Valeant acquired Salix Pharmaceuticals for $14.5 billion in 2015. Valeant tried to acquire Actavis and Cephalon and merge with Allergan, but failed.

In 2015–2016 the company was involved in a controversy about drug price hikes and the use of a specialty pharmacy for the distribution of its specialty drugs. The company's stock price plummeted nearly 90 percent since the peak. Valeant reversed the price hikes and ended cooperation with specialty pharmacy Philidor Rx Services and Walgreens took over distribution.

Valeant is under investigation by the U.S. Securities and Exchange Commission. Joseph C. Papa became CEO of the company in May 2016. Bill Ackman's Pershing Square fund held a major stake in the company before selling out in March 2017 for a reported loss of $2.8 bn.

An important part of the growth strategy for Valeant has been acquisitions of medical and pharmaceutical companies and subsequent price increases for their products.

Another important aspect to its success may have been in convincing the Ontario Securities Commission of the need for Valeant to _not_ have to follow rules and/or laws of financial disclosure. This is considered a major reason for Valeant's move to Canada, an almost childlike ease with which financial rules and laws can be ignored, exempted, or simply made to disappear.

Fortunately, exemption applications (there are over 10,000 on record in Canada in the last decade or two) are as simple as having the corporate lawyer 'gin up' a reason for needing to not follow the law, and enclose a cheque payable to the 'regulator'.
("gin up": To generate or increase something, especially by dubious or dishonest **means**.)

There is always a _given_ reason for seeking permission…and then there is the _real_ reason. (just like the written rules of investment dealer behavior…and the real, un-written rules)

In this case the regulator was the Ontario Securities Commission (OSC) and they are happy to oblige thousands of requests by companies seeking to skirt securities laws or rules. They will do it inexpensively, perhaps as cheaply as a few thousand dollars, quietly, with no public notice, procedure or process.

OSC Commissioners have the magic power of 'discretion' over securities law, and by way of further gift, they have made themselves exempt from the need to give notice, to allow public input, or to show the reasons or the test, that the legislation requires in order to have this power to skirt the law. They do not have to show their 'homework'.

Update: In May 2017 Securities Commissions also enshrined into law "immunity" from being held accountable (by civil suit) for negligence in their duties.

POOF! In an instant, Valeant is no longer required to provide financial statements in a business acquisition report. This is approved in the jurisdictions of Quebec and Ontario on July 3, 2012. The great thing for Valeant is that 13 provinces and territories have co-operative agreements (called a "Passport System") whereby if it is approved in one province, all the other Provinces accept this 'exemption' as if it had met a proper due process everywhere. Cheques may have to be written to each 'jurisdiction'.

I am starting to see why a company like Valeant would rather move to Canada, than stay in the States where I am not sure exemption to laws are as easily obtained. If you know otherwise please let me know at "Investment System Fraud" on Facebook and @RecoveredBroker on Twitter.

In Canada, the numbers of exemptions to the law far exceed any serious convictions under the law, for investment industry people, companies, or regulators. Why worry about the law when you have "hired the law?"

===========

One More Benefit to Move Your Corporation to Canada

Canada's pre-eminent truth-protecting accountant, four-decade professor of accounting, Al Rosen tells me that IFRS (International Financial Reporting Standards) were introduced to Canada in 2011.

He also says that the USA refused to move to this standard for good reason, and it has stayed instead with the old standby GAAP (Generally Accepted Accounting Principles).

In his second book, released in 2017, he gives many good reasons to worry about IFRS accounting standards, and everything he says makes me suspect that they fit well into the model of well organized financial crime.

Dr. Rosen's book title is "Easy Prey Investors: Why Broken Safety Nets Threaten Your Wealth" The street-smarts in the first chapter alone will save an investor the price of a condo.

Al's book takes a microscope and a forensic accountant's look at how investors, particularly those in Canada, are 'set up' to fail, or to be harvested by very well organized systems of financial predation.
 uphttps://www.amazon.ca/Easy-Prey-Investors-Broken-Threaten-ebook/dp/B01N138CH7/ref=sr_1_1?s=books&ie=UTF8&qid=1493570770&sr=1-1&keywords=al+rosen

This one item sticks clearly in my brain: (my own paraphrasing)

What if you could eliminate the need for credible asset valuations, and simply switch hats to a different accounting methodology which allowed management to 'make up' valuations on their own?

What if management bonus' or other forms of compensation could be based upon made up numbers that management provides, itself? Or as my friend Richard in Calgary calls it, "mark to fantasy" accounting, rather than "mark to market" valuation practices.

Update 2017: I am told that this style of accounting (magic) is now being brought into play in the U.S. If you follow Gretchen

Morgenson's writing in the New York Times, you will be well informed. Here is one example. **"Warren Buffett Invests in Canada, but Should You?"**
https://www.nytimes.com/2017/07/07/business/warren-buffett-investing-canada.html?mcubz=0&_r=0
Gretchen now writes at the Wall Street Journal.

===========

The UN Convention on Transnational Organized Crime, Article 2, defines "organized criminal group" as "a group having at least three members, taking some action in concert (i.e., together or in some coordinated manner) for the purpose of committing a 'serious crime' and for the purpose of obtaining a financial or other benefit."

With well over 10,000 salaried regulators between Canada and the USA, (SEC, FINRA, SIFMA, NASAA, CSA), one would think that authors would have no financial victimization to write about. However, when one digs deep, it becomes evident that paying 10,000 regulators is not done to protect the public from the investment industry, but rather to 'insulate' the investment industry from the public,… and to protect them from having to face our criminal codes.

By now I am hoping that you will not mind a bit of a cynical label, and an acronym. The acronym is OFC which stands for Organized Financial Crime. Feel free to silently pronounce it as a 2-sylable profanity if you wish. I do sometimes and it makes me feel better. Perhaps it will trend on Twitter as #OFC?

Already on Twitter the terms #FinancialMurder and #Unrigthesystem are being used.

===========

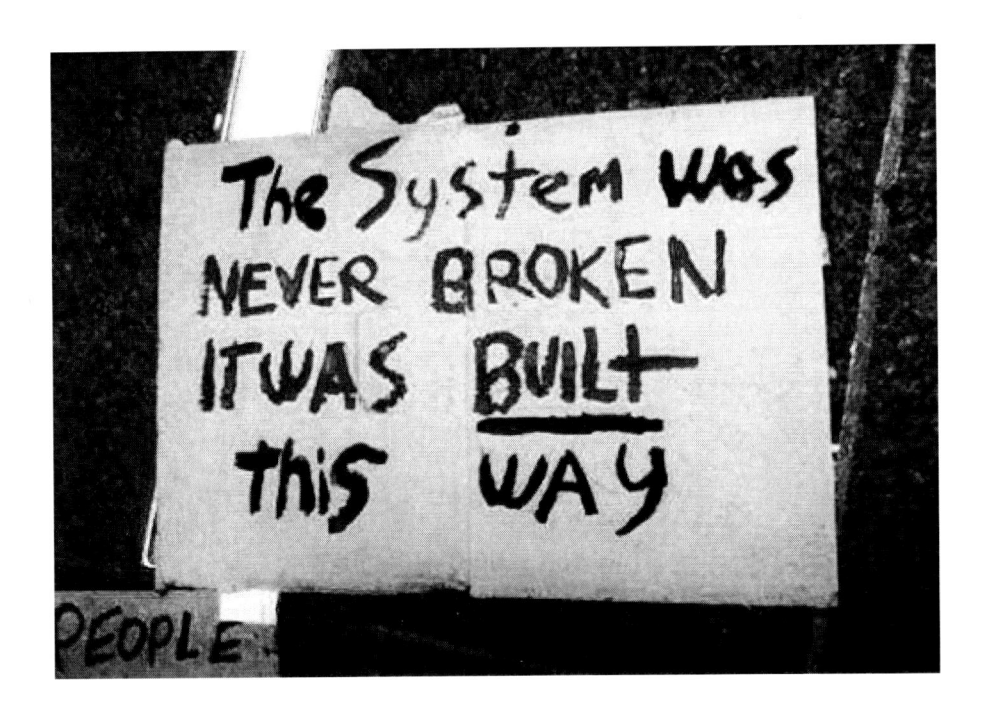

"The System was never broken it was built this way — People"

"What a great offer!....You mean that you will pay me $700,000 to make it appear that YOU follow rules? Where do I sign?" (a top Provincial Securities Regulator)

===========

Just four (4) out of the thirteen Securities Commissions in Canada pay out salaries of about 1/4 billion dollars each year to 1700 regulatory staff. FINRA (broker self regulator) in the U.S. carries a cash balance of $2 billion in the latest financial report I viewed. There is some <u>real</u> money in the regulatory game. What is with that?

Ontario Premier Kathleen Wynne made $208,974 in 2016. The Ontario Securities Commission has about 60 staff who made more in 2016 than the Provincial Premier, mostly lawyers. Some as high as $700,000.

In 2016 over 300 employees at the OSC made over $100,000, again, most commonly lawyers.   http://www.sunshinelist.ca

Why bother robbing a bank, when investment bankers can make robbing the public perfectly legal, simply by hiring one's own private…security force?

In Other Regulatory Tricks

Can you imagine what that power of 'discretion' to exempt financial laws might be worth?

How much money could YOU imagine an investment dealer creating for themselves, if they could make themselves or their product offerings 'exempt' from the law?

Let your mind go for just a moment, and let it think like a criminal might. That will allow much of this topic to start to make perfect sense…

This 'power' of 'discretion comes to them from the legislature of each province and territory in Canada. Take your concerns about financial games to your elected representative.

It is written in the legislation that exemptive relief can be granted "if the commission is satisfied that it would not be prejudicial to the public interest to do so." This is the so-called "public interest" test.

I have never seen it applied, explained, or documented, and all attempts to contact securities commissions for clarification have resulted in dismissal. One is left to wonder if the commissions are breaching the public trust in giving away the law to those who apply, or if they truly have a documented process of ensuring the public interest is not harmed.

In my more cynical moments, I have recognized that, thanks to several thousands of lawyers, who act as handmaidens to the financial industry, the wording of the legislation does not actually say the exemption must "do no harm" to the public; it simply says the commission must be "satisfied." Well played sirs… Well played.

The official reasons given for most, if not all exemption decisions by Provincial regulators read as follows:

"Each of the Decision Makers is <u>satisfied</u> that the test contained in the Legislation that provides the Decision Maker with the jurisdiction to make the decision has been met." (underlining is my own)

With top regulator salaries in Alberta, and Ontario of just over $700,000, and others at $500,000 and $600,000, it can be safely assumed they are "satisfied."

Public notice to investors exposed to risk or harm from exempted laws is not required by the regulators, nor is public input accepted into exemptions. This practice of exempting the law for financial industry players can literally be said to be done in the dark of night…on at least one exemption that I know of. It can also generally be said that it will always be of help to the financial industry, and often harmful to the public.

There is a series of 'interview ambush' video clips of Saskatchewan Attorney General (in charge of the Saskatchewan Financial Services Commission) being asked about exemptions, and his answers and behaviors indicate just how far these officials will go to <u>not even consider</u> protection of the public.

The interview follows along in the independent film BREACH OF TRUST, The Unique Violence of White Collar Crime, found on YouTube here: <u>https://youtu.be/k2K6pzFtyTU</u>

In the chapter on exemptions, one example resulted in a suicide, and some follow-up clips with the Government Minster overseeing the Securities Commission are in the last two thirds of this full length flick. See chapter 6 of "Breach of Trust", dead men can't testify… on YouTube.

(This film is definitely Stephen Speilberg quality…but only if you allow me to go back to the 1970's, when Stephen made his first made-for-TV movie about a demon runaway truck…)

Billionaire investor Stephen Jarislowski has stated, "Securities regulators in Canada do the square root of nothing." They may do 'something', but as far as public protection, I am in agreement with Mr. Jarislowsky.

I go as far as to say that I think they are well paid <u>'to do the square root of nothing'</u> as far as public protection goes. They are simply the hired guns of the financial industry when 100% of their salary comes from the same financial industry…that they are hand-picked to 'police'.

If only they did the square root of nothing. They do much worse by giving Canadians a false sense of security; a belief they are protected from fraud. I still meet people today who tell me that we have the most regulated financial system in the world. That is exactly the impression they (the financial industry) wish us to hold. Nothing could be more profitable than convincing investors that they are safe and sound…

Perhaps Canadians are protected from one, two, or two hundred of the smallest fraudsters, but they are fully exposed to the predations and systemic acts of Canada's most trusted and most organized financial criminals. Catch a few bad apples, while letting the entire diseased orchard run wild. That is the game that takes place beneath the game the public sees.

Provincial Securities Commissions are co-operative enough that if you forget to get your special exemption <u>while</u> you are breaking the law, no problem. Number six below is a copy of the back dated exemption order which, for a $250 fee, gave the Assante Corporation permission to violate the Securities Act provisions against commission rebating. For a violation that <u>they had already done</u>.

The exemptions listed below **were** all public documents at one time. All of the exemptions have been removed, or relocated so the links no longer work as of time of editing this chapter. Other researchers like myself have experienced constant revisions to Securities Commission websites, documents and so on, making it next to impossible to follow their actions which may be contrary to the public interest. You must think like a criminal for this to make sense.

1. Berkshire Investment Group (BIG) (Canadian independent, boutique wealth management, no connection to Berkshire Hathaway, BRK.A, BRK.B) needing to be exempt from the commission rebating laws similar to those exempted for Assante mentioned previously.

<http://www.albertasecurities.com/Companies/Exemption%20Orders/15182/2740521%20-%20Berkshire%20Investment%20Group%20Inc.%20and%20Berkshire%20Securities%20Inc.%20-%20OSC%20DECDOC.pdf>

2. Banks can benefit from exemptions which allow the dumping of poor selling new investment underwritings, into the bank's mutual fund customers. Anything that a bank might be stuck with that does not sell, can then be offloaded upon the trusting bank mutual fund holders. They will never receive a notice that their money was used as a dumping ground for the bank's underwriting mistakes.

http://www.albertasecurities.com/Companies/Exemption%20Orders/15182/2707101%20CIBC%20Asset%20Mgmt%20Inc%20et%20al%20NI%2081-102%20ON%20DECDOC.pdf

3. An interesting exemption since it uses the true legal language, calling its members "salespersons" (pre 2009). You will note that virtually no licensed investment "salespersons" inform their customers of that license category (nor even their new license now referred to as "Dealing Representatives".

http://www.albertasecurities.com/Companies/Exemption%20Orders/11968/_1986747_v1_-_BMO_NESBITT_BURNS_INC._S._213_ON_DECDOC.pdf

4. An application by TD so that some of the people calling themselves advisors do not have to be licensed as such. "…certain individuals who engage in securities-related advisory activities on behalf of TDIM are not subject to the following

requirement (the "Applicable Requirement") contained in the Legislation:

No person or company shall act as an adviser unless the person or company is registered as an adviser..." (POOF! And this lawful requirement is made to disappear).

http://www.albertasecurities.com/Companies/Exemption%20Orders/8705/_1678239_v1_-_TD__INVESTMENT_MANAGEMENT_INC._S._214_-_ONDECDOC.pdf

5. Here is one of the exemption orders used by Assante to start the ball rolling, and push clients' money towards their own house-brand funds. It sounds harmless upon reading the application, but the results were anything but. Massive money incentives went into place when this exemption was granted, and the incentives were not necessarily in the better interests of the clients.

http://www.osc.gov.on.ca/en/SecuritiesLaw_ord_20040220_211_assante.htm

And here
https://docs.google.com/file/d/0BzE_LMPDi9UOYWZzYXdmX25XMlE/edit?usp=sharing

6. You can even break the law and apply for an exemption after the fact.

Here is a copy of a letter from the Saskatchewan Securities Commission giving them, for a $250 fee, a backdated exemption from the law for a period of time going back to practices done in 1998 or 1999, depending upon how it is read. The backdated exemption document was granted in 2000.

https://docs.google.com/file/d/0BzE_LMPDi9UOMHR4Zm91S2FodDg/edit?usp=sharing

Note to readers: these exemption orders are written by lawyers for other lawyers to read. Most of the time non-experts cannot begin to understand the language or what the lawyers are truly trying to accomplish. It is that well hidden in legal jargon.

Each exemption carries a '<u>given reason</u>', for the exemption, (even if it is incomprehensible). It then helps if one can manage to think like a predator, a lawyer or a criminal to see the real reason. Did I just repeat myself?

When I testified in Parliament, I stated that by allowing industry players to pay the securities regulators' salaries, they 'obtain' a level of compliant behavior from regulators, sufficient to make the public interest take a back seat.

There appear to be no boundaries to what Securities Commissions will allow, and no professional, public-documented process they follow. In short, it appears to be a process which can be easily turned to benefit the investment industry, while doing harm to the public interest.

Whenever an investment product is being sold that was exempted from the law, one would think the Securities Commission would have either notified each consumer of the exemption, or been able to publicly justify the use of their discretionary powers. Not once have I seen either, in over a decade of asking the commissions.

"Exemption orders were granted about 20 times…" (according to a letter from the provincial finance minister Iris Evans) in Alberta, by the Alberta Securities Commission, when toxic sub-prime mortgage investments needed to be dumped on the public. These were those illegal investments that almost brought down the financial world, circa 2008.

They did not meet legal ratings requirements, but investment dealers had to unload them from their own inventories, so how do they get rid of them? Exemptions were gained by Securities Commissions which allowed them to be dumped on an unknowing public. This was prior to the 2008 collapse of these sub-prime products.

Across Canada they helped to drain $32 billion from investors small and large, straight into the pockets of the industry players with the bad product. (Some portion of money was recovered a decade later)

Enough money to run an average Canadian province for a year or more. Or, looked at another way, as much economic harm as 6 million 'street' or 'property' crimes in Canada would add up to, at a Government estimated average of $5000 per property crime. What was that definition of organized financial crime again? (OFC)

The further I got along in my career, the more informed I became to these entitlements that the strongest banks in the world worked under:

(A) Rules are for fools, and not for the financial industry. The financial industry makes the rules, enforces the rules, and pays and/or influences the choice of the people who enforce the rules.

(B) They enforce those rules which are helpful to self-interests, and ignore those which interfere with profits. If they think they need to go further, they simply exempt themselves from rules and laws, making the illegal, legal. If they need to go even further, they can use some of the ill gotten millions they have captured from clients, to out-wit, out-wait, out-lawyer and knock the remaining life out of any victimized client.

I noticed that the Regulator who signed off on some exemption applications to allow sub-prime mortgage investments to rob Canadian investors, later claimed that people who sold them had no idea what they were selling, and the regulator herself had "no idea" who they were selling them to. Yet she still gave them permission to skirt the law to sell them. She then got promoted to a new, more highly paid job in the industry… <u>That</u> is the <u>real</u> game being played, <u>beneath</u> the securities commission game.

The image that comes to my mind is of the perpetrators of acts against the public, saying they are "just doing their jobs," when their jobs entail doing harm to others. What they should say perhaps, is that they are 'blindly doing their jobs"…in a moral sense.

"You get better consumer protection in Ontario if you're buying a used car."
Whipple Steinkraus, V.P. Consumers Council of Canada, speaking to an Ontario Legislative Committee on investment industry protection issues, 2006. Here it is 2018 and the industry rape of society continues un-checked.

CONSUMER ACTION STEPS
Call your government representative asked him why government authorized regulatory bodies are allowed to grant legal exemptions to our laws…in semi–secrecy.

Ask the provincial Solicitor General why Criminal Code section 122, "Breach of Trust" is not applied to regulators.

Vote for those willing to recognize and stand up to the most well-organized financial crimes against society.

We don't always win by winning. We can also win <u>just </u>by trying.

===========

"There is a perception in international financial circles that Canadian markets are the 'Wild West' and it hurts Canadian companies when they try to raise money abroad. This is a very common refrain that we hear when we visit markets in New York or in Boston or in London or in Europe, a perception that somehow this is kind of a little bit more like a Wild West up here in terms of the degree to which rules and regulations are enforced." - Former Bank of Canada Governor David Dodge, Dec. 9, 2005

===========

Update January 2018: I just had reason to search the Canadian Securities Administrators (CSA) "Registration Search" page again, and I noticed that for the broker/salesperson term of "Dealing Representative, they have now removed the clarifying word of

"Salesperson" which just last year was included to inform the public of just what a Dealing Rep was.

This follows the previous change in law September of 2009 where the CSA removed ALL use of the word "Salesperson" from the Act, and rules etc, and replaced each "Salesperson" word, with the words "Dealing Representative".

Each few years the regulators (CSA in Canada) spend time and money to ensure that the public is LESS informed and warned than previously. That is what the regulators call their new and improved "Client Relationship Disclosure", except that you must think like a criminal…to understand who the improvement is intended for.
http://aretheyregistered.ca

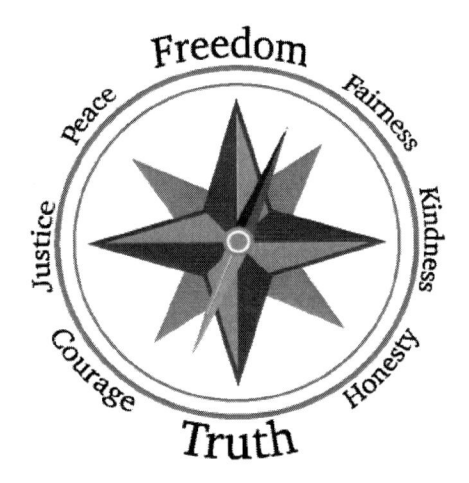

CHAPTER TEN

CAPTURING THE POLICE

"There is a crack in everything...that's how the light gets in."
Leonard Cohen

Prior to 2007 whispers and rumors began that credit products made up of sub-prime loans were not performing well. Rumors carry with them little substance, but as they grew, institutional investors were the first to get the information.

In the years prior to this, industry 'experts' assembling sub-prime credit packages into investments, needed top credit ratings placed upon them in order to sell them profitably (or more profitably than deserved).

To do this required phony bank guarantees, or guarantees which would not hold water when needed. Secondly they needed phony credit ratings, some of which were accomplished by putting the phony bank guarantees in place.

We can add banks and credit rating agencies into the circle of insiders who benefitted from doing intentional harm to the public. There is a big difference between doing accidental harm, and doing intentional harm. There is a bigger difference when it is done professionally. Tectonic are the effects upon society when professionals conspire in an 'organized' fashion.

Some 'sub-prime' investment products which could not meet the proper credit ratings went to the securities commissions to be 'exempted' from those laws. "Push 'em out the door and onto retail clients," is the Wall Street/Bay Street motto, whether through connections at the bank, the rating agency or the securities commission lawyers.

Well organized and high status crime is invisibly draining the economy, by perhaps more than every other crime in the country. Any country. Yes, even our own "best in the world' country.

According to Statistics Canada, there were approximately 8 million property-related victimizations each year from 1993 to 2004. Total economic value of these crimes increased to $40 billion per year.

Asset backed commercial paper? ABCP is the moniker used to describe some of the 2008 sub-prime mortgage paper that was sold in Canada. $32 Billion was removed from Canadian investors with these 'products' after being approved to be sold to Canadians by 'exempting' securities laws. One organized financial scam by respected men in suits can do the financial harm of six million criminal acts.

ABCP is a short-term investment, usually maturing in less than a year, but often in as little as a month. ABCP is backed by a variety of assets, such as mortgage loans, car loans, credit card balances, and other interest-bearing assets and/or by synthetic assets such as collateralized debt obligations.

Asking securities commissions what reason could be given, and what public interest is served by giving exemptions to our laws, resulted in rejection, and indignation that anyone could even question their authority.

Under such regulatory secrecy, compounded by who pays (or chooses) our regulators, society loses a considerable amount of money, and some in society lose all. I can recall more suicides and ruined lives from regulator failure to protect, than I can the number of serious prosecutions.

If you are reading this book in North America, I believe that Organized Financial Crimes by professionals (OFC) is the largest criminal drain on your country's economic prosperity. With <u>zero</u> statistical chance of being prosecuted, due to the network of political, legal, and other handmaid connections.

Consider the liability posed if securities regulators and other members of the OFC cabal, are found to be willfully blind, grossly negligent, or worse. What if some are incentivized to engage in conscious wrongdoing? Breach of Trust is a section of the Criminal Code of Canada that apparently has yet to be dusted-off, and applied to upper society crime. There are more sightings of Sasquatch in the wild, than of criminal codes being applied to financial and investment industries. Such is the insulation value of thousands of regulators and handmaidens.

<u>To capture the financial police in Canada?</u>

Step one is to make sure that financial crimes are <u>only</u> investigated against a few bad apples, and never against bad systems. Systemic crimes against society must be protected…by each system involved, whether it be financial, legal, regulatory or political.

System protection in Canadian finance is helped when the RCMP Integrated Market Enforcement Team (IMET) is invited to work within the premises of the Ontario Securities Commission (OSC). The network of 'connections' becomes tighter, preventing certain things from ever being investigated.

Step two is to capture the 'high moral ground' of self regulation of their industry. Then, once that high moral ground is obtained, establish a vast network of regulators and self regulators that insulates your operations from outside scrutiny, criminal codes, government, or other involvement. Approximately 10,000 persons in North America serve this purpose well. (SEC, CSA, FINRA, SIFMA, NASAA, etc.)

Of the financial bodies listed above, all except the SEC would be funded entirely by the financial industry. The SEC may be funded by Congress, but it's most influential persons are hand-picked by the industry, to an effect similar to paying them directly.

Step three is to convince politicians and courts that one's high moral position justifies acceptance of your very own regulator, as a body deserving of trust...without police or Judges knowing the hidden conflicts of interest. The police may not need much convincing of this, since, well, they have serious work of their own to protect society, so they are happy to turn over financial things that they are not skilled in.

RCMP unit moving under OSC's roof to tackle white-collar crime

All 28 full-time staff of the Toronto unit of IMET to move into OSC's downtown headquarters by the end of March.

By MADHAVI ACHARYA-TOM YEW Business Reporter
Mon., March 2, 2015

Police, when needed, will then be relying upon captured securities bodies to determine who ceserves exemption from justice, and who deserves application of justice. It seems to be that simple to deceive police and the courts.

The conflict that regulators hide from the RCMP is that the securities bodies serve two masters, one of public protection, <u>and</u> a second of fostering efficient markets for industry participants. This second role is equivalent to market 'lubrication'.

They do this while often being 'paid 100% by just one 'master'. The industry that the regulators are supposed to police, is the one that pays them. This is the intentional flaw that leads to capture of the regulator.

Then when a crime like illegal sub prime mortgages skims Billions from Canadians, the RCMP is called upon to look into the possible breach of public trust. They never even get to the breach of public trust, because they are being 'aided' by the regulator, who 'aided' the financial crimes themselves. These regulators inform the police that there is no crime, and…the end.

To be clear, the agency which participated in the root causes of the breach of public money, is allowed to participate in the investigation.

This is un-skillful police procedure, added to very skillful design of the regulatory systems in Canada. So clever in fact that the financial industry has succeeded in capturing even the police.

I do not blame the RCMP. They seem unaware of the potential for financial criminality behind the capture the regulator game. In fact I have yet to meet ten people in North American who have spotted such systemic acts. It is like trying to inspect the canvas beneath an original Van Gough painting. There are so many layers of paint covering that canvas, and in similar fashion, the investment industry has more 'cover-up' layers than any of Vincent's work.

The Securities Commission then 'helps' the RCMP write a 60 page report, saying that they find no criminal activity, and no reason to pursue this case. Never is it worth mentioning that they were a participant in the acts that helped remove the billions…this is another way the country is drained of tens and hundreds of billions of dollars…while those dollars keep flowing to benefit financial giants.

============

The following is from an Ontario legislature report from a standing committee on government agencies: Even this legislative investigation was fooled into not seeing beneath the paint. Not spotting the bad regulatory motives concealed beneath the layers of good motives.

This committee looked into the role of the Ontario securities commission, following the financial crash and crisis of 2008. This report was presented to the Ontario Legislature by Ernie Hardeman, MPP, in March of 2010.

From the Ontario Government report:
Decisions alleged to have facilitated the ABCP crisis

It is alleged that the Ontario Securities Commission facilitated the ABCP crisis through a series of decisions and omissions in the years leading up to the crisis.

These include:
1. *Removing the minimum purchase requirement of $50,000, effectively allowing the sale of non-bank ABCP to small retail investors;*

2. *Exempting credit rating agencies from civil liability for misrepresentation in the secondary trading market.*

3. *Allowing banks to sell ABCP, even though only one credit rating agency was willing to give the securities the required rating;*

4. *Failing to supervise the credit rating agencies that rated the securities.*

Failing to oversee securities dealers who misrepresented the true nature of ABCP to retail investors and/or broke industry "know your client" rules.

http://www.ontla.on.ca/committee-proceedings/committee-reports/files_pdf/OSC%20Report%20English.pdf

(They failed to mention #6, which is the regulator (OSC) selling exemptions to the laws so that illegal products can be sold to investors.)

$50 to $70 billion is the approximate neighborhood of every Stats Canada measured crime in the land. (except for systemic financial crimes, like this one, that we dare not measure)

$32 Billion was the take from just Sub Prime ABCP 'investments' (partial recovery was obtained… ten years delayed).

Imagine one investment-scheme, assisted by the regulators, and who foolishly, negligently (or worse, conscious wrongdoing) give financial players 'exemption' from the law. Those exemptions are then used to harvest police and Judge's pensions plans…dizzying to imagine the circle of wagons that are required to pull off schemes like this without a hitch. (OFC)

If a person were in the securities regulatory industry, and were collecting triple what a premier makes, I guess they would want to make sure the RCMP doesn't see the whole picture. "I have a great idea guys. Let's move the RCMP into our own offices, then we can 'help them to understand' our industry better…"

What began with honorable intentions to "regulate" financial markets and protect investors, appears to have spilled into a series of organizations which act like a law unto themselves. They certainly have some rather imaginative ways of bringing in extra money…

At best they have lost the capacity to balance investor protection with their (opposing) dual mandate of fostering fair and efficient capital markets. At worst they appear to be running, million dollar side-business, from their authority as regulator of a trillion-dollar industry. Like the false investment "advisor" or the, trust-selling politician, they seem to have found a way to promise trust, while simultaneously selling it out…for additional gain.

Americans and Canadians are both led into lowering their consumer defenses by securities commission promises that they 'police' the industry. This lowering of public defenses is the regulators greatest accomplishment…if I were to view it with the mind of a con artist.

If <u>only</u> they did the square root of nothing…we would be ahead by hundreds of billions of dollars.

===========

Let's consider a theoretical example:

Imagine financial inspection and regulation, as if it were the Canadian Food Inspection Agency. One of the largest stories in Canada in 2012, was about tainted beef coming out of XL Food's plant in Brooks, Alberta.

How different would the story (and the protection of consumers) be if the story went like this:

1. What if the government inspectors in such a scenario were not actually paid by the government, but paid instead by the beef industry itself?

2. What if inspectors had special 'discretionary' powers, whereby they could "exempt" certain food products from having to meet safe standards, and let them pass into our food chain, despite being dangerous or harmful?

3. What if their powers of discretion did not require them to publish a professionally followed procedure outlining how and why they came to allow consumer products to skirt our laws?

4. What if there were no requirements to inform, warn, or label any "exempted" food products sold to the public?

If meat inspectors acted like this, (and I do not believe they do) it would resemble what has occurred over ten thousand times in finance. You, as the consumer, can (and will) be sold faulty, otherwise illegal, tainted or toxic investment products, with never so much as a whisper of warning.

It's as if regulators can ensconce themselves into lucrative 'future considerations' rewards if they will merely do one thing: enter the regulatory system that polices the investment industry, and while the industry races at the speed of sound, the regulators protect the public at the pace of a Buddhist monk...in a walking meditation.

Allowing such clever design into our regulatory procedure, leads one down a slippery slope. After a period of years without anyone discovering these discretionary exemptions, it becomes free money to those working within the financial system. The regulator is, in effect, paid to sleep so society can be looted. Like a crooked night watchman at a distillery.

The total of <u>all crime in the USA</u> is measured by some government estimates to cost $500 billion per year. Therefore it might be said that clever, un-prosecuted financial players do more economic harm to America than do millions of street criminals...combined. I think I may have spotted the leak in your economy Lady Liberty...

Hopefully, we can begin to visualize the possible damage of a group of white-collar fraudsters as financially harmful as over 8 million property crimes, and nearly equal in dollar value to all the government reported crimes combined.

What if one (or one hundred) investment bankers, operating in concert with lawyers, regulators, and other assorted handmaidens, might be doing as much financial damage to our country as is done by millions of street criminals? With zero prosecution...?

If North America continues to suffer a social nervous breakdown, we must become open to consider that <u>intentional financial crime</u> is one of the causes. I must ask why the North American financial system appears designed as merely a clever looting-machine...similar to a famous Los Angeles riot, when the police were kept out.

We now live in a nation where doctors destroy health, lawyers destroy justice, universities destroy knowledge, governments destroy freedom, the press destroys information, religion destroys morals, and our banks destroy the economy.
—Chris Hedges

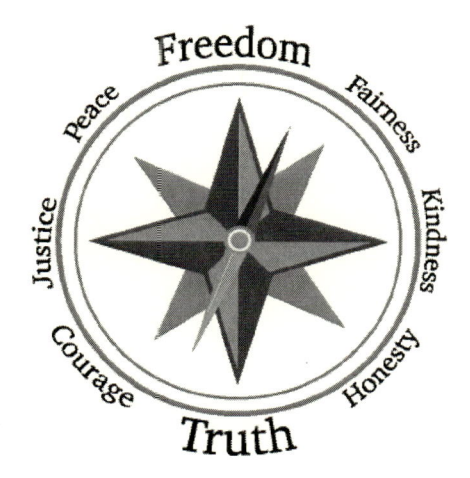

CHAPTER ELEVEN

"LAUNDERING CRIME"

"Laundering crime is the process whereby 'professional' acts harmful to society are 'cleansed and protected' from public accountability. It is the private washing of 'delicate' professional sins."

Mrs. Day was just over 80 when I was still a pup in the business. On a regular basis, she got a call from her broker at the firm I worked with, and he always had a "suggested change" to make in her account.

Whenever she visited her broker, she drove her car, some 30 miles from out of town to the office. She parked her giant of a car, something like a 1960's vintage Ford Fairlane if I recall, every time in a perfect parallel parking job, upon the sidewalk in front of the office. It was marked for angle parking, and yet she preferred to Parallel Park <u>on</u> the sidewalk.

After a few visits, we rookies realized that Mrs. Day was suffering from dementia, and was getting along on her own, without anyone doing much about it. This would have been in the 1980's.

She had an advantage of having millions of dollars, and thus lots of support from people like her broker. She was his monthly commission generating machine, and he churned her account for commissions at each opportunity. He was what the industry called a 'big producer" due to his commissions generated.

Today, the commission-trading game is mostly over. Thanks to the power of technology, discount trading and so on, we have almost entirely eliminated the value of a 'trade'. It is down from hundreds or thousands of dollars in commission when I started, to $6.00 or $9.00 (or less) per trade today.

So how is a simple broker to make a living today? Aside from changing their title from broker to "advisor", the industry has moved away from commissions, and towards product fee-generation and "advisor-type" fees. Notwithstanding that most have no such license.

Today, the broker/dealer firm would like to have zero client assets in transaction accounts, and they are actively 'culling' or firing clients who do not go along with their push into fees. Almost complete market domination allows the cabal of financial giants to abuse the public in this manner.

The big revenue generating brokers no longer have time for anyone who does not 'fit' their 'investment style', and the big broker investment style today is 'advisor' fees, plus product fees, plus…

Bring in enough of those fees and the fake 'advisor' will get an equally fake 'vice president' title on his or her business card, just like the broker earned in the Markarian v CIBC story.
(read this case for the fastest 'street smarts' lesson in professional financial abuse: search "Markarian v CIBC")

Fee based accounts earn money for the firm, on <u>every dollar</u> owned by the client, <u>every day</u> of the year. That, ladies and gentlemen, adds up to real money. A management discussion by RBC in 2001 showed how executives got $35 billion of client assets into internal fee-based products whereby the fee revenues roll in on autopilot.

No more, 'smile and dial', or 'churn and burn' to make commissions. Now a new term in industry circles is "reverse churning". Reverse churning is where a broker places 100% of Mrs. Jones account into fee based products, and then sits back doing almost nothing in the way of true money management for the client. His pay was guaranteed in the six or seven figures in a year, before the year was <u>one day</u> old. The only thing to <u>'manage'</u> is Mrs. Jones.

Thus, the new, fake investment 'advisor' has morphed into an asset-gathering machine for the investment dealer, which is today little more than a grain thrashing machine.

===========

Thought Interruption

<u>Combine:</u> An agricultural implement invented in the 1800's that 'combined' the farming acts of 'swathing' (cutting down) the stalks of grain to be harvested, and the "thrashing" process of beating and shaking out the kernels of wheat, separating the 'wheat from the chaff'.

I have not perfected the analogy, but there are similarities to an 'asset gathering' machine (the sales broker), 'combined' with a 'client thrashing' machine (the investment dealer).
End of thought interruption, back to your regularly scheduled reading.

===========

Her money is managed by robots, or proprietary funds, or advisor-fee accounts, or whatever. Just keep Mrs. Jones, (and any relatives) happy and you and your dealer can live comfortably off her account. I write this with cynicism, since it is not truly 'advice' as one would define the word, but at its worst it can be parasitic or even predatory abuse of clients.

It is a rampant form of elder abuse in todays financial world, and it is no wonder. Some of the wealthy are alone and vulnerable. It is a natural fit for a commission sales broker to become close to the vulnerable and become an essential 'friend'.

Instead of trusted financial advice, it is dressed as such, but resembles the kind of guidance your beautiful daughter might have received from someone like Bill Cosby… With apologies for offending good brokers by comparing the types of abuse, the comparison can still be made, and <u>that</u> is what is truly offensive.

It disturbed me then and it disturbs me today, because investment dealers have gotten away with the deception of passing off sales reps as fiduciary professionals. they have gotten rich doing it, and they have gotten better and better at it each year that I examine investment accounts.

The deceptive financial industry no longer 'serves' the average investor, but have become so market-dominant, that they can get away with the 'harvest' of their clients. When 90%+ of investments go to a handful of banks, there is little consumer choice left. Some wealthy clients used to make a living by farming, yet never do they figure out that when they turn their money over to the non-fiduciary advisor, they are very often 'being farmed'…themselves.

===========

After the economic (sub prime fraud) events of 2008 left the economy stunned and staggering I was fortunate enough to testify in a Parliamentary Justice and Human Rights committee. During this process Quebec MP Marlene Jennings pointed out in questioning that the new White Collar Crime Bill B52 (eventually passed as C21 after a prorogation of parliament) had some delicate banker-hacks written into it. They looked like this:

The bill was at one time called "Minimum Sentences for White Collar Crime." Its stated intentions were fine, but an amazing discovery was that a portion of the "Fraud" section of the Criminal Code of Canada was missing. Gone. Deleted. Erased. Vanished.

The Fraud section (Section 380) contains subsections that clarify and enhance the code. One of these, 380 (2), looks like this:

Affecting public market

(2) Every one who, by deceit, falsehood or other fraudulent means, whether or not it is a false pretense within the meaning of this Act, with intent to defraud, affects the public market price of stocks, shares, merchandise or anything that is offered for sale to the public is guilty of an indictable offense and liable to imprisonment for a term not exceeding fourteen years.

The Crime Bill C52 (labelled C21 in the next parliamentary session) was written with the section that applied to public markets fraud deleted.

To be clear, I am not saying that the Criminal Code of Canada was altered or changed. I am saying that anonymous co-authors of this government bill "erased" the portion of the bill that applied to public markets fraudsters (investment bankers, investment dealers, stockbrokers etc.) or, more accurately, carefully deleted these folks from the most harmful effects of the bill (jail).

How much pull must one have inside government to get your own industry deleted from the criminal code, in the creation of a bill?

In recent years I have seen others complain that oil companies participate in the writing of government environmental bills etc., and frankly, if I had not witnessed this (financial law manipulation) myself, it would be hard to believe. But I did, and so can anyone else who compares the Criminal Code of Canada with the Minimum Sentence Bill C21.

===========

Turning Criminal Acts Against North Americans into something which no longer fits the into the criminal code…is one unspoken result from having thousands of agents, agencies, lawyers and regulatory bodies on the payroll. Handmaidens…

I believe that if an academic study were done, it would find that paying industry-people to "circle the wagons" to protect and buffer even the indefensible, is in the billions each year in North America. I can come up with salaries of $1/4 billion just in counting four (4) Canadian Securities Commissions. FINRA, the U.S. broker regulator held a recorded cash position of $2 billion at about the time this book was being written. How does an investment 'regulatory' body get $2 billion in cash?   Probably not from public service or collecting and returning cans and bottles…or clients lost money.

===========

Systemic, financial Criminal Acts in Canada have thousands of persons who are paid to "launder" these acts of criminality into something clean and harmless appearing to society.

In the US, the SEC, FINRA, SIFMA and NASAA alone employ over ten thousand persons. I cannot begin to guess how many other industry trade bodies and self regulatory agents exist. You would think that one of them would talk about systemic abuse of the public. Double binds?

===========

In November 1996, 75-year old Melville Hunt and his 72-year old wife Marion transferred their mutual fund holdings to TD Evergreen Securities Inc. The funds were held in a non-discretionary cash account, (one in which all transactions must be approved by the client, just like 99% of investment accounts in North America)

On March 3, 1997, their investment advisor, sold some of their BCE shares without client permission. This is called 'discretionary trading' and is not an allowed industry practice for non-discretionary accounts.

A "non-discretionary" is the most common account in Canada. It is an account where each buy or sell transaction needs discussion between client and salesperson (aka 'advisor' before proceeding. The client has not given "discretion" to the salesperson to make all decisions in isolation. A discretionary account, on the other hand, is 'usually' an account where a fiduciary professional 'adviser' makes decisions and changes without client input. Some might say non-discretionary is "safer" for the average client since there is a required discussion prior to all trades.

This is not necessarily true, as the true difference is between hiring a fiduciary professional, which is actually safer AND cheaper for those who can find one, verses a disguised salesperson giving you direction on your life savings, with a hidden duty to his dealer and his commissions.

Discretionary accounts are usually reserved for those investors who are wealthy enough to have truly licensed, fiduciary professionals handle the daily management of it for them. If you are reading this book, there is a better than 96% chance that you do not have one of these licensed professionals....even if they say they are,.....it (the deception) is truly that encemic)

The 'cheat' by the industry is when they pose non-fiduciary, commission sales agents to the public as if they were licensed 'advisors', leading the investor to be under the mistaken belief that they are dealing with a true professional.

(few lawyers, judges and courts ever learn of the distinction between the marketing title, the true license, and the intended deception)

I spoke to Mrs. Hunt before she passed away, at a time when she was widowed and in her declining years. Shortly afterward I spoke to her son, a lawyer, about what his parents went through. He was a kind man to talk to, and he told me of his father's last days, spent in a hospital bed in the living room, dealing with finances, with lawyers and battling the special kinds of lawyers that serve banks. This while he was literally at death's door. This from the son who himself was a lawyer, but was unable to prevent nor solve his parent's victimization. This is the unique violence of white collar crime. The trusted organized criminals of today are as powerful as was the Catholic Church of the 16th Century.

I can call it victimization since I worked inside institutions like that. They have constructed a sub-industry of protection around themselves so well that they usually win. And even when they get caught cheating, they have so many layers of 'insulation' between themselves and justice, that they still manage to win over 90% of the time. Most investment victims never even spot their victimization, such is the cleverness and deceptions involved.

There are so many stories like this that I believe the abuse of the elderly, and the vulnerable by investment sellers, is an undeclared financial and social pandemic in North American. (Crime #1)

Add in the power of the banks, and legal gangs they retain to hold onto their moral high ground, (and your money:), and it becomes another pandemic of abuse and bullying to those unfortunate enough to have to live through it. (Crime #2)

If investment dealers say they owe no duty of care to clients who do not have discretionary accounts, so they admit that the majority of investors in Canada are in a "buyer beware" relationship? Sadly their advertising promises say otherwise.

In the Hunt's case, their advisor sold off a portion of their BCE shares without obtaining the authorization of the client (facts of the court finding 2001). This act in itself is illegal. But by a twist of logic, the end result (August 2003 Ontario Court of Appeal) states that since the client did not have the discretionary type of account, (since the client did not hand over complete control of the account to the advisor) they do not owe the client a fiduciary duty of care (a duty to place the interest of the client ahead of the advisor).

http://investorvoice.ca/Cases/Investor/Hunt/Hunt.htm

http://investorvoice.ca/Presentations/SCFEA/SCFEA_Elford.pdf

===========

This is a good example of the twisted legal treatment that often seems to apply to higher-status parties (banks and investment broker/dealers) in our justice system. They seem to have found a magical ability to violate the law, and yet win, at the same time. Heads they win, tails you lose…

Though the firm had broken rules by making an unauthorized trade, it did not seem to matter. If this does not make sense to you don't feel bad. I am having a hard time with it myself, and I have decades in the industry. As mentioned earlier, there may well be some contributory factors by the client that added to his or her damages, but if the argument is that "we don't owe you a duty of care if you have this (non-discretionary) type of account", I would find this a dangerous and industry damaging precedent. It is also a quite fictional fabrication, when compared with the promises of the industry.

For the investment industry, this would send a message directly opposite to that which it is trying to send, that being, "trust us, we will place your financial situation on a solid foundation, and we will use our expertise and experience to your benefit".

Rather it sends the message of, "we take _your_ money, and _our_ experience, and turn it into _our_ money and _your_ experience".

===========

Written 'stakeholder' submissions to the Ontario Securities Commission (OSC) revealed another insight into the 'winner takes all' mentality. Many submissions by financial dealers and institutions argued for _not_ having to introduce industry rules for placing the best interests of the customers first.

They argued that the principles already exist in the halls of common law, and thus do not need to be placed into the industry halls. In other words, 'we would rather force our clients to sue us…where we have 'special' lawyers who have _ways_ to deal with these things'.

Additionally, if they can limit enforcement efforts to only those with the strength to take on a billion dollar corporation, they eliminate 99.9% of their legal problems.

For those interested in which dealers do not feel it necessary to protect their customers in this way see, their submissions are here:
http://www.osc.gov.on.ca/en/38075.htm

This is a list of 'stakeholder' Comment letters Received for The Standard of Conduct for Advisors and Dealers: Exploring the Appropriateness of Introducing a Statutory Best Interest Duty When Advise is Provided to Retail Clients (comments closed February 22, 2013)

Update, 2017, regulators are...almost at the point of thinking about...maybe...considering...talking about...placing a 'best interest' standard into effect for investors. With more than 1/4 billion dollars of industry money being paid to these regulators, I think they can afford to wind that 'runaround' clock for another few decades. They have managed this quite well for the last 3 decades...

Michael Jackson did something similar called a "Moonwalk". He artfully put forth an appearance of walking forward...while what he was doing was gliding backward.

===========

Principles of common law say that professionals shall not take advantage, victimize, or abuse clients, yet financial industry people are saying they do not wish to put these principles into their own industry. Why? Because if they did they may have to follow them, whereas today the only way they come into effect is if clients can come up with the time, money and effort to go to court to gain access to the principles of paid law.

Experts have commented that access to the justice system is an insurmountable obstacle for many people. Since the regulatory system can be paid to not enforce ethical principles, financial players are often never held to account. This leaves an abused investor with

several strikes against them, making it difficult or impossible to seek justice through the courts.
1. Investors are often older, perhaps senior citizens, and having the time and emotional strength to do ten years of battle with the world's strongest financial institutions is difficult for anyone.

2. They may also be financially squeezed and unable to come up with hundreds of thousands of dollars to find help and guidance through the legal jungle. The strongest financial institutions have no difficulty with time, money, or guidance hurdles. They have your money, after all.

3. If the client is younger, or less well off, the dollar values from the abuse might be too small to justify a legal battle, so gains from hundred thousand dollar abuses of the public stays with the perpetrator as free money.

Instead of justice, the abused investor is usually steered to one of a dozen investment "authorities"—agents, regulators, self-regulators, ombudsmen, fake-ombudsmen, trade and lobby groups posing as regulators, etc. And then they are given the greatest game of 'run-around' seen since the tobacco industry of the 1960's.

REGULATORY WHITEWASH

Expert Ken Kivenko and 70 year old victim Peter Whitehouse came up with this term and description for the regulator runaround game. Ken has decades in investor advocacy work and Peter is a victim who has written hundreds of letters in attempts to gain fairness.

The K/W cycle: (of Regulatory Whitewash)

This term was coined by Ken and Peter. Both observed a consistency in government agency and regulatory response behavior. It goes like this:
1. The first response to an enquiry doesn't address the question(s) asked.

2. The inquirer asks for clarification and is again met with a non-responsive reply.

3. A third attempt at getting an answer results in a request not to ask the question again.

4. A fourth attempt results in a notice informing the enquirer that the file is closed and no further communications will be forthcoming.

I see this happen over and over…and over, when trying to help victims of professional financial abuse. The pros have rigged the playing field decades in advance of any hapless investor entering into the arena. Any member of the public has no idea they are simply entering a spin and rinse machine…to professionally and very delicately launder crimes of financial abuse. Ken Kivenko is another person who has worked tirelessly for decades to protect investors.

==========

The number of industry-paid agencies, performing in the skit of "public protection" is as long as a small-town telephone directory. In my film Breach of Trust, I show a list of about 100 such bodies. Most of those I have found are incentivized to not give equal balance to the public, but to tip the scales in favor of the industry instead.

There are few cases of individuals who tried to take financial institutions to court. Sadly, most were abused by the legal process as well, adding insult to their financial injury. The circle-the-wagons effect does not stop at just the wagons in the financial industry.

"Whacking the complainant" is so prevalent that if you Google it you will find an entire universe of legal tricks on how to do just that. Another term is victim blaming.

The personal stories I outline at the start of each chapter are *not* the tip of the iceberg. They are a mere fraction of the tip of the iceberg. For a man like Harold Blanes of Kelowna to go through the time and costs he went through, at age 90, makes him literally one in a million. Mr. Markarian is another one in one million example.

Most cases are dropped without even going past a simple letter of complaint. Such letters are usually answered by an industry-paid member and always in a manner suggesting that there is no fault by the industry member. I find at least a half dozen layers of regulatory 'insulation' that gets placed between any abused investor and being made whole by the industry.

Usually four to six layers of fake 'help' is put in front of the abused client while they are still working within and talking to the firm that abused them. (internal bank employees falsely pretending to be industry "ombudsmen", brokers, sales managers, branch managers, compliance officers, senior compliance officers, head office management etc, before the abused client is even allowed to approach the next level of a half dozen industry-paid bodies. Watching it is like standing helpless on a riverbank while a swimmer is trapped in the backwash of a weir. Most stay trapped for years before giving up exhausted…by its clever design.

I suspect I could ask North Americans to send me a copy of their "we find no merit to your complaint about XYZ investment dealer….." letters, and I would have tens or hundreds of thousands of such letters. Go ahead, post them on Facebook's INVESTMENT SYSTEM FRAUD group, or Tweet to @RecoveredBroker and we will try and make the world a bit more aware, and safer.

Other cases are settled for pennies on the dollar, IF the complainant goes to the time, trouble, and expense of taking the complaint all the way, and IF the complainant signs a confidentiality agreement, meaning that the investment industry gets to use the victim's own money as extortion money to silence it's victims.

Financial players thus get to 'decriminalize' their acts, using the customers own money to do so…*spin cycle complete…please remove any remaining items from the machine.*

Am I being too harsh? Try to imagine what I have seen in twenty years from the last millennium, and almost twenty in this millennium…

I am aware of more investment abuse-victim suicides, over that time, than of prosecutions against systemic financial abuse.

As I work on this book, I also act as an independent industry analyst, and in that capacity I deal with investors on matters involving systemic financial predation.

An experience I had today reminded me that Securities Commissions and self regulatory agencies are designed to protect the financial industry from being subject to laws which protect consumers.

Criminal violations, Competition Act violations of the public, and so on, must go through a <u>separate doorway</u>, where specially selected regulators can "sift" each one in a manner which provides a veneer of public protection, all while preventing systemic abuse from ever being discovered.

Systemic financial abuses, and the ability to harvest Canadians, and launder criminal acts, turning them in to 'clean, non-criminal acts' is protected, at all costs in Canada. I see the same game in the U.S.

Securities Regulators in North America are the equivalent of Columbian coffee beans…in both examples they are hand-picked to protect the systemic, long term harvest of Trillions.

<u>Chapter Takeaways and discussion topics for @RecoveredBroker</u>

1. The vast majority of investment regulators in North America are fully paid (or picked) by the investment industry that they regulate. The SEC is the only entity known to me which is paid by government, however it is obvious that SEC directors and top staff are hand selected by the interests of the financial industry.

2. Paying billions of dollars to your own "rental cops" is like the purchase of a simple insurance policy, giving the investment industry a blanket of coverage which protects the industry from real accountability.

3. There is no protection (and no desire for protection) within the financial system for financial abuses which are systemic, meaning the abuses that apply across the system to millions and millions of investors.

I stand to be corrected and am wide open to polite, informed and respectful public discourse on these matters. The Facebook group titled "Investment System Fraud" is dedicated to gaining a better understanding of the facts, the issues and finding honest solutions.

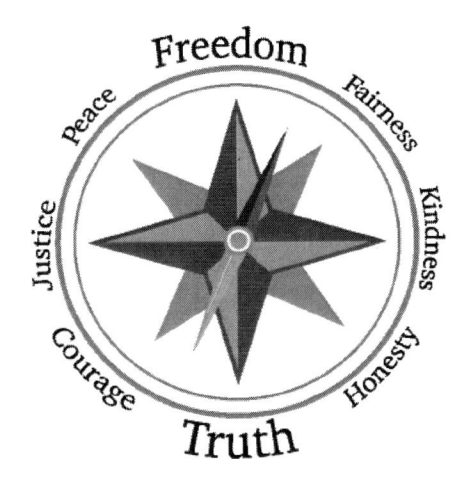

CHAPTER TWELVE

AS PROTECTED AS IF YOU ARE IN AN LA RIOT…

Imagine if you had a secret power, which would allow you to get away with any crime…

In Plato's "Republic," Socrates invokes the myth of the 'Ring of Gyges', which conferred upon its wearer the power of being invisible to others.

"If we wear such a ring", Socrates says, "No man would keep his hands off what was not his own when he could safely take what he liked."

===========

Some readers may recall the LA riots of 1992, also known as the Rodney King riots.

At approximately 6:45 pm, Reginald Oliver Denny, a white truck driver who stopped at a traffic light at the intersection of Florence and Normandie Avenues, was dragged from his vehicle and severely beaten by a mob of local residents as a television news helicopter hovered above, piloted by reporter Bob Tur, who broadcast live pictures of the attack, including a concrete brick that was thrown by 'Football' Damian Williams that struck Denny in the temple, causing a near-fatal seizure. As Tur continued his reporting, it was clear that local police had deserted the area.

The police had, for a time, decided to not enter the neighborhood where much of the damage was taking place.

The following article titled "Destruction in 1992 L.A. Upheaval: How law enforcement let the largest urban riot/rebellion rage on" sheds some light onto what happens when there is no law in the neighborhood.

<http://sundial.csun.edu/2012/04/destruction-in-1992-l-a-upheaval-how-law-enforcement-let-the-largest-urban-riotrebellion-rage-on/>

"For about a week, Korea-town and South L.A. residents were left to fend for themselves and thousands of businesses were destroyed. According to accounts by Radio Korea, Korean-American business owners repeatedly called 911, but were told that they were on their own. Korean-American men, not willing to give up their livelihoods so easily, took up arms to protect their businesses and ran into burning buildings to save their cash registers and any merchandise they could manage."

"Where were the police? According to Dr. Tracy Buenavista, professor of Asian-American studies at CSUN, many armed personnel were sent to north and west Los Angeles, concerned that the violence would spread to areas like Beverly Hills."

When the locals learned that police were not responding, many turned toward "winner take all" thinking. In my observations, this is what happens in today's financial systems. Those who are granted certain powers soon find that those powers confer something akin to the Ring of Gyges, the ability to get away with anything. Including financial murder. "No Cops equals no consequences."

I maintain that investors are left to fend for themselves among the most dangerous gangs in the world—financial gangs who pick their own members to police themselves, never do they live with, or fear criminal sanctions like other people or professions.

===========

"When plunder becomes a way of life for a group of men... they create for themselves, in the course of time, a legal system that authorizes it, and a moral code that glorifies it." – Frederic Bastiat, The Law [1850]

===========

In the case of retired Calgary firefighter Gordon Simpson, who had a bad experience with his investment dealer, and made a complaint to the Alberta Securities Commission.

He was told by the Securities Commission to go elsewhere, that he had to take his complaint instead to the Investment Dealers Association (IDA). The IDA was the old industry trade body and lobby-group that sold out the public interest with such consistency, that they were forced to 'rebrand'. Former Canadian Finance Minister Joe Oliver began his earlier days at a brokerage firm and moved his way up to the head of this IDA. When lobbyists become politicians it seems to be the beginning of the end for the public.

The supreme court of Canada had decided that this trade body "does not owe a duty of care to the public". Only to their own members. It was just another 'head-fake', with an 'industry protector', pretending to be a 'public interest defender'.

Of course Mr. Simpson's case was dismissed by the IDA, as often intentionally happens when you take a complaint to the very association of members about which you are complaining.

He appealed this "decision" by the IDA. Guess what? His appeal was denied. They would not even hear his appeal. There were two strange reasons given. One is that the IDA has their own special meaning for the word "decision", and they said (in writing) to Mr. Simpson, "a refusal to carry on with investigating a complaint was not actually a "decision" and therefore could not be appealed". (since their rules said that only a 'decision' could be appealed...)

In further argument, they stated that "Therefore, not every decision meets the definition of "decision" for the purposes of the Act."

In case that logic was not bulletproof enough, they had a backup reason to go with. Another reason given for not allowing Mr. Simpson to appeal the 'decision', was that Mr. Simpson was "not a party directly affected by the decision", and therefore he was not allowed to appeal.

This is the second time I have heard the investment dealers association pull this excuse out of lawyer-land... they gave the same foolish logic to another investor, Mr. Jim Roache of Ottawa when his case also was dismissed out of hand. Mr. Roache is quoted as having said, "If I was not a person directly affected by this, who the hell was? It was my savings, my retirement, my failed marriage..."

The Investment Dealers association was unable to grasp this simple logic (something about $200,000 salaries) and they were unable to answer Mr. Roache, or Mr. Simpson. Today, their name has changed, however that seems about all.

During my years in the industry, it became apparent that self-regulation breeds self-serving behaviors at best, and gang-like de-criminalization at worst. It allowed the investment industry to get away with crime, and the only time repercussions were expected was if the infraction affected the revenues or profits of a firm. Or, occasionally, if an industry member needed to be "dealt with" for not being a 'team player'.

The "winner take all" culture grows when there are effectively no police, no prosecutors, and virtually no criminal codes applied for systemic financial crimes. Morals and ethics are often forgotten in any situation where you can put as much as you can fit, into your pockets, knowing there will be no repercussions. As long as the Corporate pocket is filled as well, it is the modern day equivalent of the Ring of Gyges.

Police are not often invited (or willing) to look into investment crimes, and for the abused investor, going to the police is often an exercise in futility. One case I followed resulted in criminal charges, but it was a small, single fraudster and not systemic.

Most victims of criminal abuse are not allowed access into the public systems of criminal justice, but are told to go to the securities regulatory system instead. This can be the equivalent of sending an abuse victim to people who are being paid by the abuser. That is exactly how a gang would do it.

If a large profile financial crime takes place in Canada, it may be brought to the attention of the RCMP. They ran an "Integrated Market Enforcement Team" (IMET), which in principle sounded great. It was designed to consist of teams of financial and legal experts from various professions who would police high-value or important economic crime.

The year I researched them in depth (after five or more years of essentially no results) I found them to have a budget of $18 million for the entire country of Canada. This was back in about 2004 if memory serves me, and looking today I see that they were up to $38 million in 2008/2009 year, and $40 million in 2009/2010.

At that time the budget for my local city police force, serving a population of 85,000, was $17 million. It became clear to me why the IMET teams were ineffective. They were given nothing to work with. Their published budget was so small that one financial report item held an entry for <u>one new vehicle</u>. Never before have I seen a budget so small, as to require a line item to show $38,000 spent to purchase "one new vehicle", across the entire country.

I now believe (15 years later) that this force was a facade of protection—by intention of the powers above them. I see it as yet another 'head-fake', not intended to catch the top institutions in the country, but as a mere pretense of protection. We are being harvested of wealth in manners which Canadians (and Americans) may never be able to believe. Why? Because we simply do not prosecute at the top levels, where the most economic damage is done. What we do is 'pretend to police'… at those levels.

So the police will likely not help you if you have been systemically defrauded, the RCMP financial crimes division is questionable, cannot handle more than a couple of crimes per year, (while studies report that one million Canadians have been affected by fraud) and the criminal code section as applied to the greatest financial crimes has been erased.

Investment Industry trade magazines, and some newspapers, have joined in calling for honest regulatory system in a country where the regulators appear backwards at best. Note this Toronto Star article titled "Why the OSC so Rarely Gets its Man."
<https://docs.google.com/file/d/0BzE_LMPDi9UOb2pZMUwzZEl4Znc/edit?usp=sharing>

I could go on, and probably will in other areas of this book, but with what we have covered so far I hope you can see why your money is as un-protected as you would be in an LA riot…unless you happen to live in Beverly Hills.

===========

Thought Interruption

Of interest is that the official Canadian Ombudsman for Banking Services and Investments (OBSI) was 'neutered' in 2013:

"*OBSI's Terms of Reference were amended in December 2013 to remove OBSI's systemic issue investigative powers.*"

This after they got close to investment abuse investigations (at one of Canada's top banks) where they claimed that the abuses were 'systemic', ie, the client abuses applied to thousands or millions of client accounts across the country.

The Canadian system is perfectly designed so that <u>the Official Banking Ombudsman is forbidden to act</u>...in matters that involve systemic abuses of millions and millions of North Americans.

This is perhaps one of the biggest indicators of a perfectly designed system that enables crime, rather than enabling justice.

I hope the image below helps convey the 'impossibility' of expecting regulatory bodies to protect the public from harm, while themselves being financially funded by those they regulate... <u>who profit from doing the harm</u>. Can you see the problem?

When looking at one end of the figure below, it appears to form a solid structure, and yet from the other end it is seen to be an impossibility.

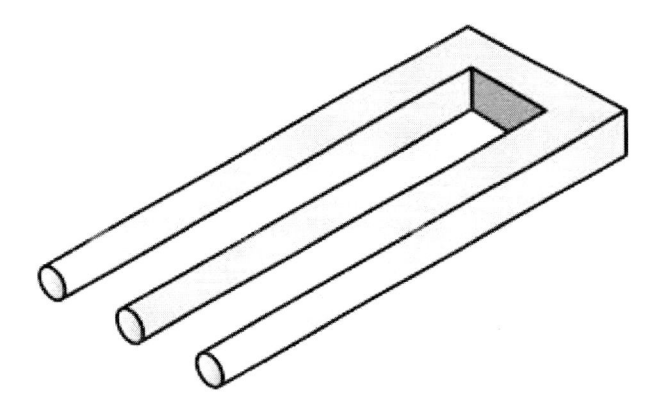

Upon close inspection the process is not what it seems and it becomes clear that it is false.

This principle conveys the current state of financial protection of the public, which <u>appears</u> to have regulators protecting the public from financial players, whilst extremely close inspection reveals only two bodies in the loop, the regulators connected firmly to the financial players, while the public protection is a mirage.

Financial regulatory regimes have become a "netherworld of nepotistic appointments".

Your financial freedom, your family's security, and your society is placed at risk due to this nepotism.

North Americans are thus forced to work ten to twenty years longer than they would in a society which policed their top looters.

As famed speaker, author, and motivator Tony Robbins so simply puts it, "each extra 1% in fees that you hand over to someone for investment advice, removes about ten years of financial freedom or of your retirement. 2% added fees removes 20 years.

It is insidious to imagine that while true licensed fiduciary professionals only charge about 1% (or less) to manage money properly, while a few hundred thousand faked advisors thrash their unsuspecting clients for 2%, 3% and even up to 5% in fees and commissions.

Now you know how banks and financial institutions can produce billions in quarterly profits as if by some magic. It is magic. It is the best sleight of hand, magic ever performed in North America. David Copperfield would be amazed at what financial institutions can 'disappear'.

It pains me to say that I was part of an industry that took and still takes advantage of the trust and the vulnerability of their customers, while promising professionalism.

At risk of repeating this, I will mention that almost every citizen in Canada and the USA is allowed to file their own 'private' criminal charges (without need for police or any 'body'). I will cover this topic in more detail in the 'solutions' chapter. Is there a Rosa Louise Parks out there…Anyone?

"Society cannot breathe when young and old are destroyed, used up as fodder for pathological systems of greed and power."
--Larry Elford 2017

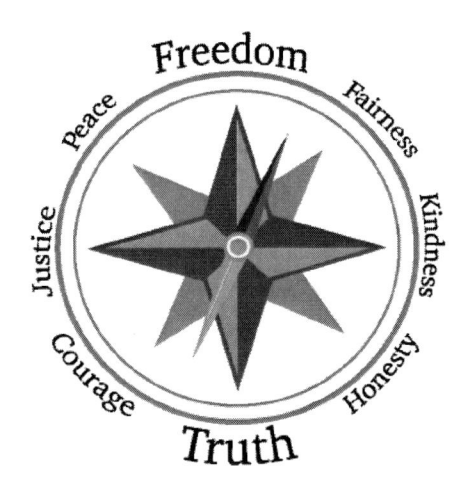

CHAPTER THIRTEEN

SEE NO EVIL

"The laws are lenient in Canada and crooks know it."

Claude Lamoureux – Former President and CEO of the Ontario Teachers' Pension Plan (from 1990 until his retirement in 2007) One of Canada's top professional money managers.

===========

The Public Service Pension Plan of Canada (PSPP) took a write-down in their 2008/2009 financial report of approximately $1 billion dollars. This is the pension plan for retired RCMP and judges. Ironically, the RCMP did not even know their pensions were being robbed, when they worked alongside the regulatory bodies to quietly close a complaint file alleging criminal activity.

The RCMP also did not seem to know that the regulatory bodies they "collaborate" with, are the very agencies who granted exemption to our laws to allow tainted investments to be sold in Canada, and to many American investors. (refer to Chapter Eleven)

Imagine if a (hypothetical) Judge could lose money four different ways in a certain type of investment, and never be aware. How well-organized would that financial scam have to be? Let's picture a hypothetical situation based on a real example to see how that might have happened.

When the city of Lethbridge invested over $32 million in improperly rated, 'sub-prime' (lower quality) mortgage investments, it never recovered its entire investment back, and it took ten years to get a partial recovery. A judge in this city would have lost one-time due to his taxes being wasted on improperly rated, and sub-legal investments. (We can also add securities rating agencies into the OFC cabal)

Loss number two for our hypothetical Judge is found in the Auditor General report of 2008/9 on the Alberta Treasury Branch (ATB). It shows that ATB put over 60% of every public deposit dollar into these sub-prime investments, to gain an increased return of .08%. That is a *ton* of risk to take for <u>virtually nothing in additional return</u>.

The Alberta government of the day did the "shoot, shut up and shovel" type public disclosure (meaning none:) about these losses, so unfortunately we have no idea how much Albertans lost on this one, but our hypothetical Judge suffered a second-blow through his Provincial taxes in this manner.

A third hit came when this Judge personally invested in these "safe" investments at the encouragement of his so-called 'advisor' at the bank.

Finally, the 2008/9 annual report of the Public Service Pension Plan of Canada, (PPSP) reveals that this judge's pension manager took a write down of just over $1 billion from these mortgage investments.

That makes four-hits, which a Canadian Judge could suffer financially whilst never figuring out how the system is rigged.

Source http://www.tbs-sct.gc.ca/reports-rapports/pspp-rrfp/2009/rpspp-rrrfp02-eng.asp#c17) (search the term ABCP)

The PPSPS is the pension plan in Canada for retired Judges and RCMP officers, among other government employees.

Fast forward to the same hypothetical Judge in a courtroom, where a giant investment dealer is being sued by a victim of misrepresentation and deception. The judge grants 'credibility' or 'weight' to the information which is most comforting to his instincts.
(see The Honest Truth About Dishonesty, film and behavioral economic studies with Dan Ariely to learn how that is possible: https://en.wikipedia.org/wiki/The_Honest_Truth_about_Dishonesty)

The judge may do this this while ignoring evidence of impropriety, license falsification, deception, misrepresentation etc. I have seen it a few times and it is an amazing thing to witness, to see human instincts of 'self' protection kick in, to taint even the judicial process at higher altitudes.

Despite losing four times with the very elements as evidenced in the courtroom, the status quo still must be revered, and some judges still unconsciously (or consciously) decide things based upon herd instinct and self preservation. Justice gets postponed for yet another day, when even our judiciary is at risk of being captured.

Securities regulators have thus allowed (by granting exemption to securities laws) a transfer of wealth from the pockets of society into the pockets of securities regulators, investment product creators and investment salespeople. It is an improper or an unjust enrichment which drains society more than any other factor I can find.

Loss after loss after loss...drains the country of wealth. Done with the help of the regulators, using (selling?) government granted powers of "discretion".

153

Then when the matter comes before the court for a 'restructuring' the first thing applied for (and granted by a judge) is immunity from civil prosecution, to all those involved in what would then be the largest crime in Canadian history at $32 billion. A different judge ensured that this was granted, again not knowing that his own pension plan was down by $1 billion dollars.....by this very crime.

By way of comparison, all crime in Canada each year is estimated to do financial harm in the neighborhood of $50 to $70 billion, vs $32 billion for one easy white collar scheme.

At an average cost of $5000 for every property crime in Canada, this $32 billion would amount to financial, regulatory and legal folks, being able to cause financial harm equal to six million four hundred thousand property criminals. For just one easy white collar scheme. A scheme so well done that even when the entire thing failed, not a single perp was nailed. Now THAT is free money.

"I'm just hoping we can keep this whole thing under control after the police find out we're stealing their pensions!"

When the RCMP IMET were dragged, (kicking and screaming) into action, who did they call upon to give them expert advice on how to close the case? (yes, I said that) None other than Securities Commission persons, who sit on committees with the RCMP IMET. Securities Commissions were the same bodies who granted permission to violate the laws. By way of irony RCMP officer's pension monies are also held in the same Public Service pension plan.

Included in complaints that prompted the RCMP into action were allegations that the Securities Commissions were complicit in removing public interest protections from these investments, going as far as acting in breach of the public trust. Thus for the RCMP to turn to these same regulatory commissions for advice on the case strikes this writer as the epitome of unskilled investigative procedure.

They were getting 'help' on the case, from the people who 'helped' allow the $32 billion to be taken from Canadians.

Either way, the forgiving tone of justifications for closing the file without finding wrongdoing read like a report written by the very people alleged partially responsible for the losses. In reality it was written by those people.

I was shocked to read Jonathon Chevreau, Financial Post, August 13, 2005 titled "Getting Your Day in Court."

It stated that the RCMP only has the resources to investigate 5% of the complaints that come to it about the investment industry!

Today, with the RCMP firmly entrenched 'inside' the offices of the Ontario Securities Commission, I have to search my memory to recall if I have even heard of any Integrated Market Enforcement Team (IMET) investigation in recent years. I suspect now that there will never be one which investigates systemic crimes against Canadians. That is where hundreds of billions are at stake…thus no human power is allowed to go there.

The startling, human behaviors mentioned in this Chapter are well explained in Dan Ariely's work.

2 minute YouTube trailer here "(Dis)Honesty - The Truth About Lies" - Teaser Trailer   https://youtu.be/dQMbDMnvxFs

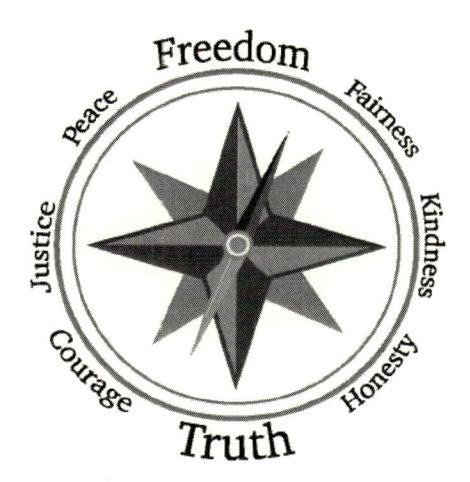

CHAPTER FOURTEEN

THE UNIQUE VIOLENCE OF FINANCIAL CRIME

When the very best get together, a herd is created, criminal or otherwise. Some call it a system. Some milk it like a herd.

"People are always saying 'I never give homeless people money, they'll probably buy crack or booze with it.' What did you think they were going to buy? A four piece entertainment centre with a nice rug and some throw pillows? If I was living in a box covered in my own urine I'd likely use substances to escape my reality too."
-- Audrey Skoog

Audrey Skoog is the manager at an emergency shelter in Medicine Hat, Alberta, and pioneer in the effort to eradicate homelessness in her community. Audrey was one of those who walked the sidewalks of Medicine Hat in order to get positive things started in her community.

===============

What would $10 billion drained each week from the U.S. economy look like? How about $1 billion a week drained from Canada?

Recessionary? Economic decline? Jobs? Homelessness? Hopelessness? Social nervous breakdown?

The nightly news shows these effects on society each day. It is like watching the stress and pain of fear, anger and poverty slowly being turned up for the entire country. All that human suffering, perhaps even the loss of the freedoms, the democracy of once great nations, just so that one small fraction of the country can loot all the rest.

Does your city look like mine? Do new business openings often bring another liquor store, tattoo parlor, check cashing store, dollar store, or pawn shop?

If you have seen more of this and fewer 'real' economic engines coming to a neighborhood near you, then you are already a victim of the unique violence of the 'trusted', organized financial sector, even if you have not a nickel invested yourself.

Economic decline, people forced to work more than one job—or work ten or twenty years past a typical retirement age—and a general loss in the country's prosperity are signs that there is a great leak in our economic 'ship'. Since we are all owners and passengers in that ship, we all have an interest in it when it starts to sink.

I think I have found the greatest leak in the economy…and it is by the people we trust to serve and to protect us. I could well be wrong, but I hope to start the conversation.

Let's look beyond the economic costs the population faces so that the financial sector (and assorted handmaidens) can prosper.

What about human costs?

Psychological—aggression, depression, addiction, self-sabotaging behaviors, domestic problems, career problems, problems with the law, violence, and suicide. The list goes on. At one point in time the police chief in my community said that if it were not for alcohol we would almost not need the police. I believe that substance abuse is a major trigger for much of the work police do. I also know that human fear pain and suffering is a major trigger for substance abuse. (Thanks Dr. Gabor Maté)

Substance abuse is just one of the problems that come as a byproduct of being financially robbed, victimized, and then morally injured when there is zero recourse for those crimes. Fear of economic uncertainty is one of man's most common fears, and economic decline due to professional looters gives an entire society reason to live in that fear.

Imagine financial abuse as like any other form of abuse—physical, sexual, psychological. Now imagine that the abusers in this case are some of the world's strongest corporations who can cheat you financially, and then beat you legally.

They can out-fund, out-wait, out-lawyer, (perhaps out-judge), and out-maneuver you in any arena.

Investors are often a victim three times.

Once when they give their trust and this is betrayed. (moral injury)

Twice when your money and their experience is turned into their money and your experience. (financial injury)

A third time when you complain to authorities and are treated to the type of 'process' any bully or organized gang would practice. (psychological trauma)

You could also be bankrupted through the process, or left with so little financial security as to be close to bankruptcy. All because one segment of the population is above our laws.

It should come as no surprise to learn that the most rapacious investment predators and bullies, when cornered, will hire only the most rapacious, 'whack the complainant' lawyers. If you have read about the brutal attacks by lawyers on victims of sexual violence when they take 'upper crust' abusers to court, then you may imagine what those lawyers will do to you if you ever try and take their investment banker clients to court.

The abuses of the financial sector may in fact do far more social damage to the fabric of society than financial harm, even knowing that financial crimes are greater than the cost of every other crime.

If you are still in doubt about that last line, just ask yourself how many trillions have been required to claw the USA out of the 2008 near collapse of the entire financial system. That was Organized Financial Crime (OFC) at its very best. They nearly brought the world to economic collapse, and yet managed to keep their jobs, get a bailout (from the public) and what, two persons were prosecuted? One? None?

===========

Sept 15th....Today in market history, 2008:
Lehman Brothers declares bankruptcy. At $639 billion, it's the largest in the history of the United States.

===========

The 'unique' violence of white collar crime is in how there seems to be no justice, no recourse, and no objective accountability at the upper levels. 'Self' regulation allows white collar criminals to police themselves, or to have 'brothers-in-arms' police them, which is the same thing. Ordinary police and criminal prosecutors 'stand down' when it comes to white collar crime. Financial players are thus free to play in completely "uncontrolled air space". It's free money.

This places your life's work, your security and your society, at the mercy of people who have friends, cronies and insiders pretending to police them.

I repeatedly witness victims of the financial industry left spinning in circles by the myriad of paid-agents hired to protect and insulate the industry, all while promising they are there to protect and defend the public. It is like watching a slow motion train wreck. Except that what is being destroyed is society.

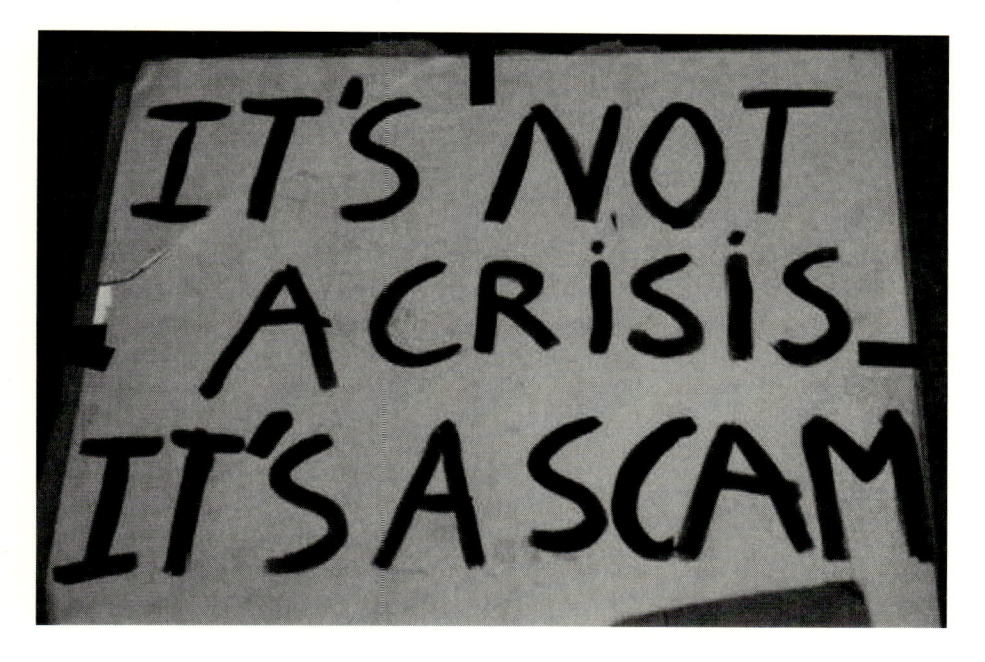

Self-regulation allows self-dealing by any group, and it results from politicians and government taking severe shortcuts in serving the public.

To wipe their hands of trouble they contract 'financial regulation' out to the very people who will profit from turning a blind eye. This is another 'insulation' effect, in that it puts distance between the politician and the wrongs of the industry. Dual insulation, in effect, when it also serves to protect and insulate the industry from application of the criminal code.

Then when victims discover their retirement cheated from them, by clever system design, they also find themselves the victim of a "storytelling exercise" by the very folks who are supposed to protect you.

The fight for justice against corruption is never easy. It never has been and never will be. It exacts a toll on ourselves, our families, our friends, and especially our children. In the end, I believe, the price we pay is well worth holding on to our dignity.
--Frank Serpico

===========

A great resource for those interested is New York Times bestselling author Maria Konnikova's book, "The Confidence Game: Why We Fall for It…Every Time",

She writes that anyone can be conned—literally. Most people respond by saying, "No, everyone but me." However, because thinking that "everyone but me can be conned," is why everyone can be conned. Precisely because we all think we cannot…so we seem to have a pre-built blind spot.

All the con artist needs do to get beyond anyone's natural defenses, is to discover enough about the victim, so that they know what some of the victims' hopes and dreams are, and then the con begins. What follows is a carefully orchestrated 'play' to make the victim think that the con has 'exactly' the same hopes and dreams, or can empathize enough with the victims dreams, to help them make it happen.

No victim seems able to resist those who can promise us our dreams. Now translate that into the daily marketing promises of the financial industry, and ask yourself if they have perhaps studied "The Confidence Game: Why We Fall for It…Every Time"
-- Maria Konnikova

"It is no measure of health to be well adjusted in a profoundly sick society."
--Krishnamurti

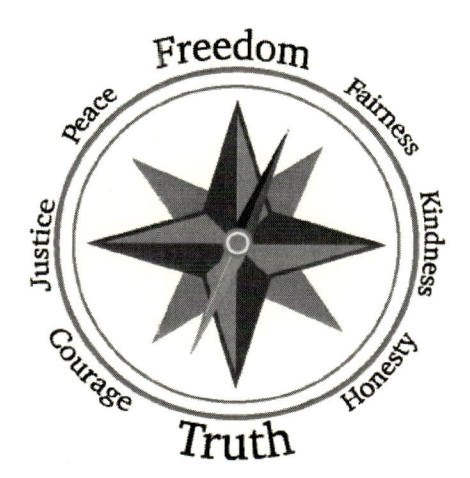

CHAPTER FIFTEEN

THE CO$T OF FINANCIAL TRICKERY

The following is an excerpt by Pam Martens of Wall Street on Parade:

The Occupy Wall Street slogan from the era accurately sums up the Federal government's actions: "Banks Got Bailed Out; We Got Sold Out." As a result of a Federal Reserve audit amendment tacked on to the Dodd-Frank financial reform legislation in 2010 by Senator Sanders, the public learned the following year from the Government Accountability Office (GAO) that the Federal Reserve had secretly sluiced more than $16 trillion in almost zero interest rate loans to Wall Street banks and their foreign peers, many of whom were counter-parties to their insanely leveraged derivative trades.

In January of this year, the GAO* provided further research on the financial relief provided to real human beings in America. The GAO study showed that as of October 31, 2016, the government "had disbursed $22.6 billion (60 percent) of the $37.51 billion Troubled Asset Relief Program (TARP) funds" that were directed at helping distressed homeowners who were impacted by the 2008 Wall Street financial crash and resulting housing bust.

Just four banks, Citigroup, Morgan Stanley, Merrill Lynch and Bank of America received $7.8 trillion, almost half of the total $16 trillion.

http://wallstreetonparade.com/2017/10/puerto-rico-relief-efforts-pale-to-that-for-just-one-wall-street-bank/

===========

Forbes says this: "The Special Inspector General for TARP summary of the bailout says that the total commitment of government is $16.8 trillion dollars with the $4.6 trillion already paid out."
https://www.forbes.com/sites/mikecollins/2015/07/14/the-big-bank-bailout/#158da6912d83

===========

By way of comparison: American taxpayers have spent $1.46 trillion on wars abroad since September 11, 2001.

Defense Department: The War On Terror Has Cost $250 Million A Day For 16 Years
http://www.ibtimes.com/political-capital/defense-department-war-terror-has-cost-250-million-day-16-years-2608639

"Who needs terror?…when bankers, regulators, lawyers and political handmaidens can harvest society more than war. Financial crime **is** terror, for those being farmed, and for a nation being looted from within its own borders…by "trusted" criminals.

===========

Investoradvocates.ca is an old-school website which I began in about 2004. I have not 'modernized' it since, so it is antique enough that there are no advertisements, cookies or pop-ups, involved with the site. It is just a 'curator-style' repository of investment industry misconduct and malpractice. Its main focus is on cataloging investment industry tricks which have become standard industry practices against most Canadian and American investors.

At this website you will find about 48 general topics in the realm of investment sales.

It began as a discussion forum in 2004, to allow people to collaborate and exchange information, and to protect the public interest in financial matters. In that regard it has not had the success I had envisioned, and came under such attack from industry participants who did not wish these tricks to be revealed to the public, that it very quickly had to be closed to public comments. It has since served as a gathering spot for articles, industry facts, traps and solutions.

If you visit this site, the section of posts under the topic
"Financial crime more than every other crime combined?" is a loosely gathered list of financial failures.

My understanding is that organized systems of finance, law, accounting, politics, lobbying, self-regulation, and industry-paid (or industry hand-picked) government regulation…come together in the perfect harvest of society.

===========

Credit to Russell Mokhiber for the following:

The FBI estimates, for example, that burglary and robbery -- street crimes -- costs the nation $3.8 billion a year.

The losses from a handful of major corporate frauds -- Tyco, Adelphia, Worldcom, Enron -- swamp the losses from all street robberies and burglaries combined.

Health care fraud alone costs Americans $100 billion to $400 billion a year.

The savings and loan fraud -- which former Attorney General Dick Thornburgh called "the biggest white collar swindle in history" -- cost anywhere from $300 billion to $500 billion.

Corporate criminals are the only criminal class in the United States that have the power to define the laws under which they live.

Mafia? No.
Hells Angels? No.
Street Thugs? No
Corporate criminal lobby? Yes. A million times yes...

Corporate crime is under-prosecuted by a factor of say -- 100. And the flip side of that -- corporate crime prosecutors are underfunded by a factor of say -- 100.

Thanks to Russell Mokhiber for the above
http://www.alternet.org/story/54093/twenty_things_you_should_know_about_corporate_crime

===========

The Biggest Organized Crime Groups in the World

http://fortune.com/2014/09/14/biggest-organized-crime-groups-in-the-world/?xid=soc_socialflow_twitter_FORTUNE&utm_campaign=fortunemagazine&utm_source=twitter.com&utm_medium=social

By Chris Matthews September 14, 2014

It's tough to go even a few months without seeing the effects of organized crime on the economy and everyday life. The most salient example these days is the rash of thefts of credit card data from big-name retail chains like Home Depot and Target.

While these threats are headline-grabbing and particularly frightening because e-commerce is a relatively new phenomenon and businesses and consumers aren't totally sure how to protect themselves from hackers, it's still a drop in the bucket in terms of overall organized crime earnings.

A 2013 survey from Javelin Strategy and Research estimates that the annual total loss to Americans due to identity theft was roughly $20 billion.

So, who are the biggest organized crime gangs around the world and how do they make their money? Here are the top five criminal gangs, ranked by revenue:

1. Solntsevskaya Bratva—Revenue: $8.5 billion (Russian Mafia)
5. Yamaguchi Gumi—Revenue: $6.6 billion (Yakuza)
6. Camorra—Revenue: $4.9 billion (#1 Italian Mafia)
7. 'Ndrangheta—Revenue: $4.5 billion (#2 Italian Mafia)
8. Sinaloa Cartel—Revenue $3 billion (Mexican Cartel)

Sheesh! Canadian organized financial gangs (bankers) alone do more financial harm than all the world's organized crime gangs combined. Not even counting the harm that lawyers do with money laundering etc, accountants with tax evasion etc, politicians, and others who manipulate systems to their own benefits.

===========

The most typical street crimes are the following:
1. crimes against life and health (murder, bodily injury);
2. crimes against sexual inviolability and sexual freedom (rape);
3. crimes against property (theft, robbery, fraud);
4. crimes against public security and public order (hooliganism, vandalism, illegal possession of weapons;
5. crimes against public health (drug trafficking).

Talking about white-collar crime, it is possible to say that in most instances this type of crime is financially more costly. It is 'estimated to cost the United States more than $300 billion annually (Berkeley, 2009, p. 201). However, this does not mean that white-collar crime does not cause harm to the individuals. In fact, it can inflict bodily harm upon people. For example, some corporations can be twice as deadly as a street offender, and thus, white collar crime can be even more dangerous than, for instance, street crime.

http://www.essay.ws/white-collar-crime-vs-street-crime-essay/

===========

The FBI has adopted the narrow approach, defining white-collar crime as:

"those illegal acts which are characterized by deceit, concealment, or violation of trust and which are not dependent upon the application or threat of physical force or violence".

While the true extent and cost of white-collar crime are unknown, the FBI and the Association of Certified Fraud Examiners estimate the annual cost to the United States to fall between $300 and $660 billion.

https://www.fbi.gov/investigate/white-collar-crime

http://www.acfe.com/

Friedrichs, David O. (2009). Trusted Criminals: White Collar Crime In Contemporary Society (4 ed.). Wadsworth Publishing. p. 50. ISBN 978-0495600824. citing Kane and Wall, 2006, p. 5

===========

Every year, the Justice Department puts out an annual report titled "Crime in the United States." A yearly Justice Department report on Systemic Financial and Corporate Crime in the United States is long overdue. That is where the serious looting occurs, and of course this is the area that power and authority cannot touch.

The total academic budget devoted to studying organized financial crime in Canada amounts to a can opener and a piece of string....no government to date has shown the courage required to even peek into this hundred billion dollar bag of worms. Is it because some government Finance Ministers have been 'sent' to us from the financial industry?

The shopping list of financial harms, as seen through the eyes of this investment forensics person, is found below, in its yet to be complete form. Even unfinished, it points to concerns of three areas of financial harm to Canadians (and Americans):

1. <u>Annual Financial 'Harvests'</u> Harms which are "built into" the systems, the investments (fees, commissions, charges etc) and into the annual cost of those products and systems.

2. <u>Individual (one-off)</u> Bad investment products, tricks or traps which the system allows, due to the self-regulatory, or captured-regulatory nature of the system.

3. <u>Systemic issues</u> which ensure that causing financial harm, or ensuring a good financial 'harvest' of people who invest and save, becomes easier for those of the industry who practice in this manner.

http://www.investoradvocates.ca The topic at this web site, tilted "Financial crime more than every other crime combined?" contains a partial list of financial harms done to Canadians by our financial services providers and allowed by regulators. The list is painful to read, and thus too painful to print here, lest we lose readers.

If we simplify things by starting with the master, Keith Ambachtsheer, University of Toronto, he started the research ball rolling on this topic for me a decade back when he published a report saying that the "haircut" to mutual fund holders is about $25 billion dollars per year in Canada. Search "THE 25 BILLION PENSION 'HAIRCUT'. Keith Ambachtsheer.

Here is a good article about this $25 Billion from the Globe:
https://beta.theglobeandmail.com/report-on-business/the-25-billion-pension-haircut/article1075979/?ref=http://www.theglobeandmail.com&

Dr. Ambachtsheer arrived at his number by carefully calculating the different rate of returns produced by professional money managers to look after pension funds and endowments etc., and he compared those rate of returns to what the average retail investor was getting on their mutual fund investments.

The difference was a 3.8% "haircut" and his report was thus titled, "The 25 Billion Dollar Pension Haircut", since this was the financial harm calculated from the approximate $700 Billion then held by mutual fund investors.

The amount of mutual funds held by Canadian retail investors has roughly doubled since the time of that report, and I have little difficulty in doing the math to come up with about $1 billion per week being harvested from Canadian mutual fund investors. Remember, that is not the fair rate for money management, but the 'haircut', the gouged amount overcharged to retail investors.

Since total estimates for ALL crimes in Canada is also in the neighborhood of $50 billion per year, it is rather easy to imagine that the biggest economic drains to Canadian society are being done by trusted financial professionals, and their systems of handmaidens.

A brief look at other methods which Bay Street Financiers use to harvest Canadians comes up with additional billions, here are just a few.

Exemptions to the law:
Valeant Pharmaceutical. $100 Billion in market losses to investors, criminal charges in the USA, while it was the OSC (Ontario regulator) that was selling them passes to skirt our laws.

Sub Prime Mortgage investments. $32 Billion skimmed from investors when the OSC again grants exemption to securities laws (no reasons given once again).

That is two. There were well over 10,000 exemptions granted (or sold) in Canada since the year 2000.

This single area of system abuse (exemptions to laws) is likely responsible for as much financial harm to the country as all other crimes. An entire section of the investor advocate website is devoted to exemptions to the law, while regulators devote millions…to keep them hidden from public view.

How much money could a hedge fund make merely by buying (or shorting) some of the companies who apply to Canadian regulators, to be exempt from our laws?

How much was made shorting Valeant Pharmaceutical by those who knew what the OSC was allowing them to do?

===========

In another example, this book has devoted considerable ink to the consumer 'bait and switch' scheme of letting hundreds of thousands of North American investment salespersons misrepresent themselves to the public. The total financial harm from this is hard to even imagine.

Here is a short list, not complete, of examples of one-off products which are aided in being foisted upon investors as a result of the industry 'bait and switch, the deception:

HERCULES MANAGEMENT $40mil
VICTORIA MORTGAGE $50mil
CANADIAN COMMERCIAL BANK $1 bil
NORTHLAND BANK $230mil
PRINCIPAL GROUP $500mil
STANDARD TRUST $50mil
TEACHERS INVESTMENT AND HOUSING CO-OPERATIVE $150mil
CASTOR HOLDINGS $2bil
BRAMALEA $1bil
CARTAWAY $450mil
GOLDEN RULE RESOURCES $350mil
BRE-X $ 6 bil
CONFEDERATION LIFE S10bil

SHAMRAY GROUP $7mil
LIVENT $500mil
YBM MAGNEX $650 mil
JEVCO INSURANCE $30mil
COREL $500mil
PHILLIPS SERVICES $2.6 bil
MERIT ENERGY $100mil
KING'S HEALTH CENTER $100mil
CINAR $1.4 bil
VISUAL LABS $300mil
HOLLINGER $500mil
CROCUS $150mil
PORTUS $120mil
NORTHSHIELD $500mil
NORBOURG $80mil

Thanks to Diane Urquhart, independent consulting analyst. Toronto.

Income Trusts sold with a deceptive yield

$8 billion of investor losses on 46 income trust IPO's and secondary offerings down more than 30%, where investment bank marketing materials gave deceptive yields and assurances of low risk to seniors seeking income and preservation of capital. Not the subject of any Self Regulating Organization (SRO) or provincial securities commission regulatory restrictions or investigations.
http://www.sipa.ca/

Exempt Market Products is the name given to a newer breed of quasi-investment that has come along recently. They are usually smaller deals like single property developments, such as a golf course or a condo development. They receive a special exemption from securities commissions in Canada whereby they do not have to file a prospectus, and can sell their 'investment' to the public with only an offering memorandum instead.

This opened the door to dealers to package and sell nearly anything to the public. Here is a list of failed or failing exempt market products, from just one Canadian province recently:

Alberta based companies to Nov 2012

Brost & Sorenson	$ 400 Million
Bridgecreek/BridgeGate	$ 75 Million
CBI Group	$ 31 Million
Concrete Equities	$ 118 Million
CPI Crown Properties/Quotavest	$ 25 Million
Edgeworth	$ 35 Million
FMC & PFK	$ 81 Million
Focused Money	$ 54 Million
Foundation Capital	$ 250 Million
Gibraltar Mortgage	$ 51 Million
Global 8 Env Tech/ CAR	$ 19 Million
Liberty Gate	$ 27 Million
Lucid group of companies	$ 58 Million
New Solutions	$ 221 Million
Platinum Equities	$ 160 Million
Signature Capital	$ 60 Million
Shire International	$ 64 Million
Stoneset Equities	$45 Million
Transcap	$51 Million
United Investment Group Inc	$40 Million
Unity Group Investments	$20 Million
Webbco International	$130 Million

This list is by no means complete. What seems complete is the lack of public protection, aided by clever regulatory deceptions and exemptions.

In my experience, the financial 'damage' of having a non-fiduciary investment "advisor", is close to 2% (and up) per year. That 2% is the added cost, but not added value, of having a salesperson-in-disguise, pretending to be a professional adviser.

It would be fraud to do this in any other industry (engineering, law, dentistry etc) but we are talking about the financial industry, and fraud does not yet apply against their 'systems'. Criminality of any kind seems yet to be applied.

Simple math reveals that a 2% reduction in returns (or increase in fees), over a 35 year investment horizon, cuts your final financial outcome in half. The real reason that financial industry frauds are not prosecuted, in my opinion, can be found in that one sentence, if one is willing to contemplate its 'inverse' significance. It helps if you are able to think like a criminal.

The inverse of skimming, cheating, shortchanging, much of society of half of their rightful future financial results…is this…the other half ends up in the pockets of those who can make this happen, including the handmaidens who help along the way. Trillions are thus at stake.

I hope this 'inverse thinking' might help readers understand why paying billions of dollars to regulatory bodies, and/or other authorities is considered a good investment…for those with an eye upon a piece of those trillions. Sorry to keep asking you to think like a criminal…

Picture life insurance products, annuities, segregated funds, new investment issues, income trusts, the list is endless…imagine how much money is harvested from investors with the same 'bait and switch' of agency-deception that allowed the mutual fund industry to skim 3.8% from fund investors.

===========

Larry Swedroe, the director of research for Buckingham Strategic Wealth says "Investors in the USA are transferring about $80 billion annually (calculated at the time of the study) from their pockets into the pockets of those who market and manage actively managed funds. The wealth transfer is larger now because U.S. market capitalization has increased to about $20 trillion."

Swedroe's conclusion is unequivocal: "Given that, each year, the active management industry likely transfers more than $100 billion in funds out of the wallets of investors, it's not hard to make the case that investors and the country as a whole would be better off if much, but not all, of the industry disappeared."

https://danielsolin.com/required-warning-actively-managed-funds/

Selected excerpt from Dan Solin, Author of The Smartest Series of Investment Books

===========

The annual estimates of the cost to the United States, of all measured criminal activity is in the neighborhood of $500 billion each year.

Sub-prime mortgages harm exceeded this amount to use <u>just one significant example</u>. I am not a student of US examples, but 109 million American investment accounts with 600,000 'brokers', many who are hiding the 'broker' registration behind their backs, are likely doing a commission 'grab' on those accounts similar to the commission grab that occurs elsewhere.

The majority of studies also rely primarily on two sources of crime data: the FBI's annual Uniform Crime Reports (UCR) and the National Crime Victimization Study (NCVS) conducted annually by the U.S. Department of Justice's Bureau of Justice Statistics.

This study estimated the total cost of crime to the country to be $425 billion per year. 1999

https://www.house.leg.state.mn.us/hrd/pubs/costcrime.pdf

These numbers do not include the cost of systemic financial crime or what one might call "well organized, trusted financial crime". Why? Because the best organized gangs tell us that we are to trust them...

<u>FINANCIAL HEALTH CHEATED OR DESTROYED LEADS TO</u>

- physical health deterioration
- mental health deterioration

On a macro (society) scale leads to:
- deterioration of the economy
- deterioration of the physical and mental health of the entire society
- deterioration of kindness, civility, trust, prosperity,
- deterioration into infighting, unrest, and possibly all the way to dark times

We (society) are fully invested today in Fear and Distraction. I won't bother to go into the minds of those who benefit the most from this investment…

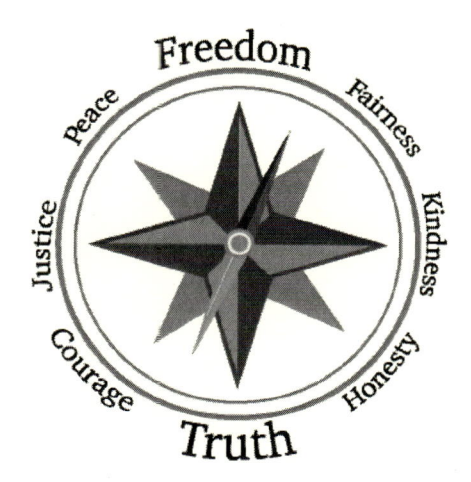

CHAPTER SIXTEEN

HIGH STATUS CRIME WORKS JUST FINE

"...and last but not least... what sets Canada apart... the lawyers in Canada... in my mind, the Canadian Bar Association is probably most powerful criminal organization in Canada.."

Former RCMP undercover drug/money-laundering expert speaking at 1:19:20 of this startling interview about how Canada is a global hot spot for organized crime and systemic money laundering.
https://youtu.be/AbAwzUlfcJ0?list=FLy8dpTRZHEz-0JBa_l0w7AQ

Search YouTube for the video titled, France is Lost, The Fix is In: Gerald Celente & RCMP Inspector Bill Majcher, from 2017.

The site may be extreme for some, but I can assure you that this former RCMP undercover officer is not an alarmist.

When a Lethbridge cop met with a suspected drug dealer he knew what to expect. (this story is not related to RCMP mentioned above)

Man sentenced for trafficking

BY SHURTZ, DELON ON JANUARY 25, 2017.

Delon Shurtz
Lethbridge Herald

When a Lethbridge undercover cop arranged to meet a suspected drug dealer last year, he basically knew what to expect.

After all, it had all been done countless times before. Meet at a specified location, exchange money for drugs, then make the arrest or continue the investigation and get the drug dealer, and possibly others, at a later time.

That was the plan last February when the undercover officer met with Roger Roy and arranged to buy some methamphetamine. The officer gave Roy $100 and Roy handed over one gram of meth.

Only it wasn't meth; the officer actually paid $100 for a gram of bath salts.

Although Roy didn't actually sell drugs to the officer, he was still charged with trafficking, and Tuesday in Lethbridge provincial court he was sent to jail.

Roy had previously pleaded not guilty to the single count of trafficking, as well as a charge of drug possession and two charges of breaching conditions of a court order, and he was preparing for trial. But Tuesday he changed his pleas to guilty and was sentenced to six months in jail. However, he was given six months credit for time already spent in custody waiting to resolve the charges.

The other charges stem from separate incidents in which Roy was caught with five grams of meth after he was arrested on several outstanding warrants in June. Then last November he was arrested again following a traffic stop and was found to be out past a court-ordered curfew. He was also found in possession of a folding knife, even though he had been ordered not to possess any weapons.

==========

A trivial story, but one which points my mind to wider systemic concerns for our society.

The ease with which a man can be prosecuted at the low end of the power or economic scale, causes me to draw comparisons of our justice systems for those at the top of power and economics.

The guilty cannot even get arrested in financial systems, when fraud, false representation and systemically harmful products are sold to financial consumers.

Such is the strength and the force-field of protection among the entitled. Criminal fraud, money laundering, regulatory breach of the public trust, it seems as if nothing can be applied against our "trusted" gangs, and yet you can easily get convicted for selling bath salts. Is the 'justice' system a system of justice, or a cleverly disguised system of power? I ask because I care and because I seek to understand it.

Observations like this began to make me think about how crime appears to be prosecuted differently for persons of high or of low 'status'. Although I was always told that justice is blind, I began to see otherwise.

Something appears to either be broken, or it is "fixed" at very high levels.

As I observed high profile sexual assault cases (Bill Cosby and the Stanford student/swim athlete in the US, and a sexually aggressive radio host in Canada) and I began to see similarities between how the law treats high status sexual abusers, and how they treat high status financial abusers. It made me wonder whether it was the principles which were being judged, or the status of the personalities.

What I saw was less interest in the wrong, and doing what is right, and more focus on protection (or fear?) of the 'higher status' person. It appeared to be a 'power' system for some and a 'justice' system for others, based upon wealth, status or influence.

The lesson history teaches, in any injustice, is to simply notice of the status of the alleged abuser, versus the status of the abused. That is step one.

If an abuser is a person or institution of high social standing, or a corporation, history tells a thousand tales of a different breed of 'justice' than if the abuser is on lesser social standing. Justice rushes to prosecute a lower status offender, but abuse or attack by high status offenders seems a different story.

In many financial abuse cases I have read, I recall the words, "the plaintiff was a victim of their own misfortune", which is a often simply a 'storytelling' exercise by storytellers (lawyers), to try and blame the victim, and never allow blame to fall upon the professional, or upon a corporation.

I have noticed this statement used against 90 year old victims, vulnerable victims who took the words and advice of their "professional" and never were they informed that the 'professional' was a commission salesperson wearing a fraudulent costume. No matter the crime, victims simply cannot seem to get the rich or the powerful arrested. Why? I believe this is due to the combined power of well Organized Financial Crime. (OFC)

Victims of financial assault are most likely to be judged not by standards of right and wrong, but by standards of wealth or social status. Million dollar lawyers line up to defend a corporation or a high status offender, since it is the fastest road to…more millions.

These lawyers do not always play by rules of the justice system, or of honesty, but may tend towards getting the win. Getting the win is the money ticket when defending high status abusers. Does that make justice no longer blind?

In 2017 my local newspaper had this from The Associated Press:

"The judge imposed a forty month prison sentence. "The conspiracy perpetrated a massive… and stunning fraud on the American consumer that attacked and destroy the very foundation of our economic system."

What I found interesting was that although this statement could be made about millions of crimes in the financial sector, for some reason, these words were said about an auto manufacturer (VW), and seemingly cannot be spoken about investment bankers. No matter how many trillions are cheated from society.

That is an indicator that there is a hidden system of 'protection' that prevents criminal sanctions from being applied upward against financial power. It again raises the question of whether we have a system of justice, or is it a hidden system of power at the very top? I feel that it could be a little bit of both, based upon my observations.

===========

GETTING JUSTICE

September 16, 2013
Not with a Bang but a Whimper – the SEC Enforcement Team's Propaganda Campaign
By William K. Black

Professor Bill Black writes the following (2013) in reference to getting justice against the most trusted of financial gangsters:

How many C-suite officers of Wall Street firms were individually sued by the SEC? The SEC says it took action against the following elite financial institutions:

Bank of America: No officers sued
Bear Stearns: No senior officers sued
Citigroup: No officers sued

Countrywide: CEO sued, settled for "record $22.5 million penalty and permanent officer and director bar. (10/15/10)" [Bill Black: most, perhaps all, of the penalty was paid by Countrywide's acquirer and insurer. According to the SEC's complaint, the penalty represents a small percentage of the CEO's fraudulent gains. The CEO was already retired by the time the SEC sued.]

"Credit Suisse bankers - SEC charged four former veteran investment bankers and traders for their roles in fraudulently overstating subprime bond prices in a complex scheme driven in part by their desire for lavish year-end bonuses. (2/1/12)" [Bill Black: None of the officers sued was close to being C-suite level.]

Fannie Mae and Freddie Mac: "SEC charged six former top executives of Fannie Mae and Freddie Mac with securities fraud for misleading investors about the extent of each company's holdings of higher-risk mortgage loans, including subprime loans" [Bill Black: all six executives are C-suite or very senior.]

Goldman Sachs: No senior officers sued

IndyMac: "SEC charged three executives with misleading investors about the mortgage lender's deteriorating financial condition. (2/11/11) - IndyMac's former CEO and chairman of the board Michael Perry agreed to pay an $80,000 penalty." [Bill Black: The penalty figure is not a misprint. IndyMac made hundreds of thousands of fraudulent "liar's" loans and sold them to the secondary market through fraudulent "reps and warranties." It was the largest "vector" spreading mortgage fraud through the system. The three executives sued were C-suite level.]

J.P. Morgan Securities: No officers sued
UBS Securities: No officers sued
Wachovia Capital Markets: No officers sued
Wells Fargo: No senior officers sued

http://www.ritholtz.com/blog/2013/09/not-with-a-bang-but-a-whimper-the-sec-enforcement-teams-propaganda-campaign/?utm_source=The+Big+Picture+Updates&utm_campaign=1a127ab75c-big_picture_email&utm_medium=email&utm_term=0_662cf1de86-1a127ab75c-39137365

===========

"There is a shortfall in enforcement in Canada. That's probably the politest way to say it," says John Coffee, a professor at Columbia University Law School.
http://www.canada.com/calgaryherald/features/brex/story.html?id=a260e707-209c-4e31-9f6e-191a50aeee6f&k=92467

Professor Coffee also said there are over 300 times more penalties imposed, even when adjusted for size of each economy, in the USA over those imposed in Canada.

===========

For me, this book is part study in human depravity. In that vein it is related to Maslow's Hierarchy of needs. (more in Chapter 21)

It appears that many of us humans take a detour at the level of personal safety and security, going to extremes in areas of power or money as they relate to our personal security. Like any other potential addiction or mental 'hoarding' issue, power and money, is subject to the need for "more", in many of us who suffer from insecurities in this area. If this occurs, it places some of us on a slippery or addictive slope, without the necessary tools to prevent our moral or ethical decline.

The depravity can advance to a willingness to ignore harms to others if it serves the need of gaining more money, property, or prestige. Soon one finds oneself freely able to commit harm to others in the name of this need, even when done under the guise of a "professional" capacity.

The end result can put any of us in or near the category of a sociopath. Where "normal" human instincts such as guilt or anxiety about doing harm to others are weakened or deadened. Imagine a highly developed reptilian portion of the brain, the amygdala, far out of balance, lacking a developed maturity.

As I research the financial services industry, I observe that as many as one in ten persons could fit into this category. Experts in sociopathy or psychopathy (pardon my blending or misuse of terms) suggest that something like one in every twenty or twenty five people we meet in our day is likely to suffer from either.

The numbers are far higher in industries connected to great money and/or power, and yet again higher, the further one climbs the ladder within those sectors.

Even at one in every twenty five, it would mean that 280 million people exist in the world today who would not suffer an anxious moment, not even for a second, if they were to do you great financial or other harm. Now just imagine 280 million people gravitating toward the type of professions or occupations where this 'defect' is rewarded.

The rewards are simply too great and the risks of this kind of behavior are statistically zero in some industries. It is free money. Take all you want. No police will come. 'Self-regulation' simply becomes 'gang decriminalization' and financial self-regulation can bring about the ruin of entire economies…and societies. All ruined for persons who may themselves be mentally stuck at the lower levels (second level) of Maslow's hierarchy of needs. Even for a billionaire, "too much" is still not enough, if they suffer from a never-ending need for "more". They may be just like Meth addicts, stumbling the streets of our cities, breaking into cars…except the damage organized financial gangs do is many times worse.

===========

Industry muzzles its victims
Gag Orders keep bad advisors' names out of the press

Select excerpts from an article by Jonathan Chevreau
from the National Post, Thursday, October 23, 2003

One of the frustrations with this job is some of the most potentially instructive stories can't be made public. Since the stock bubble of 1999 burst, many tales of investor abuse involving leveraged loans have come to my attention.

Too often, the consumer/victim of abuse starts to go down the legal path in an effort to recoup their lost retirement capital. But the closer they get to expose the villains in court or the press, the more likely they will be offered a partial settlement.

Once settled out of court, everyone agrees to shut up. The chance to warn other investors is lost because of gag orders the lawyers are allowed to attach to settlement agreements. The perpetrators are free to go their merry way and find new victims.

===========

As Bev K. an investment victim in Ontario said so clearly to me:
"Everyone connected with the investment industry is looking for excuses NOT to protect seniors' financial interests in the investment industry".

What do I say? I agree. Virtually everyone in the bank/financial game is hard at work, harvesting the wealth of seniors, as well as any other investor that lands in their crosshairs. And they are so well protected and insulated by the web of financial, political, legal and regulatory players who share in the spoils, that society is caught in a financial trap. A trap set by the very servants who have promised to protect us.

===========

The video found at the link below is an interesting take on what they call a judicial 'haven' where our most 'trusted' criminal class risk virtually zero chance of running into police or prosecutors."

It looks at the U.S. Department of Justice, and the appearance of it being a captured agency when it comes to handing out justice (or none at all) to folks like Goldman Sachs.

It is titled "The Veneer of Justice in a Kingdom of Crime" and found on YouTube:
https://youtu.be/eHgbRYgpGGs?list=FLy8dpTRZHEz-0JBa_l0w7AQ

===========

Finally, from Zero Hedge comes this insight into our systems of power:

Ponzi Pays - Why Armed Robbery Is For Suckers In Today's Judicial System

by Tyler Durden   Aug 12, 2017

That there are large sentencing disparities between white collar criminals and armed robbers shouldn't be a surprise to anyone. The American legal system exhibits a strong bias toward individuals with resources who can afford top lawyers to negotiate a lenient sentence for, say, defrauding 600 investors out of $1 billion.

But according to data provided by Dynamic Securities Analytics in partnership with Ponzitracker.com, the gaps in sentencing might be larger than one might expect.

Ponzi scheme operators who stole more than $100 million in 2016 were sentenced to 14 years, about 168 months in prison, or 21 days for each $1 million stolen.

By comparison, federal sentences for robbery were 117 months (9.75 years) with a median loss of $2,989, which works out to about 40,372 months in prison for each $1 million stolen.

In other words, robbers served 50,000x more time per dollar than your average financial fraudster.

http://www.zerohedge.com/news/2017-08-12/wanna-make-1-million-month-try-stealing-100-million-dollars

The fascinating thing about this article is that it illustrates the judicial discrimination when it comes to sentencing disparities between Ponzi scheme criminals and armed robbers. It could also open a conversation about 'well organized systemic financial crimes', as compared to Ponzi schemers and armed robbers.

I suspect that when sentences for crimes done by a cabal of bankers, lawyers, regulators, accountants and legislators, it might be that armed robbers face justice by an infinitely higher measure than do those in the powerful cabal.

Organized systemic crime pays…

===========

When you hear platitudes about how well protected North American society is from financial fraud artists, I hope some will think of the word "Sinecure", to have another 'frame' with which to see things through:

Sinecure (from Latin sine = "without" and cura = "care")

Sinecure refers to a position that requires or involves little or no responsibility, labour, or active service. The term originated in the medieval church, where it signified a post without any responsibility for the "cure [care] of souls", the regular liturgical and pastoral functions of a cleric, but came to be applied to any post, secular or ecclesiastical, that involved little or no actual work. Sinecures have historically provided a potent tool for governments or monarchs to distribute patronage, while recipients are able to store up titles and easy salaries.

Many of the top regulator positions fit in this category in my view. The sinecure regulatory job is secure…IF the regulators in those positions keep their mouths shut about abuses and harms being done. Sinecure positions are the perfect handmaid to abuse, when the position is influenced, appointed or paid by the industry that the sinecure is supposed to police.

===========

"All you needed a gang of lawyers and you could safely steal whatever you like. Lawyers are the hitmen of our times."

David Lagercrantz from "The Girl In The Spiders Web"

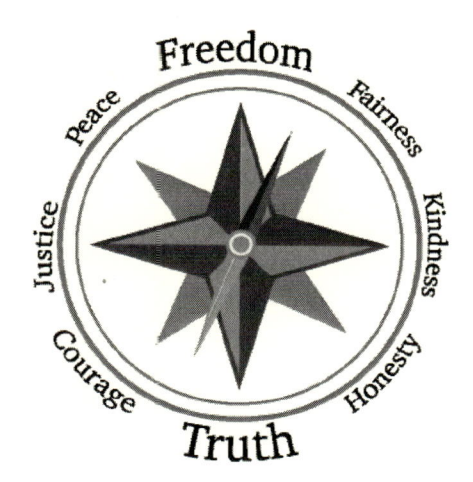

CHAPTER SEVENTEEN

CRASHING SOCIETY

The 21ST CENTURY ECONOMIC DEPRESSION,

20 LOST YEARS, 2008-2028

"The short answer is that Wall Street, for the last thirty years or so, has been skimming prodigiously from the top."
-- Benjamin Landy

===========

Of the greatest fears common to most humans on the planet appears to be the fear of economic insecurity.

Added to the fear of economic uncertainty is a level of societal stress when it is found that some of the most trusted persons and institutions in North America are actually working <u>against the interests of those they are sworn to serve.</u>

This book is focused on financial players and authorities who claim to regulate and protect the public. If the public is financially abused, without protection, or recourse, it can trigger emotions and chemicals in the human brain that are the same as, or similar to those triggered by any other kind of abuse. Physical, psychological, sexual, etc.

To have an ever increasing portion of society, running on cortisol, adrenaline, and a host of brain chemical-cocktails adds to the level of fear and panic among people.

I maintain that living in a hierarchical world where those at the top can abuse, rather than serve, the rest, leads to an increasing news diet of people "going Postal"....I could be wrong to draw the connection, but I lay it out there for others to expand upon.

===========

Excerpt from The Guardian, Sept, 2017

The economic cost of Hurricane Irma could rise as high as $300bn (£227bn) as the storm lashes Florida. Analysts said about $2tn of property lay in the storm's path. Barrie Cornes, an analyst at the stockbroker Panmure Gordon, put the overall economic cost at $300 billion.

The insurance industry is still assessing the cost of Hurricane Harvey, which caused severe flooding in parts of Texas last month. Initial estimates suggest the final bill could be as much as $100bn. That compares with economic damage of $176bn inflicted by Hurricane Katrina in 2005, which included $82bn of insured losses, according to the Swiss Re Institute.

https://www.theguardian.com/business/2017/sep/10/economic-cost-of-hurricane-irma-could-reach-300bn

Would you choose another Hurricane Irma to visit Florida, or the financial equivalent harm done by 600,000 fake financial 'advisors'? Both can do a few hundred billion in harm to the nations financial health, but at least Irma does not promise to be your trusted servant while doing the damage.

The above numbers are all in the range of figures that I get to see harvested from North America by professional financial players, acting in packs…gang-like.

There are many ways to measure the societal harm of Organized Financial Crime (OFC)
1. $50 - $60 bil/year, in Canada, about as much as all other crime, combined

2. Your life of saving and investing, cut in half

3. 10-20 years of additional work for millions of Americans

4. Society pushed toward poverty while a fractional percent of the population become insanely, and/or unjustly wealthy

5. Personal Moral Injury against the rest

6. Social nervous breakdown

The further twist in subject matter is that this is not what the average person thinks of when we mention "organized crime".

This book is interested in what some might call "trusted' organized crime. Crime that is done by highly respectable persons who work in very respectable professions, even regulators. Financial crime which is done by bankers, lawyers, regulators, politicians, accountants, auditors and so on. Organized Financial Crime (OFC)

Prem Sikka, esteemed Professor of Accounting at Sussex University in England labels it the "Pinstripe Mafia". Prem has become a world authority on money-laundering, and related areas of financial and accounting crimes against society.

Organized crime is found within section 467.1(1) of the Criminal Code of Canada, which states:

A "criminal organization" means a group, however organized, that:

(a) is composed of three or more persons in or outside Canada; and,

(b) has as one of its main purposes or main activities the facilitation or commission of one or more serious offenses, that, if committed, would likely result in the direct or indirect receipt of a material benefit, including a financial benefit, by the group or by any one of the persons who constitute the group.

(Excluding a group of three of more persons that has formed randomly for the immediate commission of a single offense.)

http://www.rcmp-grc.gc.ca/soc-cgco/what-quoi-eng.htm

Historically, the unit cost of financial intermediation (financial 'middlemen') has been somewhere between 1.3% and 2.3% of assets. However, this unit cost has been trending upward since 1970 and is now significantly higher than in the past. In other words, the finance industry of 1900 was just as able as the finance industry of 2010 to produce loans, bonds and stocks, and it was certainly doing it more cheaply.   (BEZEMER HUDSON ECONOMIC STUDY)

This is counter-intuitive, to say the least. How is it possible for today's finance industry not to be significantly more efficient than the finance industry of John Pierpont Morgan?

The short answer is that Wall Street, for the last thirty years or so, has been skimming prodigiously from the top. The total economic cost of financial intermediation grew from under 2 percent in 1870 to nearly 6 percent before the stock market collapsed in 1929. It grew slowly throughout the postwar expansion, reaching 5 percent in 1980. Then, beginning during the deregulatory years of the Reagan administration, the money flowing to financial intermediaries skyrocketed, rising to almost 9 percent of GDP in 2010.

This is exceptionally counter-intuitive, as Philippon points out. Over the last forty years, information technology has increased efficiency and lowered costs throughout the economy. Retail and wholesale trade, for instance, have both shrunk by about 20 percent as a share of GDP since 1970, thanks to better technology and improved economies of scale.

===========

My personal observations, go something like this:

For every 1% increase in the share of GDP taken up by bankers and investment bankers, I believe that we witness perhaps another ten million North Americans pushed into, or closer to poverty, hopelessness, helplessness, and some form of financial, emotional, and social crisis. This leads directly into mental health issues and other forms of injury. Watch the news anywhere in North America and you might see the signs in today's society.

As I write this my daughter is on a holiday in Las Vegas the weekend of Oct 2, 2017, where a sole gunman injured or killed over 500 people at an outdoor concert at the Mandalay Bay resort. I make no direct connections, but there are observations of 'distress and dis-ease' that can be seen in today's society.

I believe that if a few sectors of the world, are allowed to financially abuse the majority of life on the planet, and to skate freely from accountability by being powerful and above the law......that causes an extreme amount of stress and duress on humanity. Powerful abusers may 'frame' the backlash with false labels including the "terror" label at times, because it is easier (and more profitable) than being accountable for their own abusive behaviors.

Look at the flip side and ask if some of the victims would also call it terror. Ask yourself who does the label "terrorist" more aptly apply to? The <u>cause</u> of millions and millions of other people's terror...or the <u>effect</u>, the retaliation...the blowback so to speak.

If we allow society to be less "fairer"....we can expect more mental stress and what some label as "terror". I try to never believe the media label, the political label, as they are often involved in "framing" the story in a way that is advantageous to their interests, and distracts from their own 'causation(s)', putting the blame on others and taking the spotlight away from their own acts of power and greed.

Perhaps the simplest way to convey the terrible impact the crisis had is to reflect on the conclusions from research carried out by Oxford University - that the crisis led to more than 10,000 extra suicides due to the consequences of a far higher number of people losing their job, having a home repossessed or falling into serious debt. That is a shocking statistic. Clearly, financial stability is a precious public good that warrants nurturing and protecting.

Andy Agathangelou, Founding Chair, the Transparency Task Force speaking about the social costs of financial crisis in the UK,

Please feel free to shoot this entire section full of holes. I am not trying to convince you of anything, I am merely here to better understand some of the things I see in today's world. I look forward to connection with others who also seek to understand, and we will learn together.

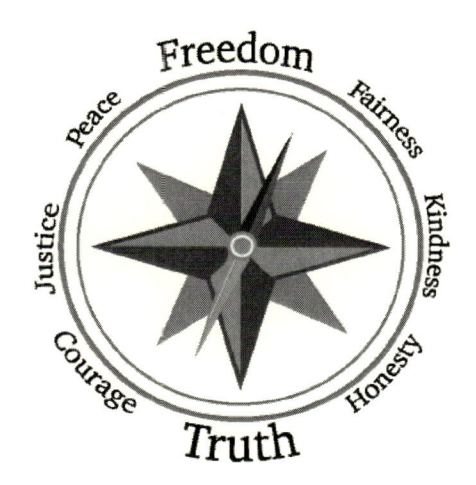

CHAPTER EIGHTEEN

CRASHING A HELICOPTER

This Chapter serves as a mental break from stories of doom, gloom and people who profit from harvesting society. I hope to give you a rest with a story of how to crash a helicopter. There are some similarities to crashing a life and I hope you won't mind the distraction.

After this chapter, the book transitions into a more positive tone, with solutions, and steps that can be taken to prevent your family, or your society from falling for the many traps set by systems of money and power.

The first time I crashed a helicopter, no... the *second* time I crashed a helicopter...WTF?

I was in the Oldman River valley about "Five West" (five miles west of the airport) as I informed the tower.

It is a beautiful spot to fly to quickly, and without bothering anyone, do practice in the sky. The area is the original site of Fort Whoop-Up, a supply trading post where goods came north from Fort Benton, Montana, and also travelled east and west on the Oldman River. Many barrels of rotgut alcohol were peddled here to take advantage of the natives. Some of this 'drink' included anything and everything, including printing ink to give it the right look. It might be the oldest spot in my area where I can look back and imagine predatory white men taking advantage of the vulnerability of others. Not much has changed.

I loved to go and train my brain, making sure my hands and feet could make the helicopter move in 6 directions at command. Forward or backwards, lateral sideways flight, vertical up and down, pitch of fuselage up and down, roll of fuselage side to side and yaw of nose left or right. It is a great brain-expansion exercise to be able to do this, and is the most fun I have ever had.

I was in a Bell 206 Jet Ranger, so it cost about $600 per hour to operate, but it was the still the best therapy I have found in the world.

On this day I was practicing landing and taking off from what are called 'confined areas'. Picture the Vietnam era helicopter pilots, desperately trying to find a space in the jungle to touch down and pick up their buddies. Trees everywhere, no openings, and they let the blades of the workhorse 'Huey" helicopter settle down into the trees, trimming them like a giant upside-down Whipper Snipper.

With helicopter blades wide and thick enough to make a small Cessna aircraft wing look tiny in comparison, legends abound of Huey pilots trimming the jungle like a weed whacker as they settled in to land. Well, my confined area practice was just like that....except it was a perfectly clear area at least 200 foot square, big enough to turn a semi-rig in.

Anyway, here I was, having fun landing, taking off and circling back for another landing, to hone hand-eye coordination with the machine.

Upon lifting above the 40 to 60 foot Cottonwoods one more time, I was surprised to find myself out of wind, or a little bit short of the lifting power that I expected and needed. The helicopter nose was starting to turn slowly to the right......which is not a good thing, because that means...I have some fast thinking to do.

(clock starts here, of the mental cockpit recording* of the event......*tick, tick, tick, 0.03 seconds elapsed....*)

What follows is my personal thought process during the event:

Blades in North American built helicopters turn to the left, or counterclockwise, just like European built helicopter blades typically turn clockwise right? I have no idea how the two regional types of helicopters can be made with such a simple, but huge difference in direction....but it must be like the driving on the right left thing....??? Wait, shit, back to the matter at hand.....when nose goes right, this means that the tail rotor effect or its power needs to be increased to stop the turn....or demand for lift needs to be less. (less torque effect on helicopter) "Think Man!"

tick, tick, tick....0.90 seconds elapsed...

Anyway, blades turning one way at a high rate of speed and power, cause an equally strong turn-reaction by the body of the helicopter in the opposite direction. A drift of the nose (a spin if it gets out of hand) to the right must be avoided, lest it gets away on me, and the helicopter 'spin' of death begins...

tick, tick, tick....1.50 seconds elapsed...

I did what every private helicopter pilot in the world would do in this situation. Naturally I clenched every muscle in my body slightly, in an instinctive fear reaction. Just slight enough that I was not aware at the time, however I recall it now, after much time for processing.

tick, tick, tick....1.60 seconds elapsed...

Clinching every muscle in my body, as a reaction to the "OOPS, something is not quite right with this picture" causes the muscles in my hands and arms to tighten just enough, and combined with the body's natural reaction to draw inwards, ever so slightly as if preparing oneself for a hard blow…well I did all those things.

Since my hands and arms are in control of two essential controls to what the helicopter does in the sky, those actions caused me to simultaneously (but not consciously…yet) PULL UP on the collective in my left hand, and in control of the amount of pitch (blade angle) that I put on the blades, which controls the amount of **lift**, they will generate, which affects the amount of **power** my turbine is required to produce…which affects the torque, which affects the spin.

tick, tick, tick….2.01 seconds elapsed…

I am pulling up on the power required, and at the same time pulling back with my right hand to 'clinch' and protect. The pullback with the right hand causes the disc to tilt back slightly, (disc is a name for the flat 'spinning-plate' image that is produced when a helicopter blade turns. It is turning so fast that it appears not as individual blades, but as a solid 'disc")

tick, tick, tick….2.20 seconds elapsed…

Tilting the disc backwards, towards the rear has the effect of slowing the helicopter, or making it go backwards if desired. That has the effect, at the wrong moment, of causing the helicopter to 'lose lift' and losing lift has the effect of making the helicopter drop, which has the effect of making my brain tell my left arm to pull more power, which has the effect of stopping the dropping…..(first mentally conscious act I have had yet……

tick, tick, tick….2.30 seconds elapsed…

Pulling more power causes more torque reaction on the helicopter body, which causes the nose to rotate further, (or faster) to the right. Too much thought…running out of options.

The nose turning more to the right (or turning slightly faster) reminds me now of my foot pedals, which control the spinning rotor at the tail of helicopter, making them effective at keeping the nose pointed where I wish. This is perhaps the second time I recall conscious awareness of my own thoughts... all else was pure reaction. Now I notice that unconsciously or otherwise, my left leg has already pushed the pedal to the floor......it is as far as it can go. BEEP, BEEP, BEEP (alarm bells going in head now......perhaps more involuntary clenching....don't recall.

tick, tick, tick....2.40 seconds elapsed...

I will spare you the lesson, on why the left pedal to the floor means I can have NO more power (no more "push' effect) from the small rotor on the tail......which means I will have more rotation of the helicopter body to the right (or faster rotation to the right), which is already starting to scare me. It feels like being in a canoe that is bent out of shape in two or more dimensions (moving, tipping and turning at the same time).

tick, tick, tick....2.50 seconds elapsed...

A helicopter can get bent out of shape in three (make that FOUR) directions so when things get bent out of shape in a helicopter, the inexperienced brain has a really tough time recognizing what 'might be' going on, and what to do about it. Veteran pilots can correct me on any of this, I don't mind.

tick, tick, tick....2.60 seconds elapsed...

Where was I... Oh, I was in a confined area, surrounded by 60 foot cottonwood trees. I was supposed to be climbing above those tree-tops, but at the moment I was no longer climbing, and perhaps slightly declining, which is causing the horizon to rise up in my field of view which is bad.

tick, tick, tick....2.70 seconds elapsed...

198

A rising horizon signals the brain that I have a declining (or falling) helicopter, which is usually a bad thing, so once again, some bad auto-reactions kick in causing me to want to pull more power (conscious) and clinch my arm in an unconscious fear reaction.

tick, tick, tick....2.80 seconds elapsed...

Lets take a few hundredths of seconds to think and regroup... I'm alone inside a spinning, dropping, forward creeping (slowly) helicopter, with treetops coming at me in the windshield...

Hitting trees with a helicopter is frowned upon...and expensive.
Hitting anything with a running helicopter is frowned upon.

...and my left foot is 'pedal to the metal' which means it is to the floor, as far as it can go.

I have reached the end of ......my limits.....(useless thought enters: Hey, I know what this is called from my lessons! This is properly called "Loss of Tail Rotor Effectiveness, or LTE for short". It occurs when there is not enough 'pushing' power left in the tail rotor, to stop the torque effect of spinning blades from causing the fuselage to counter-spin in the opposite direction)
Older Bell 206's did have some of this, come to think of it...
tick, tick, tick....2.90 seconds elapsed...

I have no other cards to play so to speak (experts will disagree with me here, however I must point out that at the time I was a private helicopter pilot, flying alone with perhaps 100 hours experience. Experts will now nod and agree.....I had not enough skill, yet, to have many other cards to play.

Actually, I did try one more thing, and I am sure that this is what brought me down. At 2.91 seconds, the thought occurred to me that I must be doing something wrong, and I must act now to rectify it, and so I took a wild guess that perhaps I had jammed the wrong pedal to the floor unconsciously...that could solve everything...and I tried the other pedal out of sheer desperation. Nope. I had the correct pedal to start with, and trying the other one just cancelled my flight ticket. Put a fork in me, I am done like dinner.

tick, tick, tick....3.0 seconds elapsed...

I had one other conscious recollection, that of using the trigger finger on my right hand, to click the microphone transmit button, and make a distress call over the airwaves, "ZULU PAPA GULF, IN THE RIVER VALLEY", "ZULU PAPA GULF, IN THE RIVER VALLEY",. (conscious act)

tick, tick, tick....3.2 seconds elapsed...

I have no recollection of the amount, or number of turns of 'rotation' of the helicopter, the rate of descent, the rate of drift towards or away from the trees that were coming at me.....nothing.

tick, tick, tick....3.5 seconds elapsed...

...no recollection of moving any controls until I found myself in a firm, but level-skid landing, within my clearing of trees. The collective in my left hand was bottomed (meaning I had somehow managed to lower it *after* touching down...after having found the unconscious presence of mind to raise it sharply at exactly the right moment. (to cushion the landing...thank God helicopters can do this stuff)

*tick, tick, tick....3.90 seconds elapsed.......*with the helicopter now "down and clear", somehow safe and sound.

The reason I knew I had unconsciously raised the collective at the precise moment before touchdown, was that from a height of 40 to 60 feet, the fall without cushion of any kind would have broken the machine. It would drop like a 2000 pound weight from a six story building. Pulling up at the last fraction of a second must have happened unconsciously, since that is exactly the way to cushion a vertically dropping helicopter.

Helicopter blades spinning above one's head, act like a pair of airplane wings moving through the air. A helicopter stores a great deal of energy in a rapidly rotating set of blades. During free fall, that energy in the blades can be cashed-in and used like a set of air-brakes to slow or cushion the descent. <u>Once only</u> can you call upon and use this energy, and then you are down. So you had better get the timing right.

If the pilot pulls up on the collective at exactly the right moment when that cushion is needed, the blades will twist into a position of 'full lift' (twist to full angle of attack to the air, instead of simply spinning flat and slicing through the air) and you can effectively 'catch' the 2000 pound machine with the strength of that lift energy. It acts like the final flare of wings that a goose makes just before it touches down.

Don't ask me which, but either some unconscious training reactions on the controls happened, or the hands of fate plucked me out of the sky and set me down with a slight bounce. Either way, I shut the helicopter down, and tried to make radio contact to let the tower know I was OK. I heard them talking to other aircraft about my call, but I could not transmit to them from the floor of the valley. So after a very careful check of the aircraft, and inspection of the tail rotor, I lit the turbine, took off without incident, and gained enough vertical height to transmit to the tower.

It is at this point that I have to admit that a Bell 206 Jet Ranger does not carry any kind of flight recording device, and that my estimates of time elapsed came entirely from, estimates, and the recording of these events from my memory. I have had a few years now to replay these events in my mind, and mentally process the steps I took, and the mistakes I made.

The story of crashing a helicopter is inserted only to give a personal glimpse into my life, which was a pretty darn good life, I must admit, and it also serves as a bit of a metaphor for crashing my financial career, unintentionally, by my choice to stand firm and 'refuse to abuse'. It also serves as what I hope to be an interesting story, and a break to the plethora of financial negativity in the book. There. I just used 'plethora' in a sentence. Scratch that one off my bucket list.

I refused to abuse clients who trusted me, and I had every confidence in financial system controls and procedures to prevent and protect the public from abuse.

It turns out that I was as wet behind the ears on this 'protect the public' thing, as a rookie pilot in a shiny Jet Ranger. Both require careful operation of a dangerous and highly unstable system.

I was trying to walk my truth, inside the most well organized system of financial abuse ever invented. I had every expectation that procedures and practices were in place to prevent abuses of the public, like they are in other systems. I had no idea just how wrong I was. I also had no idea how far I would fall, nor how hard the landing would be.

Crashing a helicopter is far safer than trying to tell the truth within a culture that is earning billions from deceiving the public. What a lesson to have to learn. What an interesting opportunity to be presented with. What a gift! What a ride!

I may have crashed my life a fair bit, by trying to reveal some truth in a system lubricated by lies. But I am still alive, and the truth of what I tried to reveal is still here. In fact, as I edit this today it is 2017, and a few more credible media outlets have just begun to cover some of the deceptions and the fraud-like games that I was concerned about for the last two decades.

Reputation for integrity is the <u>only</u> thing investment banks have to offer, and they are short sighted enough to put it entirely on the poker table against any soul who stands up to tell the truth.

That might be the gift. The invitation into a poker game with billionaires, where I put everything I have onto the table, including the truth, and they put their reputation up against it. That is the dumbest move that either of us should be making, but hey, I am just learning how to fly this thing… I wonder what this button does…

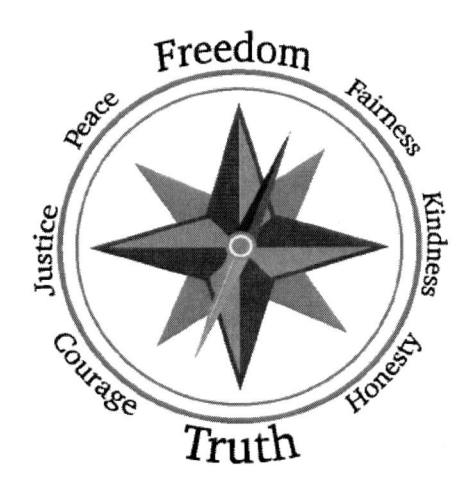

CHAPTER NINETEEN

LITIGATION: THE ART OF STORYTELLING*

"Sometimes the law is used to 'prevent' justice."
Quote from a wise woman, sitting between myself and a disbarred lawyer at a luncheon.

===========

Whistleblowers choose their key life actions using a higher moral principle than 'themselves' and their own self interests …and perhaps a bit less street-smarts.

I believe my chance for justice was probably dead before I even got close to the court house.

When I filed suit against RBC for what I felt were violations of rules, codes, ethical codes of conduct, I was not prepared for the amount of delay, denial and deflect, that the bank was willing to deliver.

After waiting approximately 12 years from filing the lawsuit, for justice to be done, I learned within six months of the scheduled trial date, that my lawyer was being forced to step away.

In a rather surprising move, this small town, humble, very intelligent lawyer was being appointed to the position of a judicial master, in the city of Calgary. A few raised their eyebrows at this, and commented that they wondered if the appointment had anything to do with the RBC counsel being a former partner of the premier of the province.

I had less than six months to find new legal counsel, and they prepare for a trial that had been 12 years in buildup. I was assured that no court would expect this much preparation to be possible in under six months and there was no doubt that there would be an adjournment to allow time to prepare.

My replacement lawyer was shocked and surprised when stepping into the courtroom for the application for adjournment for trial preparation time, to find that not only the courtroom had been changed, but that the judge to hear the application had also been replaced. He found this is to be unusual, but not as unusual as finding that there would be no adjournment and that he would now have only four or five months, to prepare for an $18 million dollar ($10 mil payable to charity in the claim) trial against the largest bank in Canada.

"Code Red" warning horns blaze in the background as a description of what that felt like when I learned of it. Perhaps the greatest work done in the halls of justice, does truly take place _in the halls_, as some say.

I now realize that the million-dollar lawyers who defend billion dollar banks, have special tricks and tactics up their sleeves, and some have decade's worth of personal connections within the legal system. Not all of them within the law. In hindsight this now seems to be part of the value that the million dollar lawyer brings to the table. The ability to use connections to steer or alter a given course of events. That and to also be a good storyteller.

Looking back, I wish I had chosen a jury to hear the trial and not a judge. I feel I might have dodged the very large possibility that the bank lawyers might have shared a few drinks over the years with folks who are now judges. Folks they can 'relate' to. Juries would may not be as easily 'influenced' by the magnitude of money, power, status, whatever the influences that are allowed to enter the justice system via the human condition.

I have nobody to blame for my naïveté. I simply was foolish enough to place my trust in yet another 'system'. Today I have learned that systems, whether financial, political, judicial or any other, are not places that one should place complete trust, certainly if the issue involves an imbalance of wealth, power or influence.

Most systems give far too much 'benefit of credibility' to the 'aura' (or connections) surrounding wealth, power, or influence. The justice system seems no different in this, at the upper levels. I guess the good news is that we can say that Justice is no longer blind…

My first lawyer did give me fair warning when he said, "Larry just make sure that you are aware, if you decide to play hardball with these guys, that the balls will be very hard". Having no idea what exactly that could mean I proceeded to put my hope in our 'system' of justice. Not such a great idea…but what a learning experience!

Little did I realize that I would be facing professional-league storytelling and victim blaming, as well as 90 mile per hour fastballs coming at my head. I was never in the game. Never even laced up my shoes.

According to top legal minds, 'litigation is storytelling'. If you Google this term, you will find thousands of hits about the art of storytelling, yarn-spinning, to win in court. Who knew that one of the foundations of our free and fair society stands upon something as flimsy on storytelling and theatrics?

The legal industry can do a bang-up job of cherry picking facts, polishing up those cherries, and creating a fabulous story to tell the court. The higher status criminal or abuser is then given the benefit of the doubt in court, by virtue of, well…status, for one thing. A million dollar legal team also carries weight that seems to help with the status thing. Again, personalities before principles comes to mind.

To see this (status affecting justice) in action on any day, simply follow any high profile sexual assault trial. The trial usually involves a high status abuser, and it often becomes clear, that justice in never quite totally blind to the status of those in its court.

The first day of the trial I should have known something was wrong when the judge said something to the effect of, "Whether it is tires, cars, whatever, it is all sales, and everybody knows that." The problem with his statement is that he was the referee in a trial where the crux of the matter was about people who represented themselves NOT as the salespersons which they were licensed as, but as professional advisors, which they held no legal license nor duty for. Fraud was the underlying issue, yet it was precisely the issue the courts seem unable to touch, for the highest-of-status fraudsters.

The judge was teaching us his opinions on matters before hearing the facts of the matter. Day one.

The defendant had used (and still today uses) false representations to make investors think that their sales agents held the professional standards of financial 'advisers'. Nothing could be further from the truth, and the judge illustrated either a bias, or a very failed understanding of this concept, by these and other comments made.

From that day forward, it seemed that he had a predetermined outcome in his mind as to how things should work out in the end, and his job seemed to be in figuring how his judgement would be worded to accomplish that outcome. I am a biased source of opinion on this, so bear with my observations.

Of course this view sounds like 'sour grapes', as I read it myself. The only saving grace I can claim, is that the truth still remains the truth, whether my case was won or lost. The truth is bursting at the seams today, (post-trial of course:) that indeed, more than one hundred thousand "advisors" in Canada and perhaps many more in the U.S. hold no such registration, but are choosing to misinform the public. That is known as fraud to the world outside of finance…Inside finance, fraud is not spoken of, it is "hushed", by lawyers says my experienced friend Joe.

On the last day, after showing with considerable detail that each RBC salesperson who testified was not a holder of a license or registration for the "Advisor" term they were using, the judge's comments were to the effect that lawyers call themselves by many titles—solicitor, lawyer, advocate, and so on. He did not see the concern for the public in my revealing the RBC advisors that did not have an advisor license.

What this Justice chose to ignore is that it is generally understood that regardless of what title a lawyer may use, they usually actually <u>have</u> the legal requirements to use such terms and to represent clients in court. RBC salespersons in this matter <u>held no such license or registration that they promised the public.</u>

The Judge acted as if his role was more to <u>prevent</u> the scheme from seeing the light of day. The very same judge then went forth and protected TD bank in an unrelated "advisor" fraud case months later.

Within 18 months advisor deception was the lead story on CBC National news March 29th, 2017. See "Copy of CBC NATIONAL NEWS. FINANCIAL SALES TITLE TRICKERY MAR 29 2017" on YouTube. It is amazing to witness how a few CBC reporters can spot fraud and identify it quickly, while a Federal Judge seems only able to spot the personalities in his court, and not so much the principles.

The abused investor (or employee in this case) meanwhile stands watching his entire life, perhaps his life savings, go up in smoke, because "litigation is often storytelling". Legal experts never told me this before the fact. I am telling you now. Our systems of justice may be as easily rigged by well 'connected' lawyers, as is rigging an Easter egg hunt for your two year old daughter.

I also learned that the right legal team can spin anything, (and I do mean anything) to find at least two, perhaps three or more possible meanings (stories) with which to use against their opponent. Lawyers train hard in finding possible alternate meanings from a set of facts. Keep that in mind if you ever think about wasting ten years of your life and half million dollars to pursue justice. It matters very little what <u>you</u> know <u>for certain</u> to be the truth, as there are <u>always</u> another three ways to look at it, or spin it if necessary, and the other side will know that long before the shell-shocked victim.

Two weeks in court against the strongest bank in Canada was like being run over by a bus, every day, for two weeks…with alternative facts…or alternative stories, woven from cherry-picked facts.

I can now imagine a 16th Century Witch Hunt must have felt like.

"In no other legal battle --- mugging, home invasion or a car theft -- is the victim forced to prove their own personal legitimacy as a prerequisite for being believed." This is Charlie Angus commenting about another type of abuse. His words seem to apply to the victims of high status financial abusers.

There is a legal tactic called "whacking the complainant", and although still taught at some law schools, it is considered unprofessional and unbecoming to win cases by destroying victims. That does not stop the weakest of lawyers…or those addicted to their own greed.

Reverence to the system, allows the truth to be as carefully concealed, and danced around as if it were a flower arrangement in the middle of the dance floor. While protocol allows the victim to be destroyed. Anything from soup to nuts, will be brought into court to make it sound as if you are the worst possible person in the world… while evidence of bank or investment dealer malpractice is forgiven or not 'granted credibility' by the judge.

One example the Calgary judge was able to use to brand me a liar, was that I gave a 'different' reason to my doctor for asking for anxiety/depression help, in the 1990's, than the answer I gave to my medical flight examiner…15 years later. The relevance to my fraud allegations against the bank escapes me, but such is how the law can be used to prevent justice.

The sharp lawyer brought those two things into my trial, without me realizing until months later than the two contradictory statements were separated by 15 years' time difference.

I hope this does not sound too much like sour grapes, just know that you can also ask others who have had the misfortune to witness this for themselves. All I ask is for readers to keep an open mind as I try and describe normally hidden places, and concealed methods of 'how things work'.

Abuse and bullying of a victim is an amazing and horrifying thing to watch in action. Simply astounding to see how clearly and cleverly the courts can become a place to 'prevent' justice from occurring. <u>Preventing justice</u> for the highest of status guests while <u>pursuing justice</u> for the rest? Is this the deal for those who can afford upper-elevation justice?

Trial at this level is a carefully orchestrated dance in which the status quo is maintained, the boat is not rocked, and justice is not always the outcome sought. What seems sometimes sought is that the 'right' people win, and the 'not-right' people get punished for even daring to question power or status. Look back across history if needing other examples of this.

Sadly, the 'right' people are often those in the upper echelons of power, influence and money. Again, the saddest news here is that lady justice seems to have regained her eyesight…in recognition of high status defendants.

Justice, like violence is often dispensed "downward" from the strong towards the weak. It appears that it is not polite for the weak or underclass to ask justice to travel upwards. That appears frowned upon by the system. There are just too many willing handmaidens who stand ready to protect persons and systems of status.

Justice may operate like gravity in that sense. At least it appears to become so, just as soon as one crosses the line. That line is often found somewhere around $100 million dollars and up, for one-off crimes, and any smaller amount if the crime can be applied across an entire society through systemic means. Systemic schemes that cheat an entire population also seem 'invisible' to current systems of regulation or justice.

===========

It is simply "career smarter" for those inside the system, to "protect upwards" in the direction of the powerful, and to "prosecute downward", in the direction of the weak. Career-smart is explored by behavioral economist Dan Ariely, in his book and documentary project "(Dis) Honesty, The Truth About Lies".

I learned volumes in his film about human self-preservation instincts, about the need to 'fit in' with ones peer group, or risk being left 'outside the walls'. It is a book/film that I think everyone should see. Thanks Dan, for this ground breaking work.

Lawyers have told me that even judges tend to bend in this gravitational direction, due to the less messy aftereffects, (the embarrassment of appeals, reversals, etc) if they protect the higher value entity in their courtroom, and prosecute the lower value entity. There is simply less "callbacks", or blowback to their work when they take the easier path.

I have not witnessed these "fact-bending" instincts in any judge that I have witnessed handling cases well below the $100 million mark, or cases that are not connected to systemic financial abuse. I have seen nothing but impeccable and honorable judicial behavior in every court room I been in. It is only at elevations of $100 million and above, or in systemic crimes where things seem out of control.

===========

"Power brokers control things"… is a quote that came to me today, as I was writing this, and I think it applies directly to the types of lawyers that the billion dollar banks retain. They do not go looking for legal help in the yellow pages. The kind of legal help that is willing to "do anything", is found on very private lists. These are the lawyers who do not put their pictures on bus shelters and billboards.

It is pretty much like I imagine how one would go about finding a "hit man", and the analogy is not very far off when one observes the harm that rapacious lawyers are willing to inflict.

They are, in effect "hit men" for hire to top corporate bidders. Between that thought and the idea of a gravitational pull to settling cases in favor of the powerful....it seems as though the justice system has a lot going on beneath those black robes.

It is interesting to note that at about the same time that RBC was in court denying wrongdoing, or ill treatment of the public, they were quietly negotiating a 'settlement' and a $20 million penalty with the OSC for wrongdoing and ill treatment of the public…(my trail was in Fall of 2015)

This was a Wells Fargo moment for Canadian banks, which allowed RBC to settle their wrongs for pennies on the dollar, rather than admit their wrongs in civil court and have a public precedent set.

"During a routine compliance review in January, 2015, RBC self-reported to regulators that they had found inadequacies in parts of their compliance systems which resulted in a number of RBC investors paying, directly or indirectly, excess fees they should not have been charged.

The Ontario Securities Commission (OSC) will hold a hearing on Tuesday to consider whether it is in the public interest to approve a no-contest settlement agreement between the OSC and RBC.

The amount of fees overcharged to investors has not been disclosed.
CLARE O'HARA   GLOBE AND MAIL WEALTH MANAGEMENT REPORTER
JUNE 23, 2017

https://beta.theglobeandmail.com/report-on-business/rbc-faces-scrutiny-following-report-of-excess-investor-fees/article35454155/?ref=http://www.theglobeandmail.com&

===========

The CBC National News then revealed on March 29th, 2017 (GO Public CBC) that over 120,000 Canadian investment 'advisors' fail to hold the proper registration and duty of care to represent themselves as advisor/adviser under the Securities Act. Justice Sullivan of Calgary was able to ignore this despite evidence presented to him through two separate trials, just two years prior.

===========

Anything that can be corrupted already is, we just don't yet know how.

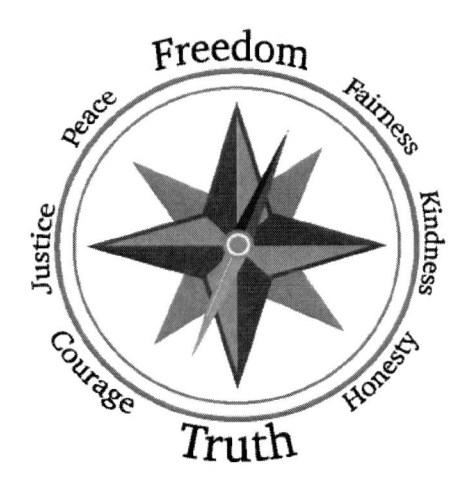

CHAPTER TWENTY

MORAL INJURY, CRASHING A LIFE

"Everyone has a plan...until they get punched in the face."
Mike Tyson

===========

Who do I blame, for the broken switch in my brain?

I saved most mention of myself until the latter part of the book, because this book is not about me.

I am merely an observer to systemic abuse by financial professionals, and I was too stubborn to stay silent and hurt the people who gave me their trust. I had a little bit of respect for myself, a great deal of respect for my profession, and a reverence for the trust my clients gave me.

===========

I slept in the back of my truck, the night after testifying in Ottawa, to a Parliamentary committee about investment tricks that rob billions from Canada.

(link to standing committee: https://openparliament.ca/committees/justice/40-2/53/larry-elford-4/only/)

I was on my way to flight training at the heliport at Cline River, a 10 minute flight from the Columbia Ice Fields in Jasper National Park, Alberta. My reason for being there was part of my need to change just one thing in my life. That one thing turns out to be 'everything', as they say.

I was in the process of changing my life circumstances, or giving up some or all of my earned comforts in life, in pursuit of a quest for 'character'. Flying helicopters was a wonderful mental pursuit to work on, to try and live life, now that my search for ethics and answers had 'removed' me from the investment industry.

The higher quest was to see if yet another type of secretive abuse could be outed, and exposed to the world before I expired. Typically it takes 50 to 100 years or more for human abuses of other humans, to be discovered, uncovered, outed, and resolved.

Recall how long it took to bring the tobacco industry around from doing harm to others. For billions of dollars, millions of handmaidens will help keep abuse alive…for decades.

Think about how long other abuses have remained hidden, when the abuse is done by powerful men.

My discovery of abuse was in the area of financial abuse by fake "trusted professionals". What a discovery to make in a first-world country. I found it first in Canada, and then learned of it in the USA. Today it is a daily headline in the UK, Australia, and other countries.

My profession was dealing with the trust and the money of vulnerable people who came to me for help. At somewhere between five and ten years into my career, I gradually became aware of another 'secret' business inside the investment advice business.

This newly discovered 'business', is the hidden, predatory, but more profitable side of my profession. The visible side is the business of earning investment clients trust, as well as their money, to invest. The hidden, more profitable side revealed itself as I made the discovery (with Stan Buell of SIPA.ca) that nine out of ten financial salespersons hid their salesperson license while their Broker/Dealer firms went to any lengths to also hide the salesperson's weaker agency-duty to customers. A circle of deception came in focus.

This second (hidden) business was thus in 'farming' the client, while the first (promised) business was in 'serving' the client. It was simple sleight of hand done to over 100 million American investors, and over 10 million Canadians. Bait the customer with promise of a professional adviser, and then switch the delivery to that of a 'counter-party' salesperson. Almost pure fraud.

"Agency duty" is the key to realizing whom the sales agent truly works for. Their sales-advisor duty is to serve and protect the dealer and the brokerage firm's financial interests. Hiding this, and concealing the license, allows broker/dealers to dupe the public into believing something quite different is happening to them and their life savings. It can be a predatory, self serving relationship that is sold to millions of North Americans as if it were a highly professional "advice" service.

===========

All the fraud takes to keep hidden from public accountability is one clever vowel-movement… and about 10,000 paid regulators.

===========

By now you may understand why I say that shortchanging 100+ million North Americans out of their rightful investment returns is the highest paying, lowest risk work in North America.

It also occurs to me that the lowest paying, highest risk work is that of telling the truth about those who are cheating and/or shortchanging 100+ million North Americans.

So what is wrong with my head that would cause me to give up a $100 million book of investment clients, a six figure income, and the ability to fly my own helicopter to the mountains, or to a picnic by the river?

What's wrong is that it hurt me to discover as a young man how much of my 'profession' was harvesting customers. It hurt even more after I spoke out, despite all codes of conduct which promise that a crooked financial industry is not allowed. A promise that truth will correct financial wrongdoing. It did not correct anything except my career, along with anyone else who spoke up.

It (organized financial crime, of the white collar variety) is so endemic, that it might rank up there with Hydrogen and stupidity, as one of the world's most common elements. Trust me, I know stupidity…and I now know systemic financial crime.

I found myself on a journey that is part rescue mission, part compulsion, part ethics experiment, part psychology study, part socio-economics. It included experiences in law and politics at higher altitudes. What a ride. What an opportunity. Where else do you get a chance to potentially be of help to millions of people…while repeatedly being punched in the face?

Where else do you get a chance, somewhere between slim and none, to change something that effects nearly every person on the continent? I got that chance, through no request of my own. I was given that gift. A curse actually—but a gift if I could make it into a gift. I will let you know how it turns out.

I no more enjoy investigating systemic crime or abuse than I imagine a homicide detective enjoys studying serial killers. The simple fact, however, is that financial crime 'is what it is,' and I 'am who I am.' And both of those things came together to make me the unique person that I am, to tell this story.

I got here by no specific planning or intention, but through a series of steps, often missteps, each one gradual, and each one leading me closer to where I stand today. When I took the very first step of refusing to be a "team player", as my RBC sales manager repeatedly asked of me, little did I know it would lead me here. By no means do my skills make me the best person, or even a good person, to be doing what I am doing. I just seem to be one of the people who is trying.

Those who know me have probably noticed how deeply involved I have been in this for the past couple of decades. It was, after all, my profession, and one for which I was in some way responsible.

I was disturbed to awaken and find myself in a dystopian financial world where the highest rewards go to the most ruthless among us. Where six, seven, and eight figure salaries can be easily earned if you are willing to hurt, cheat, or harvest people, but the same salaries are not quite as easily (or as rapidly) earned for those who would help people... or for those who refused to harm and harvest their clients.

I was also disturbed to observe that some of the highest paying work in the legal industry goes to those who work *preventing justice* from applying, rather than applying justice. To see a lawyer brag of billing one million dollars...for legal "work" that pushed a man to suicide, just to protect the guilty.

I found myself in a job where to lie is to win, and to tell the truth is to be threatened or fired if it might affect profits. Yet to lie could also get you fired, according to the rules and codes of ethics. This causes a double-bind, which puts all the risks and pressures upon the investment salesperson, with no risk to the investment firm. Heads they win. Tails you lose.

I am disturbed to see that those who tell the truth, or help others are valued the least, and in fact might even be the most punished in the world. Think of those who are famous for trying to tell the truth—NSA whistleblower Snowden, military truth-teller Manning, WikiLeaks Assange. Go back in time and view what the powers of the day did to King, Ali, Mandela, Gandhi, or other history makers. Jail was often their reward for good deeds done...when crime is on the throne.

It is frightening to be part of a business model where lies, cheating, willful blindness, is the most highly rewarded activity. It feels like a world where wrong is right, and right is wrong. If this is the case, then a few million professionals are trapped in a double-bind. On the one hand they are told they must follow the rules, the laws, and the codes of ethics of honorable conduct, and on the other they are often punished, devalued, or even terminated, for doing this.

It puts millions of financial people (and closely related industries) in a position in where no matter which direction they choose, they may lose. If you take the high road and refuse to sell out your self-respect and your profession, you run the risk of not meeting the demands of your bosses and being terminated.

If you sell out and go for the easy money, you will be the terminated scapegoat if the sellout becomes public. Your firm will hold you out as a bad apple, and let you take the fall, despite the corporation being the management-push behind every 'systemic' abuse of ethics regarding clients. The systemic abuses are a million times more dangerous to society than the one-off bad apples.

Purchased regulators provide the "assist", making sure that the "right" people are sanctioned, and the guilty people are protected. It all works rather smoothly, to protect the industry, and not the public.

Double-binds, if powerful or stressful enough, have been known to weaken one's natural resistance to health problems, both physical and mental. Psychological studies have connected the dots between mental health problems and people who are placed in unsolvable double binds. If you look closely, you can see it in our overall society today.

From years of working in the financial industry I am well-versed in the types of financial misconduct used against investors. Most dangerous is its use against seniors.

Those who speak against this misconduct can then be subjected to unique forms of employment abuse by this powerful industry that desires to keep its trust exploitations secret.

Victims, whether clients or employees, may then be subjected to legal targeting and bullying, whereby the power and money of the industry is used to legally harass and beat the investment victim or employee. Your own money may be used to hire million dollar lawyers, simple hit-men, to beat you from getting your money back. That is just how the big guys roll.

Lives end up ruined, finances decimated. Few victims obtain justice or fairness from the system, and often speak of how the system was yet another source of psychological trauma, piled upon financial injury.

It is no wonder then that victims end up in dire circumstances. Depression, addiction, isolation, self-sabotaging behaviors, relationship struggles. All types of socio-economic woes can come about when financial corporations are allowed to deceive and cheat the public with impunity.

Those who have lived with me have seen what the unique violence of white-collar crime does to those who get caught up in it, including trying to reveal, protect or prevent others from its effects.

I have felt a bit like the boy who cried wolf for a number of years, although in the past decade, economic events of the world have shifted to justify some of the howling. I have also felt like the 'Cassandra' figure of Greek mythology, who was blessed with the ability to foresee catastrophic events of the future, and cursed so that no one would ever believe her prophesies.

I have learned the devastating personal effects of financial abuse, employment abuse, corporate abuse, and legal abuse. I'm speaking in hopes that my children and their children may not have to face similar struggles. Similar secret abuses. Every abused person should step up, lest the <u>one 'super power' of the abuser</u> remains intact.

What is the <u>'super power'</u> of every abuser that lets them get away with abuse for decades in some cases? Secrecy.

It is the ability to use power, threats, and 'status' to keep the spotlight from shining onto their abuses. Watch any of the great film work about those who speak truth to power. Academy Award winning film "SPOTLIGHT". Tobacco whistleblower film "The Insider", and NFL player injury film "Concussion".

I apologize to all who have known me over the past twenty years. I am sorry I have not been myself, and at times I have not even been bearable. I have been a non-stop broken record of warning/complaining in advance of much public evidence to support the need to complain.

I have been mono-focused on the most interesting and fascinating "system-mechanics" puzzle I have ever encountered.

The puzzle is to understand the social, political, financial, moral, legal and ethical dynamics that come together to allow millions of Canadian and American investors to be abused. Victimized by persons posing as 'trusted' financial, legal, political and regulatory professionals.

Yes, some are trustworthy, however the majority seem to have found themselves caught in the corporate 'double-bind' of "do what we say or else…" The compelling evidence that suggests that the majority are captured in this manner, is that the rest are too afraid to even speak about it. That tells you of the balance of power involved.

My apologies to the ten or twenty percent of those professionals who do not victimize their clients. You know who you are, and you are not offended by the truth. I have spoken too many of you. Perhaps my speaking out with this book, will finally allow you to use your voice for public benefit as well.

To me the puzzle is one of simple system mechanics—the mechanics of how financial, legal, accounting, justice, political, and regulatory systems fail, and what causes them to fail cooperatively. Fail the public in a way that players within those systems gain, while society loses. It is a bit like looking at an airplane wreck after the crash and trying to decipher what went wrong to bring it down. It is work that is both fascinating and horrifying.

My forensic investigations are focused on what I believe to be intentional wrecks, <u>harms caused knowingly</u> by people who know better, but can't, or won't act better. I have never seen air crashes where a pilot, engineer, or someone in the system profits from mechanical failure. But in the investment field it is now common practice to make more money distributing toxic or poorly designed products and advice to the public. More on that in Chapter 26.

Each failed investment can always be blamed on "markets". Its like having an endless "do not go to jail" card, for those who profit from investment client sabotage.

It is always more profitable to 'water down' the products, to thin out the soup. Keep in mind that financial products are intangibles, often unable to be seen, touched, tasted or sampled like the soup. Only experienced market savants like Warren Buffet can 'feel' the intangibles of an investment, based on decades of experience.

The average member of the public is as blind and as vulnerable to those intangibles as a newborn kitten.

In the financial arena, corporations can make billions by taking advantage of the intangible nature of their products, and the blindness of their customers. Back that up with 'purchased' systems of regulation, accounting, law and politics, and they not only 'can't lose', but also 'can't even get arrested'.

The fascinating discovery (for me) is in how any backyard mechanic can look at systems or mechanisms, and diagnose obvious problems. They spot those problems, and make part replacements to put the system back to 100% operation. Just like the mechanic in coveralls does when you take your brakes, tires or wheel bearings in for repair.

But what if the guy was not wearing coveralls? What if he wore a suit instead? What if he could spot the problem, like any mechanic might spot it, but he/she had financial or systemic incentives to **not** fix the problem?

What if he is told, like I was, to "Shut up…or else"?

What if the system he works in preferred not to fix all the broken things? What if there was more money to be made in a bad system, an off-balance system, a crap-product-production machine? Those flaws can provide 'opportunities' for untold billions to be made.

Unlike the braking system on your car, where any mechanic can spot the problem, and fix the problem…financial, political, judicial and regulatory systems have no mechanics responsible to keep the system clean and in top operational condition. There may be entire departments, and upper level staff who need to be replaced, or tossed out, and yet there is little to no willingness to make those repairs. No mechanics equals no accountability.

Systems do not repair themselves. System players often profit more from not repairing 'themselves'. Investors often get the worst regulatory and other related systems of handmaidens that money can buy…and that breeds the worst (read most profitable to insiders) investments that can be unloaded on America. Doubly so for Canada.

The broken 'thing' could be the judge who makes decisions based upon relationships, the politician who does similar, or the Securities regulator who is paid $3/4 million…by the people he is supposed to police. Double binds are everywhere. With no mechanics on the job to spot them…or to fix them.

So I live with what was my career. It is now changed so that I am no longer a hard working investment professional that I once was. I am now an expert in investment industry misconduct and malpractice. I am an educator, a speaker, a writer, and someone who helps himself only by helping others. That is what I used to get to do in the investment industry, help myself by helping others.

That used to be the capitalism model in my father's day, "to those who do the greatest good, go the greatest rewards'. Today the greatest rewards go to those who do the greatest harm, and this is not a sustainable model for society. This is the age of looting, raping and pillaging society…by gangs of trusted professionals.

===========

Now I am trying to turn what feels like post-traumatic stress, into post-traumatic growth. Another term, 'moral injury,' I learned in 2016, comes even closer to describing what myself and many others have felt. Others just like me, who work for government or corporate entities in which secrecy may be of far greater value than truth.

Consider that I worked for the largest bank in the country, one of the largest in the world. It boasted of having up to 70,000 employees worldwide. Today it is closer to 100,000. But it forbade each of those from speaking the truth, if the truth was not what management wanted spoken. Imagine the moral injury within any one corporation when silence is required, even if causing harm to society. Imagine the size of the Class Action payoff if the employees ever find their voice…

My friend Deb, who helped me proof this book, pointed out that Canadian Banks now generally require departing employees to sign a new document called a "disparagement agreement", whereby the departing employee is forbidden from ever saying anything that might be considered 'disparaging' against the former employer.

Writing this book, speaking to public audiences, sharing my experience in hopes of saving them some of the pain and abuse, is as much about my own recovery as it is about helping. As Rachel Naomi Remen says, "Only service heals".

===========

Thank God that change is accelerating of late, with new information coming faster in the age of instant communications. As I write this, "fake news" is now considered normal, to go along with fake food, fake regulation, fake politicians and so many other things now being identified as less than portrayed. My father, who passed away just 20 years ago, would not ever recognize the world in which we live today.

Just one decade ago (2007) I could not engage in open discussion with people about the greed and corruption of our banks, brokers, and regulators. Now it is not uncommon for ordinary folks to bring it up with me on the street, or to protest in the street, against our 'trusted' criminal class.

The truth is emerging. But it is still worth a billion dollars a week (in Canada) to keep it buried a while yet, so don't expect the industry to give up any of those billions soon. (ten billion per week is my U.S. cost-to-society estimate) GOOGLE "Cost of 2008 economic crash". it is measured in Trillions, and of course it was blamed on…the markets…not on system criminality.

===========

"If there's injustice in the world, I believe those of us that have the ability to witness and record it, document it and tell the world what is happening have a moral responsibility to do that. Then, of course, it's left up to those that are receiving that knowledge to make the moral choice about whether they want to stand up against the injustice or observe it." - Kumi Naidoo, Greenpeace International

Perhaps one of the reasons I do what I do, besides the circumstances I landed myself in, is that I was supposed to learn about the next level beyond being the best broker I could become. Here is a positive-experience story that I am starting to feel common elements in, as I work to protect and inform millions of people about financial abuse.

The following story is distant from the realm of financial abuse, but closer the realm of a emotional healing of that thing in our head that is hard wired for fairness, as all healthy human brains are.

A female humpback whale had become entangled in a spider web of crab traps and lines. She was weighted down by hundreds of pounds of traps that caused her to struggle to stay afloat. She also had hundreds of yards of line rope wrapped around her body, her tail, her torso, a line tugging in her mouth.

This is her story of giving gratitude.

A fisherman spotted her just east of the Farallon Islands (outside the Golden Gate) and radioed for help. Within a few hours, the rescue team arrived and determined that she was so badly off, the only way to save her was to dive in and untangle her.... a very dangerous proposition.

One slap of the tail could k ll a rescuer. They worked for hours with curved knives and eventually freed her.

When she was free, the divers say she swam in what seemed like joyous circles. She then came back to each and every diver, one at a time, nudged them, and pushed gently, thanking them. Some said it was the most incredibly beautiful experience of their lives.

The man who cut the rope out of her mouth says her eye was following him the whole time, and he will never be the same.

===========

Compassion for those beyond oneself and immediate family is connected to advanced societies, whereas self-serving, self absorbed behaviors is the mark of societies in decline.

===========

Maslow's pyramid:

- **Self-actualization**: morality, creativity, spontaneity, problem solving, lack of prejudice, acceptance of facts
- **Esteem**: self-esteem, confidence, achievement, respect of others, respect by others
- **Love/Belonging**: friendship, family, sexual intimacy
- **Safety**: security of body, of employment, of resources, of morality, of the family, of health, of property
- **Physiological**: breathing, food, water, sex, sleep, homeostasis, excretion

=========

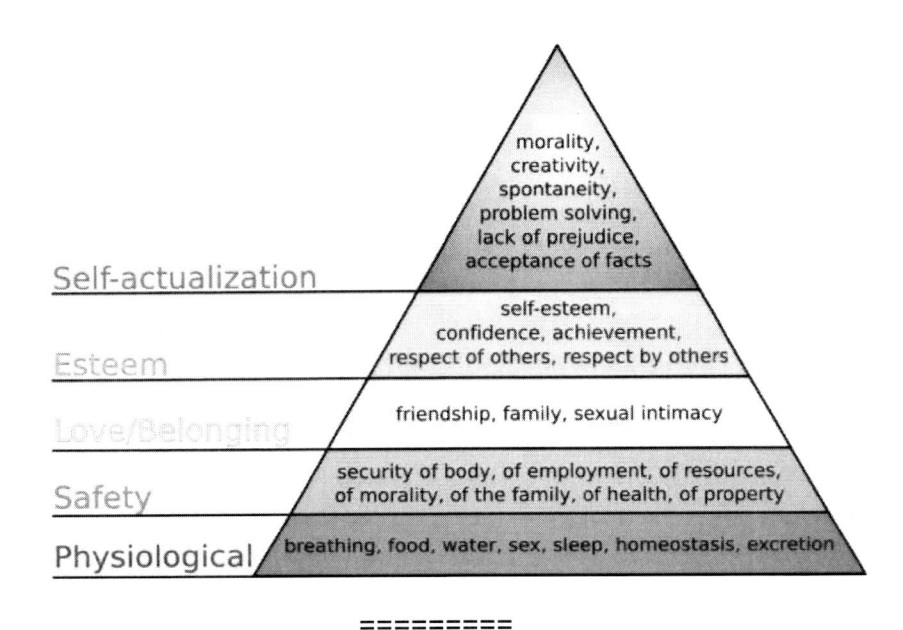

Maslow's hierarchy of needs is a theory in psychology proposed by Abraham Maslow in his 1943 paper "A Theory of Human Motivation"

Maslow studied what he called exemplary people such as Albert Einstein, Jane Addams, Eleanor Roosevelt, and Frederick Douglass rather than mentally ill or neurotic people, writing that "the study of crippled, stunted, immature, and unhealthy specimens can yield only a cripple psychology and a cripple philosophy."(Wikipedia)

I learned that Maslow's hierarchy of needs <u>now has one more level</u>, which Maslow added as an afterthought about 20 or more years after he achieved fame with his original pyramid. (the new Maslow pyramid is shown just a bit further along, page 264)

He originally thought that the highest level of human attainment, (if that is the wording), was the level of self-actualization. Self-actualization is understood to mean, to become the very best example of humane behavior that I can possibly become.

Twenty years after he introduced his five level hierarchy of needs, he added the sixth level, "self transcendence".

Simply put, it is the level where we 'get over ourselves' and begin to think and act to benefit others. Of ascending to a set of beliefs or practices which are beyond "just ourselves." Grandparents are good at this, having spent a lifetime working, they come to the point where the greatest satisfactions in life come from putting children, grandchildren, friends, neighbours and community ahead of themselves.

Meanwhile, elements of the second level of Maslow's pyramid can be seen as a place that some of our weaker souls, perhaps many billionaires appear stuck. Many of us are stuck in never having "enough".

Which is to say stuck in fear. Fear of not having enough. Fear of not being enough. We all feel this fear, I suspect. I know I did. I do. But again, I am thankful for the gift of desperation. For the exact circumstances which would cause every single thing in my life to change dramatically, and which has put me on the journey that I find myself on today.

===========

"Financial stress is one of the triggers leading to emotional, mental and physical illness. "

I live in a time where I can actually stand back and witness a growing percentage of our society coming under stress and duress.
Economic strain is so evidently a cause of society stress, it is as clear to me as if I were to witness an 8 year old boy poking a stick into an ant hill to watch the panic. I now get to see society panic on a weekly basis.

Abuse is defined as:
Any act, or failure to act, which results in a significant breach of a vulnerable person's human rights, civil liberties, bodily integrity, dignity or general well-being, whether intended or inadvertent, including sexual relationships or financial transactions to

which the person has not or cannot validly consent, or which are deliberately exploitative.

I simply refused to become 'that person', that abuser, that 'trust manipulator' that my financial institution needed me to be, to feed it's addiction to more.

If I do not grow up, get over myself, and do what I can to help others, then I have not learned anything from the challenges in my life. Those challenges, with the gift of hindsight are merely opportunities for me to learn, to grow and to mature.

===========

It was 2017 before I learned the term AFS, which stands for "acute financial stress", and what this type of pain and suffering was then causing society. Allostatic load came into my vocabulary sometime around 2015, informing me about the 'overload' circuits in the brain which can become 'burned out' after too much use, or stress to them.

My wife cried when she watched the video on Allostatic Load, of literally burning out stress circuit-breakers in the brain. The causes and effects described were a little too close to what I (we) have experienced.

Below is a link to this information that I hope will help others:
THE GOOD, THE BAD & THE DAMAGING: CHRONIC STRESS & ALLOSTATIC LOAD
Matthew Hill, PhD
Brain Architecture, Stress, Resilience, Addiction
June 2010

Dr. Matthew Hill, from the University of Calgary, draws on neurobiology to discuss toxic stress, its effects on the brain, and later manifestation of disease. Dr. Hill specifically focuses on how early stress in life can have long-term effects on brain architecture, promoting a disease state which can manifest symptoms in the long-term.

http://www.albertafamilywellness.org/resources/video/the-good-the-bad-and-the-damaging-chronic-stress-and-allostatic-load

===========

In my own words, Allostatic Load (AL) means that some folks who have had very traumatic experiences, or traumatic lives, may actually have destroyed or damaged 'circuit breakers' that allow certain brain functions to be turned on or off. Allostatic load can burn out the switch, so the brain may lose control of that function. It may no longer be able to turn on or off the things that healthy brains turn on or off at certain times, and under certain conditions.

In scientist wording: (Bruce McEwen)

The notion of <u>allostatic load</u> (AL) to indicate the wear and tear that is inevitable after innumerable cycles of allostasis, or when there were disorders of allostasis, such as ineffective activation or termination events. (stress that never goes away.)

Allostatic load follows a basic trajectory of distress (intense short-term or chronic stress) that then causes any of the key allostatic systems in the body (e.g., blood pressure, cardiovascular, metabolic, inflammatory, etc.) to remain (more or less) in a state of dis-regulation.

This dis-regulation, particularly when chronic, can lead to significant damage to these and related biological and psychological systems, and in turn, leads to significant negative health outcomes including diabetes, heart disease, cancer, depression, alcoholism and post-traumatic stress disorder.)

This provocative model for the development of chronic diseases provides a plausible explanation for the fact that in the midst of some of the most remarkable medical advances ever, the 20th century also marks the emergence of chronic diseases with non-communicable conditions accounting for **nearly two-thirds of deaths worldwide.** (abuse of society, including financial abuse, is literally killing people at a rate we have not yet recognized)

In the U.S., chronic diseases are the main causes of poor health, disability and death, and account for most of health-care expenditures. This epidemiological transition, the third after the Age of Pestilence and Famine and the Age of Pandemics is widely called the Age of Chronic Diseases. In other words: stress damages our bodies and minds, and shortens our lives.

http://hexaco.org

The ability of financial corporations to skirt criminal laws, while abusing nations is <u>killing people</u> as well as society.

===========

'Moral injury' was the first 'corporate induced' psychological injury that I believe I experienced.

The term came to my attention in 2016. Post Traumatic Stress Disorder (PTSD) was a new and interesting topic of discussion, which came upon the public radar in the first decade of this century. (2008: Grey's Anatomy introduces a TV character with combat-related PTSD)

It explained a great deal about stress related harm, but it seemed rather specific to people who have seen, felt or suffered immediate trauma. Soldiers, police and emergency workers. Their trauma was not my trauma.

What about whistleblowers and others in situations which cause chronic stress that can last for years, or decades, without rest or respite?

Moral injury was studied in response to the number of suicides of returning war veterans, many of whom could not cope with the things they were forced to do, or see, or support, in the name of war.

I first understood moral injury as the type of injury a military whistleblower might suffer when he/she saw or participated in doing immoral things in the course of their operations. This was new and useful information for me.

It might include a drone pilot for example, sitting in an air conditioned trailer in the Nevada desert, flying remote control (drone) missions over places halfway around the globe. How does that person drop bombs and film the aftermath, the bodies, the damage, the children, and then get in their new Mustang convertible and drive home to their family on the base, or in some Nevada community?

What did they just do? What did they cause? Was it right? Some of these people had to do or see horrific things, and then go home and pretend as if nothing had changed in their lives. Does "just following orders" erase the feeling, or is it another double-bind which can do serious psychological harm?

I first observed the double bind in the brokerage industry, at a time when I was struggling to earn the trust of my clients, and to keep my head above water. My office mates with a few more years experience than I seemed to have found the Holy Grail, and made commissions as easily as taking candy from a baby. Sadly, most were literally taking advantage of the trust and the vulnerability of their clients, which is in principle, the same...as taking candy from a baby.

I was forced to declare bankruptcy in 2016, due to not being able to pay for the six figure legal costs of the bank. I had sued them for their unethical practices and constructively dismissing me in 2004 and I was beaten in court like a rented mule.

The court process, was an experience all its own. But the bank was not content to let me go with that beating, and seemed determined to set an example of my audacity to question their ethics. I learned that <u>extreme bullying</u> behavior is another attribute of Organized Financial Crime (OFC), much like it is to runaway systems of power.

It didn't seem to matter much, that the things I claimed as harmful and wrongful to the public, were starting to become public. They had won their case in court and that is all that mattered. They had a finding of legal "Fact" and no amount of "real facts" could change that. (Alternative facts are in our courts as well as the White House)

All they now had to do was to make certain that my voice was silenced. To do that they financially hunted both myself and my wife, through legal means, which if one has not gone there, is truly just psychological harassment, piled on top of career destruction to "hush" dissent. It felt like being pursued in an action thriller movie, without the guns, the girls and the positive outcome.

My friend Joe had to remind me that lawyers are the hitmen, helpers and hushers, in todays organized financial and corporate crimes.

Psychological torture can take a myriad of forms; Employment threats, workplace bullying, wrongful termination, mobbing, singling persons out for management retaliation, financial, and many other tactics. Search 'workplace bullying' to learn more, such as the startling fact that many victims of bullying at work are the best workers. They are often viewed as a 'threat' to less competent or lazier colleagues.

We live in a time where members of the public can no longer be punished with physical torture, however harmful forms of psychological torture are free and fair game in the world today, for tens of millions of corporate employees.

The psychological abuse may not ever stop, ever, for those who have spoken outside their company, or organization about criminal acts or abuses of power. See CBC 'Go Public' 2017 stories of abused bank employees, where 3000 employees stepped forward on this topic. They had to hide their identities…or else.

I participated in a research report (2017) for the Small Investor Protection Association of Canada, (www.sipa.ca) that uncovered that 96% of persons selling investment products in Canada did not hold an 'advisor' registration, nor did they hold the professional duty of trust and care that they advertised to the public.

That is the kind of information which an investment selling bank would not want its customers to know. It is also illegal to conceal or withhold ones license and registration from customers view. Unfortunately, I learned that 'illegal' is often a mere technicality, when done by those with great power. This is another aspect which seems common to moral injury, as that wise woman once said to me, "sometimes the law is used to 'prevent' justice".

I learned what it must feel like to be a victim of any other type of assault, who is then forced into a courtroom against a higher status abuser. The psychological beating, the victim blaming and the storytelling by cunning lawyers leave a person empty and in as much pain as was the assault. The result is more psychological torture and trauma, this time at the hands of clever, rapacious lawyers hired to do the legal assault.

One forensic medical expert report suggested that the corporate retaliation brought upon myself over a period of years, for trying to get my company to follow its own ethical codes, was akin to psychological torture. But none of those reports mattered either… in court at least. All were given no 'weight' in that judge's arena.

What was given the most weight? Status of the abuser relative to the abused. Ahh, now I get it…"the law can be just as easily used to prevent justice…"

The court process felt to me as yet another example where 'personalities' could be treated as being more important than 'principles'. I observed that sometimes justice may be more concerned with 'whom' is in their courtroom, than with the principles at stake. I cannot say this occurs frequently, but after a few decades of trying to understand high status financial abuses, I see it occurring more frequently, the higher the dollar values become.

Prior to entering the courtroom, I was required to engage in something called arbitration, where a mediation process is attempted before court time is granted. The interesting thing is that the mediator, is a retired judge, who works for a private company, now hired by most Canadian banks to 'mediate' (hired referees?) complaints against the…um, banks that hire them.

One of the memorable questions this retired judge asked me about my case was, 'how is it that you are the only voice in Canada speaking of these complaints….where are the other voices?"

By that, I took it to mean, if you are the only person saying what you are saying Larry, how do you expect me to believe you? I did not have the presence of mind to reply in the manner I wanted, so I remained silent to that question from the retired Judge, but here is the answer that came into my mind.

The question is not <u>how many</u> people are saying what I am saying, but in <u>how correct</u>, and accurate, what I am saying might be. For a judge, or anyone, to question a premise or issue, based upon it's 'popularity', told me a great deal about the status, the politics, and the 'which way is the wind blowing' measuring process that must come into a judge's mind.

By early 2017, I was finished with the nine months of bankruptcy proceedings and ready to be released from this form of financial purgatory, yet RBC had yet other intentions to continue the beatings.

They contested my release from bankruptcy and wished to pursue avenues which involved my wife, so it was a continual state of low level fear that we lived in. Fear and legal expenses that RBC seemed quite happy to pursue, simply to send more psychological messaging, according to many who guided us along the way.

We still did not fear the truth. What we feared, at all times was that bank-lawyers, with decades of experience and inside-judicial connections, could manufacture stories, paint inaccurate pictures of blame and doubt, and bring "weight" to fabrications simply due to the way in which the system is geared.

Stories can sway judges when told by million dollar lawyers. Multiple million dollar lawyers is even better at getting a judge to go along with the story. It felt like a show of force to bring four or more lawyers to beat a former employee, not a show of justice. It was a show alright.

The fear we lived in was due to the discovery that the rules of fairness and common decency need not apply in higher stakes cases, and that one has to know that the banks have decades upon decades of legal connections (and political) with which to call upon to get the job done. Any job it seems.

Banks simply do not hire the nice lawyer down the street from you. They can draw the slickest legal talent straight from Hollywood Central Casting.

The truth and principles that I stood for, are now coming out as I write these words, and it hope it (the truth, and some of these words) will survive long enough before being buried yet again. Share your own voice with me @RecoveredBroker and perhaps we can change things for the next generation.

============

My physical weakness did not become apparent to me until about January, 2017, when I made the discovery that basic health truly requires at least two functioning mechanisms. It requires not only a physical strength and ability to get up, get around, and get things done, but also a sufficient mental strength and willingness for each thing that needed doing. Right down to getting out of bed or something as simple as brushing one's teeth.

I had never thought of this dual requirement, because I had never suffered for more than a day, from failures of mental strength, and those days were always connected to an event of one kind or another which 'explained' why a person needed to lay in bed and do nothing for a day. Everyone needs a 'mental health' day. No one should suffer a mental health life, due to corporate greed and criminality.

It became apparent to me that I was isolating and sleeping and tired for far too many hours of the day. I had slowly cut myself off from many things that required mental effort. I learned that going out in public requires mental, and not merely physical effort.

Looking back, it should have been more obvious to myself, but who wants to admit that they are either getting old, or getting weak, and furthermore who is willing to think about getting weaker in the head.

When I left the industry in 2004, I had gotten rid of a cell phone, and here it was 2017 and I still did not use one. I told myself that this was the privilege of my free life, however underneath, I knew it was also a form of separation, of isolation, of knowing that I wanted to be left alone, to be separate from as much of the concerns of the world as I could.

I typically did not answer the house phone as well, since it was simply easier to let a machine take those calls, and to reduce yet one more source of interruption, disturbance, or stressful news.

Going through bankruptcy required digging up mail and bank statements going back years, and this provided yet another clue to a subtle self-isolation. I had not even opened mail from banks etc, from about 2004, until 2015 in many cases. One reason was knowing partially what they contained, and another was not having enough emotional energy to give a damn what they contained. Has anyone else ever felt that way I wonder?

It scares me to write these things since I had taken such careful steps to hide any weaknesses. Now I am not sure if hiding them helped me or simply served to hide yet another form of abuse that perhaps others may suffer from. The secret power of abusers is the ability to keep their abuse a secret. How many victims recognize that they themselves may be protecting their abusers?

I was now doing what I term 'morbid isolation', while still managing to function in the world. To 'suit up and show up', when required. But as soon as done, I would be back home, and back to the three "R"'s. Research, rumination and writing.

I know that true morbid isolation probably is far worse than what I was suffering, and I do not wish to minimize what others go through, but for me, what I was going through was morbid, so that is the term I use to describe it.

People who are abused, even just financial abuse, can often feel a sense of shame, as if it is somehow their fault. As a result, many of them will hide their victimization, which only aids the abuser.

===========

Today it feels like I am losing my mental strength, or my stamina to keep moving forward. It was been more than two decades now that I have worked to expose abuses by financial professionals and investment regulators.

The progress has been rather minimal, as a hundred million North Americans are still being lied-to about their financial "advice" provider, and too many are cleverly 'harvested' of their financial and retirement security. I can now look back at ten to twenty years of individuals standing up and speaking the same things I am saying today, and each book, each speaker, each whistleblower is silenced, and the truth buried yet again.

It has never even slowed the pace of harvesting the public, by those in power and those who sit at the regulatory/political/legal controls. The machine is simply too large to stop.

Oh, how certain I was at the very outset, that doing harm to investment clients for more money, was against every principle of the financial business I had entered. That it would be impossible to not find <u>every management hand</u> offering help and assistance to correct the situation and make the client's 'whole' again.

I was 24ish and was I unprepared to encounter the best organized systems, preventing discovery of rigged, unethical financial behavior. I found every single management hand turned against me, despite private assurances that they thought what I was doing was right. Each one of those managers was caught in their own 'double bind' circumstances. Silence by each and every one keeps a bank with thousands of employees able to abuse and entrap every one in that double bind.

Now I am almost 60. The investment industry alone, continues to (pick) pocket the equivalent of <u>all financial harm done, by all measured criminal acts, in the entire country, combined</u>. Every year this occurs according to simple records and observations.

Financiers must thank their lucky stars daily, that nobody funds academic studies into the costs of systemic, white collar crime. It is the best organized, most carefully protected game on the planet, to my knowledge. Please prove me wrong if you know otherwise, or add to my knowledge if you can.

It is slowly coming to light, and more members of the public are beginning to see the system-rigging. To learn how the system is 'fixed', against them ever getting fair, honest and good faith services, as promised.

If I can help to prevent this systemic, hidden financial abuse from ruining society for my children and grandchildren, then this little struggle will have been worth it. Even if I only make a dent. (so far the only dent I have made is from banging my face into the fist of corporate criminality…)

===========

Almost forgotten was another medical evaluation I went through after leaving RBC. It was a SPECT scan of the brain, done at the clinic of Dr. Daniel Amen in Newport Beach California.

I went there long prior to my trial process, in efforts to figure out what, if any harm was done to my brain, by a never-ending work environment of chronic stress. (endless psychological double binds)

This was before I learned that the brain was as subject to overuse, to stress, to abuse, as any physical muscle could be. It was around the time that the science of 'neuroplasticity' of the brain was becoming more understood.

I wanted to know not only if my brain had been harmed by years and years of the stress induced by being a financial whistleblower, but if I could take steps towards healing, or reversing the effects of that harm. There might be hope in neuroplasticity…

I believe it was my adventures with alcohol, which I have been loath to discuss, which prompted this journey to California and this personal search for answers. I had found alcohol to be a socially acceptable and approved corporate environment lubricant, and sadly I discovered that it relieved the daily stress of being put in an office environment filled with double-bind mental traps.

After a lifetime of not being a drinker, and hating the taste of the stuff, to find myself discovering the 'ice wines' of the Okanagan regions of Canada at a charitable fundraiser I was hosting, I had found a wine that did not taste like vinegar to me.

The rest are just details of my adventures with alcohol, other than to say that success happens when preparation meets opportunity. In this case the preparation was in years of the chronic stress of being a boy crying "WOLF", while not quite realizing that the firm was making ten or twenty times more money by acting like wolves. The opportunity was when the magic chemical of alcohol was added to that 'stress-prepared' brain. I did not say it was a good opportunity…

Alcohol is one of those magic elixirs, which ensures that people with deep pain, abuse issues, unresolved moral issues, or those put into double bind situations where no outcome is satisfactory, can find an easily obtainable chemical treatment of those anxious feelings. Instant chemical peace of mind…with a catch.

The trouble with adjusting ones feelings with a chemical, is that it is fake. Chemical peace of mind is no more peace of mind than is peace of mind from sugar, porn, gambling, shopping, sex, adrenaline, or a myriad of other risky or self sabotaging behaviors one can engage in. Even money is a drug to some.

But alcohol is socially approved and provided at most corporate events, and here I was, neurologically 'prepared' with years and years of mental stress, handed the 'opportunity' to trigger my brain, with the sweetest wine on the planet. It hit me with a chemical kick, at the exact moment in time that my brain was crying out for relief…life is like that sometimes.

Another kick. Another gift?

The use of alcohol to treat stress, pain, abuse, insecurity, moral injury etc., would occupy the next six or seven years of my life and bring about (or magnify) some of my worst attributes and behaviors. It also brought about some of the best lessons ever taught to me, lessons I would not have learned without having gone on the journey, or taken the fall.

Doctor's at the Amen Clinic in California (SPECT Scan brain imagery) said that they could actually see and measure the changes to portions of my brain, from long term chronic stress. Mental stress causes physiological changes to the brain, neurons die, new ones wire new pathways, new traits, new habits.

No one (to my knowledge) at that time was talking about how a workplace could actually do harm to ones brain, to physically alter the structure, the wiring, the firing.

This was fairly new to my eyes, and I studied everything I could about mind and brain, to try and understand myself better.

My wife and I knew that I was not simply the same person I used to be, and I needed to learn...if I was to heal.

So it was enlightening, and motivating to see scanned images of my brain, lit up in various colors which illustrated areas of activity, over activity and under-activity. Brain scan images, combined with psychological or psychiatric evaluation of a person, was a practice began by Dr. Daniel Amen, due to his unique skills and experiences in psychiatry.

He became the world's first psychiatric professional to believe that in order to better understand the mind and mentality of psychiatric patients, that quality images of the brain could shed new light into issues that people suffer in the mind.

Every other medical area (except psychiatry) were using scans to better see what internal body organs might be doing or not doing, so why not scan and examine the brain if it might help?

Ironically, as I read some of Dr. Amen's books, I discovered that his ideas were a little 'too advanced' for members of his profession to handle at that time. In response to his threat to some livelihoods, (or egos), etc., he was promptly chastised by his professional organization, which tried to run him out of the business in a gang-like fashion. Ironic in that this was exactly why I had visited his clinic. To learn about my own industry reactions to myself, for similar reasons of fear and threats to other egos.

Psychiatric profession "bullies" lobbied to have Dr. Amen's license to practice revoked, such were the fears of those who were not able to grasp or apply Dr. Amens advanced diagnosing techniques. It was eye opening to discover another example of career bullying for those who try to advance their professions.

===========

Dr. Amen cannot help but cry, and his voice shakes with emotion as he gives this TEDx Talk at 12:40 mark, on 16 Oct 2013.
https://www.youtube.com/watch?v=esPRsT-lmw8

His video will change your understanding of the brain in just the 2 minutes from 12:40 to its end. It changed mine forever. It explains (to me) the greatest unanswered questions facing America this very weekend that I write these words (October, 2018, Las Vegas sniper)...it explains some of the worst violence in American history...today's history. Dr. Amen describes it in just 2 minutes, and he did so in 2013, search "Daniel Amen TED Talk 83,000 brain scans".

===========

Here I am, a couple of decades along on my journey of discovery.

Discovery of everything I can learn about the financial "advisor" name-game. (bait and switch)

Discovery of everything I could learn about management and corporate abuse. (The hard way of course:)

Discovery of too much about legal abuse.

Discovery of everything I can learn about mental abuse.

Discovery of too much about moral injury.

Discovery of everything I can learn about alcohol abuse.

Discovery of too much about regulatory abuse.

Discovered too much about moral blindness. ("shoot, shut up and shovel")

Discovered far too much about political moral blindness: (Rule #1 is "Never rock the political boat while you are **in** the boat…stupid", and Rule #2 is to "shoot, shut up and shovel instead")

Discovered a great deal about what this can do to the human brain. Human bodies. Our shared society.

It is Jan 26th, 2017 as I write this. I am scheduled to undergo questioning under oath by RBC, for use in determining if they can destroy my family's financial affairs along with my own. No stress there. I feel like I am slowly discovering how to breathe under water, and that is yet another discovery that I will be thanking RBC for. (The desperation of these folks just keep handing me gift, after gift…. after gift)

===========

"GIFT? Are you truly nuts Larry?"

Not according to Mark Mason, author of "The Subtle Art of Not Giving F*ck"

Mark writes in an entertaining yet unusual style that is quite easy to understand. One of his findings is that "happiness is often the result of solving really important problems in life, not in having an easy life".

Here are three paragraphs from page 21 of Mark's book to give you the flavor of what his book is like and why it too, is a gift:

This book doesn't give a f*ck about alleviating your problems, or your pain. And that is precisely how you will know it is being honest. This book is not some guide to greatness it couldn't be, greatness is merely an illusion in our minds, a made up destination that we obligate ourselves to pursue, our own psychological Atlantis.

Turn your trauma into power, and your problems into slightly better problems. That is real progress. Think of it as a guide to suffering and how to do it better, more meaningfully, with more compassion and more humility. It's a book about moving lightly despite your heavy burdens, resting easier with your greatest fears, Laughing at your tears as you cry them.

 I hope you discover the book for yourself and urge you to look past the implied profanity in the title. It contains everything that Eckhart Tolle and many other masters of the study of life, have been trying to tell us.

It does so in a language that comes from the heart, and the street, so it explains details in startlingly clear and understandable fashion.

I liked Mark's book. No I loved his book, and I purchased multiple copies of it to give to friends who seemed ready to hear what he is saying. I have not done that in years, discovered writing that I would buy in bulk to share with others. His book, smacked me in the head on so many pages that I had to mention it here.

It was my son who found it and gave it to me, and I think he is turning out a darn sight smarter than his dad. They (kids) all are these days.

Tony Robbins is the other person who I came across, and learned from. His approach to tough times and to personal trauma is to use those difficulties for growth. To fuel through the pain. To become stronger human beings and to thank those who helped you, by pushing you to overcome. So my abusers, the banks, regulators, and all the rest are to be thanked for giving me this challenge. Thanks also to Tony for his contributions to helping others.

===========

Lastly…

I will tell you what moral injury feels like to me.

Moral injury feel like something is very wrong. Every day. It also feels like that something (that is wrong) is very important. To not just me, but to everyone. Whether it is or not is beside the point. The point is the nagging feeling of "wrong". (billion- dollar robberies that stir the emotions of a hundred million confused North Americans helps to justify those feelings, but does not do anything to lessen the injuries:)

One has a strong feeling that something is not right, perhaps connected to situations where evidence exists that indeed, something is <u>very wrong</u>. After all, there is much that is wrong in the world, and some of us get swept up by it. Some in it. Some get swept away.

It then triggers feelings of unfairness, when the situation is unraveled and understood. That unfairness might be regarding the environment, animals, children, work, war or anything. It just feels like there is a grave injustice being done and that you know what that 'thing' is, that does such injustice. (hint: it is never what the nightly news tells you)

I learned that the brain is hard-wired for fairness. Fairness is related to kindness, which is related to compassion, which is related to all good things including love. For those like me who have difficulty with the word love, having walled myself off from feelings, just picture the feeling of hate, and imagine the opposite.

Then add in the feeling one gets when 'selfishness' is added to unfairness. Unfairness by itself is not necessarily a debilitating feeling, most of the time. Many life situations are unfair, beginning with the early death of people whom should have not had to die. I can accept this although it makes my heart heavy.

But when one adds 'selfishness', and pure human greed into the equation, as a <u>cause</u> of unfairness, this multiplies the emotions many, times in intensity, as well as in chemical makeup of those emotions.

Why? I don't know but I think it has to do with the injustice, the indignity, perhaps the "forced-into-submission" feel, of living with, or being witness to unfairness, when done by governments, corporate systems, or by persons who abuse power against others. It seems that it is always the use of power against the powerless.

Now we are back into the realm of moral injury, the emotional and psychological harm done by persons who have done the harm knowingly, willingly and selfishly to others, in order to feed their own dopamine needs.

The thing is that 'power' comes with the responsibility over what that power can do. Or at least it should in a safe world. We seem to have morphed to point where right, wrong and responsibility, do not matter, and that the only thing that does matter is 'who is bigger'? "Might" becomes "right".

Who is stronger and thus who gets his way? By force if necessary. It is not a moral question or one of justice, right or wrong, but simply who can overpower. That power wins in a world run without values.

===========

I now know that the world would suffer less terror…if only it were fairer.

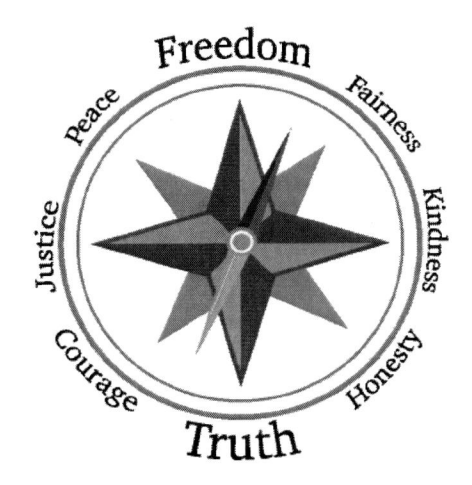

CHAPTER TWENTY ONE

SPOTTING THE SUBCLINICAL PSYCHOPATH

Bullying often stops when psychopathy is discussed, rather than admired...or elected.

What a shock to find myself as a young man of 24, inside the most "trusted" industry—the financial industry—only to discover over time, that a very high percentage of those at the top had an invisible weapon. It is the same invisible weapon that some psychopaths have when they mingle in society. Their weapon is the inability to feel anxiety while harming someone else.

Combine that with an ability to be charming and earn trust, and we all know what can go wrong. I worked 20 years inside a business where many had that power, that inability to feel remorse. (it is either lack of remorse, or the fact that most are trapped inside the classic industry 'double bind". (Do what we say...or else)

*Quotation by Robert D. Hare, Canadian Psychologist, born 1934: "I always said that if I wasn't studying psychopaths in prison, I'd do it at the stock exchange."

From his book Snakes in Suits.   http://www.amazon.ca/Snakes-Suits-When-Psychopaths-Work/dp/0061147893

Dr. Robert Hare is one of the world's foremost experts on the condition of psychopathy.

===========

Mobbing: One of the Worst Kinds of Workplace Bullying

Workplace bullying is a major issue in workplaces and can take many different forms. One of the ones that is the hardest to deal with is what is known as 'mobbing'.

Mobbing is when a worker enlists co-workers to 'collude in a relentless campaign of psychological terror against a hapless target.'

According to experts, the target of the bullying is typically someone who is different from the rest of the group and is often the most conscientious employee. The best employees are seen as a threat by the psychopath, and this can cause them to be singled out for 'elimination'. They also point out that 30 per cent of all workplace bullying is mobbing, and the trend is growing.

Some say that workplaces that are organized by bureaucracy or hierarchy are the most susceptible to this type of bullying.
From http://www.teamsters362.com/mobbing-one-of-the-worst-kinds-of-workplace-bullying/

==========

I believe that our world will be a safer place for all, when we understand that to some humans, power and money are addictive, and can be as compelling as drugs are to the street addict.

Destroying societies, lives or ecosystems is of zero concern to those who are hopelessly addicted to obtaining their own personal 'fix'.

"Power makes people feel both psychologically invincible and psychologically invisible," adds Adam Galinsky, a professor of organizational behavior at Northwestern University's business school.

"Having power changes you physiologically, reducing your body's internal feedback that tells you which actions are good or bad," says Prof. Carney. "Power temporarily intoxicates you."

"Leading you to feel that all your ideas are brilliant and that any evidence to the contrary is unconvincing."

http://jasonzweig.com/what-conflict-of-interest-how-power-blinds-us-to-our-flaws/

During my journey I have had the opportunity to work with, and observe many persons whom might meet the definition of psychopath, or sociopath, depending upon which description you prefer.

(Sociopaths are often called psychopaths and vice versa but there are differences between a psychopath and a sociopath. Psychopaths, for example, are far more likely to get in trouble with the law while sociopaths are much more likely to blend in with society. And while sociopaths and psychopaths do share some traits, sociopathy (antisocial personality disorder) is generally considered less severe than psychopathy. From https://www.healthyplace.com/personality-disorders/psychopath/psychopath-vs-sociopath-what-s-the-difference/)

My experts tell me that the proper term used today is "anti-social personality disorder", but I will stick with the old terms for now due to the greater audience recognition.

I am of a belief that these, and many other disorders of the mind, are found in various strength within all humans, and not merely an attribute reserved for the ill.

I believe all of us exist on a continuum, a line which measures the range from the very healthy at one end of the scale, to the very sick at the opposite.

When I was growing up, mental health was thought of as something where a person was labelled either healthy, or insane, and we did not have a very good understanding of its variations. My own (incorrect) understanding of mental health was that each person's mental health was either "on or off", making them mentally ill or mentally healthy.

Now I realize that no one on the planet has perfect physical or mental health. None even have perfect dental health…

We are all on a continuum of health, on the line somewhere, even if it is not a visible scale in many cases.

I first observed the subclinical psychopath (or sociopath) when I found myself immersed in the largest bank-owned brokerage firm in the country, and I learned that the office manager was hand selected from within the office sales staff. They were called 'brokers' at that time and they lived and thrived only on what they earned in commissions each and every day.

These guys were the very best at the "eat what you kill" game. The alpha males.

The most important measurement of investment office activity revolved around just three things: commissions, commissions and commissions. It was the topic of every morning sales meeting, each meeting (of consequence) with management, every incentive or corporate reward, and was printed off each morning and revered like a spiritual power.

It was used to measure the value, or 'worth' of each broker in the office, and for every perk/reward that could be withheld or forthcoming. Needless to say that the alpha male was the most cunning, most powerful who coveted this status within the office. Now experts recognize it as perhaps the most insecure.

The office ranking of commission sales people was a very competitive, dog-eat-dog environment, and the firm's investment customers were the dog food.

My office manager was described by others as either psychopath or sociopath, depending upon their own understanding of the words, and it was the first time I recall hearing either word used to describe someone with whom I rubbed shoulders with each work day. I began to learn more about this sliding scale of desperation or depravity. I began my journey of discovery of how the most fearful or insecure persons among us often gravitate to the 'rat race' and become the biggest rats. Perhaps in an effort to compensate for the internal feeling of lack, or 'not enough'.

I can identify with the feeling of not being 'enough'.

Corporate power and personal wealth is usually an acceptable pursuit, and at times admired by society. However I have come to see it as another addiction when taken to extremes. I believe that myself and other people who have not yet reached a state of maturity or enlightenment, find ourselves affected and directed by some of these fears and feelings.

===========

Hyper-success as a mental disorder?

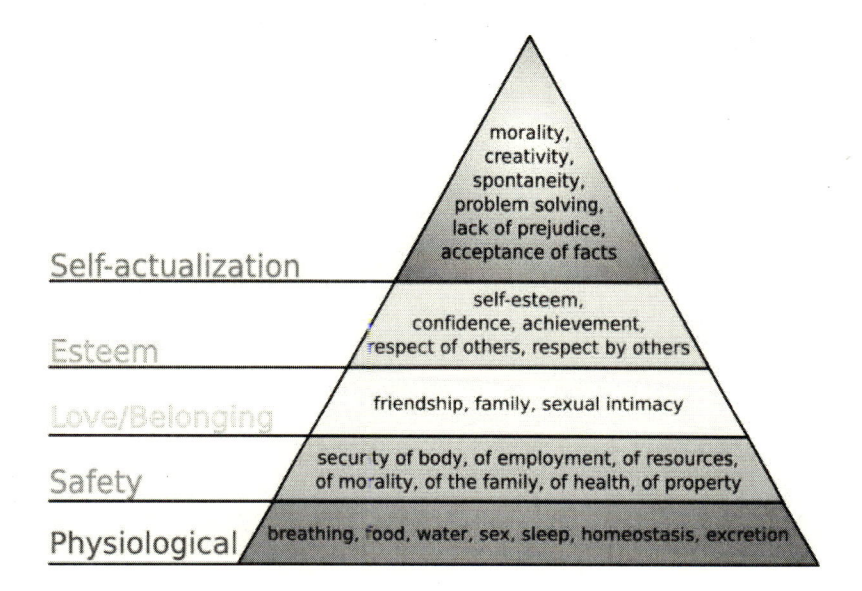

```
                          /\
                         /  \
                        /morality,\
                       /creativity,\
                      /spontaneity,\
                     /problem solving,\
                    /  lack of prejudice,\
Self-actualization /    acceptance of facts \
------------------/------------------------\
                 /      self-esteem,        \
                / confidence, achievement,   \
Esteem        /  respect of others, respect by others\
-------------/--------------------------------\
Love/Belonging/  friendship, family, sexual intimacy  \
-------------/----------------------------------------\
            /   security of body, of employment, of resources,\
Safety     /    of morality, of the family, of health, of property\
----------/------------------------------------------------\
Physiological  breathing, food, water, sex, sleep, homeostasis, excretion
```

Can we revisit Maslow's hierarchy of needs for a moment, and then take a look at his 20-years-later-discovery, and changes he made to his hierarchy of needs pyramid?

Maslow's theory was fully expressed in his 1954 book *Motivation and Personality* and he developed a simple theory and way of illustrating concepts of human behavior. It described five levels of human needs stacked on top of each other, to illustrate our 'ascendance' from mere survival, to becoming the very best we are capable of being (self actualization) at the top of the scale. (Wikipedia)

Above is what his original pyramid of needs looked like, circa 1954

What if a tiny fraction, say less than 1% of 1% of the world, are sufficiently mentally 'tweaked', let's say, for them to cause a majority of the rest of life on the planet to be stressed, either physically, mentally or financially. Financially stressed to the point of never being able to rise to level two of this hierarchy? Never able to feel safety.

Imagine if 1% of our population, had an internal mental imbalance, or an addictive need for 'more', strong enough that they were willing to do anything, legal or otherwise, to fill this need? To make all of society suffer, if necessary, so they themselves could feel "enough".

Even when some accumulate billions, it still cannot satisfy the person who is mentally stuck on "not enough"... emotionally unable to move beyond level two (safety).

One of the gifts of my journey is that I now know that financial security is a mental or emotional state, and not a numerical state. Unless you have what it takes mentally, no amount of numerals will ever provide it.

It does not seem fair...to financially harness and torture an entire planet, just to satisfy the emotional or mental needs of a few unwell people.

With the discovery that a healthy brain is wired for fairness, when I witnessed human suffering caused by greed, as I did in the sales offices of RBC each day, I had to leave or become more ill myself.

===========

People often wonder why wealthy, powerful people want more wealth and power. They don't. What they want is dopamine. That need never goes away. -- *Dave Collum, Investment Expert and Cornell University Professor of Chemistry and Chemical Biology*

===========

Myself, and many others, have observed that fear of survival in our younger years, and found ourselves in a corporate dominated world, where 'production or attainment of money' was the only measure of self actualization, or personal worth. I wanted to be just like the office manager, who appeared to 'have it all'.

What I did not know then, was that the greatest degree of fear and insecurity would drive a person to become the big sales achiever, or "producer" as they were called within the firm. I got wrapped up in the world of mostly men, who measured their "self worth" by the only visible scale at that point in their lives, which was their "net worth".

Looking back, we were nothing but a bunch of morally and emotionally confused children, chasing after the financial goals put in place by a giant corporation, like three year olds at an Easter egg hunt. Some of us excelled at that chase. Some became managers, some got corner offices, and some purchased fine homes and automobiles to announce to the world that we were 'somebody'. A few even got the fake "Vice President" sales-title at investment firms.

I now realize how ridiculous and childish this pursuit was, for the benefit of a hungry corporation.

I see my industry now as a collection of the most scared and driven people, starved for recognition, stepping over each other (and their clients) to try and "be somebody". I now see the wealthiest sometimes (not always and not a fair overall generalization) at times like those who are hoarders…mentally stuck on Maslov's level 2 with never enough.

Hoarding might be a symptom of a mental disorder that is partially triggered by fear. Whether money, empty jars, bags or any of the things that a hoarder will accumulate, while other people are pursuing normal lives, hoarders do not feel they have enough, of that particular item, or enough of any item for that matter. For a while for me it was cars and winter tires. You can never go wrong with a good set of winter tires…

This can then start to form a type of addiction, whereby more is not enough, no matter what it is. Which brings me back to Maslow and my interest in his pyramid. It turns out that he and I made a similar discovery, he long prior, and unknown to me. I stumbled upon it much later in my career and it was then I learned that Maslow also stumbled onto something which caused him to alter his famous Hierarchy of Needs.

===========

In his later years, Maslow explored a further level on his hierarchy of needs, while criticizing his own vision on self-actualization.

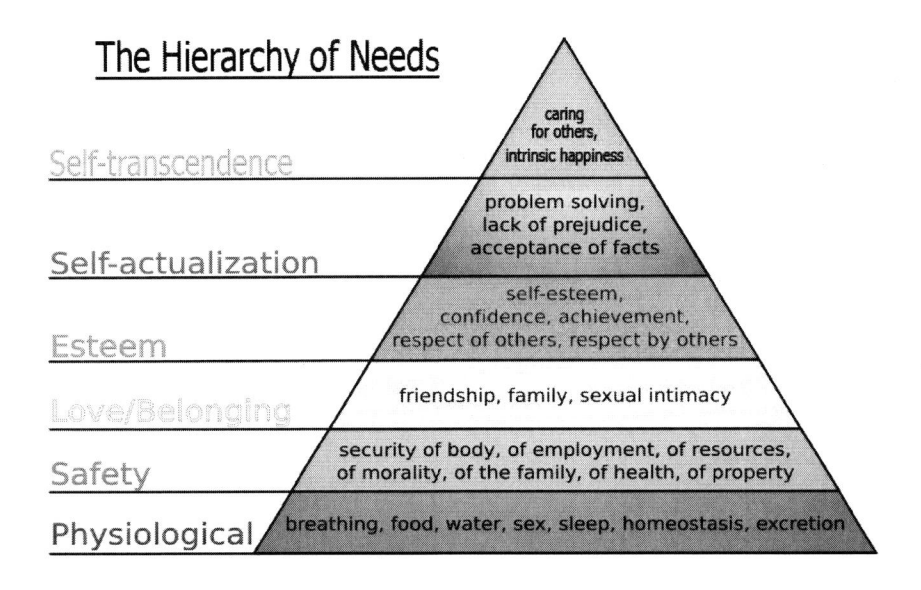

The Hierarchy of Needs

- **Self-transcendence**: caring for others, intrinsic happiness
- **Self-actualization**: problem solving, lack of prejudice, acceptance of facts
- **Esteem**: self-esteem, confidence, achievement, respect of others, respect by others
- **Love/Belonging**: friendship, family, sexual intimacy
- **Safety**: security of body, of employment, of resources, of morality, of the family, of health, of property
- **Physiological**: breathing, food, water, sex, sleep, homeostasis, excretion

He reasoned that moving to higher levels of awareness, consciousness, spirituality or humanity required us to strive to "get over ourselves", or has he called it "self transcendence".

I think it is brilliant, and fits perfectly with everything we have learned about our most highly evolved and conscious people.

Those who care as much or more for their surroundings, their fellow humans, the environment etc., as they care for their own comfort or welfare.

Those are who we should emulate in this world. Not those who have billions and yet remain mentally stuck at or below Level Two.

Taken to extremes, it begins to resemble a sort of anti-social personality disorder or something of psychopath or sociopath-like behavior. It feels like it, as I see the fabric of society being tattered by persons and corporations who appear lost in their abstract addictions to "more". More of what? It doesn't seem to matter. Just as long as it is much more than the rest. More relative to the next guy. Money as a mental disorder? Or the awakening to the life freeing discovery that having "enough" money is a state of mind… and not a state of numbers.

If we allow the most powerful positions in the world to be occupied by such persons, perhaps sick persons, then I now understand why an entire planet, humans, animals and the environment must suffer, just so those undiagnosed persons can feel better about themselves. Is that too negative or pessimistic?

<u>If I could change just one thing in the world</u> today, I would set our human-awareness clocks ahead 100 years by asking society to "spot or learn about pathalogically-selfish personalities". I feel that this should be as common in a safe society as is spotting the drunk driver of today. I hope it will even be a subject taught in early school grades.

I also hope that our most shining examples of self transcendence will also be studied/taught, or re-discovered. They were in the last century and now we seem to have lost our hero's.

Just imagine how different our society would be, if psychopaths were noticed, understood, and helped to become valuable members of society, instead of electing them to powerful offices, or otherwise letting them destroy society simply to feed an inner illness.

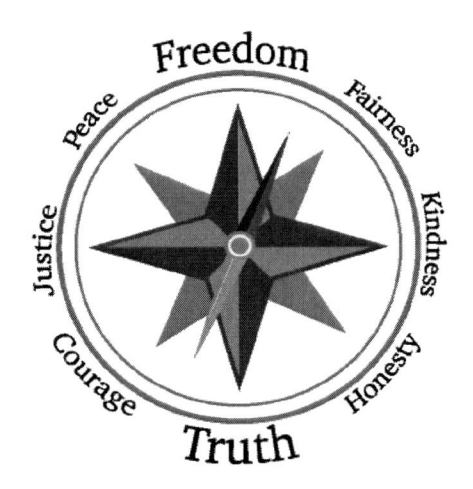

CHAPTER TWENTY TWO

MEDIA AS HANDMAIDENS

Q: What is the difference between the looting of Zibwabwe and the looting of North America?
A: North American media covers the looting of Zimbabwe...

===========

shill:
An accomplice of a hawker, gambler, or swindler who acts as an enthusiastic customer to entice or encourage others.
From Wikipedia

A **shill,** also called a **plant** or a **stooge,** is a person who publicly helps or gives credibility to a person or organization without disclosing that they have a close relationship with the person or organization. Shills can carry out their operations in the areas of media, journalism, marketing, confidence games, or other business areas.

A shill may also act to discredit opponents or critics of the person or organization in which they have a vested interest through character assassination or other means.

In most uses, *shill* refers to someone who purposely gives onlookers, participants or "marks" the impression of an enthusiastic customer independent of the seller, marketer or con artist, for whom they are secretly working. The person or group in league with the shill relies on crowd psychology to encourage other onlookers or audience members to do business with the seller or accept the ideas they are promoting.

Shills may be employed by salespeople and professional marketing campaigns. *Plant* and *stooge* more commonly refer to a person who is secretly in league with another person or outside organization while pretending to be neutral or a part of the organization in which they are planted, such as a magician's audience, a political party, or an intelligence organization (see double agent).

Shilling is illegal in many circumstances and in many jurisdictions because of the potential for fraud and damage; however, if a shill does not place uninformed parties at a risk of loss, but merely generates "buzz," the shill's actions may be legal. For example, a person planted in an audience to laugh and applaud when desired (see claque), or to participate in on-stage activities as a "random member of the audience," is a type of legal shill. *Shill* can also be used pejoratively to describe a critic who appears either all-too-eager to heap glowing praise upon mediocre offerings, or who acts as an apologist for glaring flaws.
(see also: Industry-paid securities regulators)

===========

I accepted a challenge from a reporter, after I told him that 96% of people who claim 'advisor" status in Canada do not hold the license, nor the legal duty of a registered adviser.

I set out to see if I could find a single licensed advisor/adviser in downtown Calgary, and to share the results. After two hours on the government authorized registrant check site (CSA) I found that 100% of the advisors/advisers in three downtown Calgary bank-owned investment offices held no adviser license or registration. Instead the category of license/registration was in a salesperson capacity, (Dealing representative registration).

After I delivered this interesting info to the reporter, and he ran it past his editor, and found it was not very welcome news after all... for their largest advertisers.

===========

It is best to learn early that the 'clients' who pay the Piper, so to speak, are advertisers who pay to promote things in the media. The reader is the "product" that is being delivered to the advertiser, but it can take decades to realize this.

It is an upside down way of viewing the media, especially the 'news' business. If you do not believe, simply spend some time checking it out. Seriously, it will be one of the better investments you will ever make. (Google, "news reporting as advertising" to read some views)

As Hearst, (or Orwell, or Lord Northcliffe) is reputed to have come up with "News is what somebody somewhere wants to suppress; all the rest is advertising". True words regardless of whom to credit.

I ran across this candid description from Jon Rappaport, of the changes inside the media game over his career.

I thought it did a better job than I could of telling how media have become captured and caught in the same financial double-bind as everyone else who needs their job to survive. The managerial-psychological trap that says "be a team player, or else..."

Jon was kind enough to give me permission to reprint his story, and for that I thank him.

===========

A Media Experience story, By Jon Rappoport
January 23, 2017

During my 34 years of working as a reporter, I've had many informal conversations with mainstream journalists. They were illuminating. Here, from my notes (1982-2011), taken after the conversations, are what these guardians on the watchtower revealed:

ONE: "Investigative reporting has been dying. There's no money for it. If I work on a piece for three months, while my paper is paying me, suppose at the end I come up dry? It happens. I can't make my case. I've got nothing to show for it, and my paper is out whatever they've been paying me. They don't like that.

The other thing is, investigative work makes my bosses nervous. They don't know where it'll lead. Worst case, I might come up with something that'll put the paper in a bad light. It's like an intelligence agent in the field who wanders off the reservation. He's got an assignment, but he sees something better, more important, and that's where he goes. He ends up finding out something about his own agency. Something bad.

I've seen that happen. A reporter finds out his own paper has been covering up a heavy scandal. It's an intrinsic part of the story. What's he going to do now? Go to his editor and tell him what's going on? Chances are, his editor already knows. Now the reporter's jammed up. He's in a bad spot. A guy I know came to me with that exact problem. You know what I told him? Burn your notes. That's what I said."

TWO: "Most reporters who cover major issues are de facto intelligence assets. Some know it, most don't. They're all taking their information from controlled sources. It's like somebody giving you talking points as if they're the honest truth. In these talking points, you're told who the players are in a story and what they're doing. But they aren't the important players, and what they're doing is just a cover for what's really going on. It's all about misdirection.

I've managed to get a few stories published about illusion vs. reality. But the thing is, no one follows up on that. It's in print, and then it dies. One night, I had a little heart to heart with my editor. I told him it would be a lot easier if I just had a desk at the CIA in Langley. He agreed. He said we could move the whole paper there. But then the spooks would realize they didn't need us at all. They could put out the paper themselves."

THREE: "We're in a business. We're selling a product. That's our role. If our bosses don't like what we're submitting to them, they let us know we're giving them the wrong product. Our company makes product A and we're giving them product B. Most reporters wouldn't even understand what I'm saying, because they're mentally in the camp of product A. That's where they live. So as far as they're concerned, they have lots of leeway. I don't like talking to those guys. They're dumb."

FOUR: "I can write an article that's critical of what a drug company is specifically doing, but I can't criticize the company. If I did, my editor would read me the riot act. He knows if he published that article, his boss would get a visit from the company. They would threaten to pull their advertising. Everybody would be in serious trouble. There is a fine line. Sometimes, the evidence against a drug company is huge, and we can get away with a critical article. But most of the time, it's a no-go area. I could lose my job. If I did, I would have a hell of a time trying to find another position on the same level. I might be subject to an industry-wide demotion."

FIVE: "I thought I could quit working for my paper and get hired by somebody else, who would give me more freedom to write the stories I wanted to. I made a few quiet inquiries. Turned out I was wrong. They're all pretty much the same. I could get hired by some small paper and write whatever I wanted to, but I would make very little money. I'd be screwed. They don't cover this in journalism school."

SIX: "Sometimes an order comes down. By the time I get it, it isn't sounding exactly like an order. It's more like 'this is what we're doing'. We need to go after a politician and bury him. That kind of thing. Nobody is complicit. You can't find somebody and blame him for issuing the order. It's vague enough that everyone escapes blame. And you don't want to talk to your colleagues too much about it. You don't want to be seen as making waves. It's sort of like a game plan in football. You're going to execute the plan. You're not going to start talking about what a lousy plan it is."

SEVEN: "I'm a guy who's expected to put out baloney for our audience. I can slice it a few different ways, but it's the same basic thing. After a few years, I can do it in my sleep. I know the routine."

EIGHT: "You talk about who's really running things behind the scene. I know something about that. But I can't write it in a story. That would be called original research. I'm not allowed to do that. I can only quote authorities on two sides of an issue. And the guy I quote first---he carries the point of view of the story. The other guy is the doubter. I place him in the weaker position. I get to choose, but I already know what's needed and required."

NINE: "Reporters in my business have two choices. They can lower their IQs and become cynics, or they can maintain their intelligence and get booted out. That's what it comes down to. Anybody with an IQ over 90 can see we have agendas. The whole business is agenda-driven. The main job of a reporter who wants to keep working is developing a cover---pretending he's speaking the truth. This is a cover for his real identity. A guy who pleases his bosses.

Several of us had the whole Bill Clinton-Monica Lewinsky story before it was published. We wanted to go with it, but we were told to sit on it. So it was our job to agree with that assessment. We had to pretend we didn't have enough proof yet. We had the proof, but we had to make it seem like we were responsible journalists and needed more. That was a bunch of crap. The agenda was to protect ourselves from the wrath of the White House. That's what the editors and the publishers were talking about among themselves. Sure--- protect the president. But the real thing was the fear that he and his people would strike back at us and do us damage."

TEN: "My decision to get out of the news business was pretty easy. I wanted to write a story about the influence of the Council on Foreign Relations on government policy, since World War Two. The way I was told to forget about it was like a cop talking to a drug dealer. All of a sudden, I was the bad guy. I really got into it with my editor. I saw what a phony he was. The thing is, I knew he had a cozy thing going with the CIA. Several people knew it. In my years in the business, I got a first-hand education in what selling out means. I came pretty close to the edge. There's a weird adrenaline kick to it.

You see your whole future laid out in front of you. It's very rewarding, in terms of money and status. If you just play ball, it'll be a smooth ride."

ELEVEN: "What the teachers told me in journalism school was a load. All I needed was one honest talk with a professor, and I never would have bothered with the whole thing. I was naïve. During my career, there were days I thought we were really on the right track. Somebody wrote a great piece, and it was published. But then we fell back. We put out provable lies. And they were big ones. It was like being psychologically whipsawed. A few great days, and a lot of bad ones. The worst thing for me was government sources. I was like a horse with a feed bag on, and they were filling it up with rotten food. They knew it, I knew it, and we just kept doing it."

TWELVE: "I saw what I called 'the inch-below' thing. An inch below what we were reporting was the real story. It was about power players and what they were doing to make profit for major corporations. It kept coming up. Crimes. People should have been arrested. I could have written great stories. But nobody wanted them. I would have proved intent. I'm talking about wars. Not little stuff. Whole wars, and the money. The profits. In court, a lawyer could have taken what I had and made a great circumstantial case. The jury would have been convinced. When you can't publish these stories, you sink into boredom after a while. Tremendous boredom. That's why some reporters become drunks."

Jon Rappoport has worked as a free-lance investigative reporter for over 30 years. He has written articles on politics, health, media, culture and art for LA Weekly, Spin Magazine, Stern, Village Voice, Nexus, CBS Healthwatch, and other newspapers and magazines in the US and Europe. In 1982, the LA Weekly submitted his name for a Pulitzer prize, for his interview with the president of El Salvador University, where the military had taken over the campus.

Thanks Jon!

===========

"A society grows great when old men plant trees whose shade they know they shall never sit in." -Greek Proverb

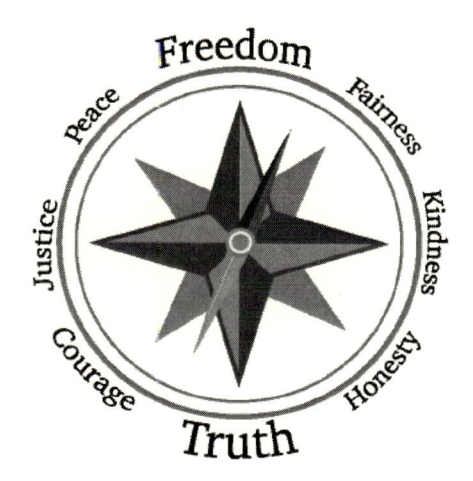

CHAPTER TWENTY THREE

SOLUTIONS and FINANCIAL SELF-DEFENSE

The reasonable man encounters circumstances and adapts himself to them. The unreasonable man persists in trying to adapt circumstances to himself. Therefore all progress depends upon the unreasonable man.
--George Bernard Shaw

==========

My friend Derek was driving a truck for a living, and came to me with questions, about his investment accounts. I did my best to pass along what I knew without blowing his mind to the risks and predatory industry practices.

But Derek was sharp. No slouch in the thinking and understanding department, and he kept wanting to know more. He really wanted to learn and gain control over his financial future.

He felt bad picking my brain as a friend, and did not want me to feel used, so he asked me if I would coach him, teach him, take him under my wing, and help him to gain confidence in how to handle money properly.

To make sure he was not taking advantage of my time, he kindly suggested that he should pay a fee when we sat down and talked about his situation. He wanted to learn, but he was not one of those who wanted me to whisper 'the solution' in his ear and make all financial problems go away. That is a good sign. He asked me what I might charge to have investment conversations with him, and I flippantly replied, how about $20 per hour?

It is a pleasure to run into people who truly wish to take some time to gain understanding, so it was not work for me, but rather nice to have him as a sounding board to my own thinking.

Fast forward about five months later, and Derek is now teaching me. We sit down and discuss things as friends, and I learn as much from him now, as he does from me. The teacher has become the student, and the student has gone from being 'baffled by the industry spin game" to being a street smart and confident investor.

A few hours of honest conversation is all it took. It is that easy, or at least it was for Derek. It took me about 20 hours to fly solo in my first helicopter. Some younger, quicker guys were flying solo in about 13 hours training. It is different for everyone. As Jon Rappaport said so well in the previous chapter, "All I needed was one honest talk…"
Find that talk.

The moral of the story is that I hope you will sit down with someone who has:
- a) nothing to sell you by way of investment products,
- b) no hidden conflicts of interest or relationship that work against your interest, and
- c) can talk to you like a favorite Uncle would talk to you (not like a sales agent working for a bank, mutual fund or life insurance company)

A visit to those salespeople is fine, but keep in mind that they are salespeople, and that they are trapped in a double bind, where their dealer dictates what advice they give you, and likely not your best interests.

Most people in investment sales are captured and motivated by what they "produce" in commissions for the firm…"gather" in assets for the firm… or place into fee based, or house brand products which earn the firm fees.

It is an invaluable thing to be able to visit someone, just like visiting an accountant, a lawyer, and get some sensible 'advice' time. No biased advice.

A FEE ONLY planner, (with no products to sell, or persons to refer you to) might be the best investment you ever make. It will cost you no more than a visit to a therapist, and it can make all the difference to your future.

Five or ten hours spread out over a year, will help a person go from lack of truth, lack of confidence, to aware and confident, if that is their goal. That is what I like to see in investors.

Then, perhaps a follow-up conversation, once or twice per year to stay on track and handle questions that arise, and POOF! The fear is gone. The mystery is taken out of money, and it is no longer like sitting down with a sales gal who is compensated by how complicated they can make things, so the investor has no alternative but to throw their arms in the air and surrender to the salesperson.

Simple, simple, simple, is how investing must be, or it is not investing.

As Einstein is said to have quoted, "anyone who cannot explain something to a six year old, with a crayon, does not know what they are talking about." That is what builds strong and confident investors.

Derek inspired me to begin a monthly public discussion event in my town, called MoneyTalks.

It is a casual meeting, where anywhere from six to 20 people gather and we discuss topics related to money, investing, the economy, interest rates etc. It is free and it is priceless.

It is a blast to go over financial topics, and bring each one down to a level of understanding that everyone gets. It is a non-threatening environment where no sales agents are allowed, no products can be pitched. We can dissect anything we wish to learn more about) but no conflicts of interest are allowed in.

This is a meeting that I think will always have a following, just like my old car club still meets to talk about horsepower 40 years later. It is how expertise is shared and world class experts are made in any area. Stick with those who have nothing to gain by lying to you and selling you crap, and who simply want to engage in conversation about those things that most interest them. Start one of these in your area and you will be amazed at what great connections you will make, and confidence you will gain.

I enjoy protecting people from the world's top financial predators. It is exactly how my mind was trained to think. It came from years of having to seek and find the financial problem or opportunity. Thus it is the most natural discussion in the world for me.

===========

Investing is no more complicated than cooking if you can only stay away from the people who are paid to make it complex. I have

always stuck to the belief that only three things are necessary to create overall investment success, in the long run.
1. Quality Investments
2. Diversity among investments
3. Time to let them work.

A wise man named Dennis, at a MoneyTalks session questioned me on the third element. He suggested that some retired folks do not have the luxury of time, and I had to agree with him. Some investors need a return on investment and they need it <u>now</u>. They still need the first two however, and the third is a nice thing to have if you wish to watch your investments grow over the years.

The other element which deserves comment, however, is that term, "Quality Investments".

Over the long term, (30 years plus) the quality of both investments, as well as investment advice has changed considerably.

I will use a comparison with grocery shopping to try and make my point. Many of us understand the change in food store items over the past 50 years, and there has been much learned, about nutrition and processed food. Processed products are now found everywhere on grocery shelves with long lists of ingredients, many of which sound like chemical names. We know there is a great deal of 'junk' in these products.

We are cautioned by nutritionists to consume less of these products, and more of the healthier foods that are found on the perimeter grocery stores. Everyone understands what is meant when talking about 'real' foods like milk, eggs meat, vegetables, fruits and so on.

I hope that makes sense to you, because similar could be said about investment products. Just thirty years ago, most investors held stocks or bonds in companies whose names and operations we could all recognize and understand.

Today, there are many investment products that "look like they were cooked up in a meth lab", to quote Diane Urquhart, former head of research for a major investment dealer. Diane is now retired, and she and her husband Hugh, spend their time volunteering, educating and protecting the vulnerable, through investment consulting to various groups. They work tirelessly on things like helping to protect disabled former employees of defunct tech firm Nortel, whose pension was being cheated away from the very people who needed it the most.

Nortel was another 400 billion dollar Canadian sacrifice to the gods of systemic financial crime. I won't even try to go there at this stage of the book but is one of our largest inside-job robberies. It was also Canada's largest company by market capitalization.

Diane and Hugh have done constant investor protection work for the two decades that I have known them, with such dedicated intensity, as to exceed anything accomplished by 13 Securities Commissions in Canada. They are an example of those whose work has become a labour of love, and they do great things in silence for the country. Just like other hero's I have met on this journey.

Diane made an important point about 'synthetic investment creations'. One which any investor today needs to be aware of. That and the dealer push (I should say **PUSH!!!**) to get their sales force to put every investor into fee-based accounts.

Back to ingredients. Recall just one generation ago, and if you cannot recall investments then, ask an older person what an 'investment' looked like. They will mention a bank, insurance company, electrical, gas, or telephone company that one could invest in. Examples still exist from the thousands of companies on any stock exchange.

However, when I do forensic analysis on modern day investment accounts, the thing that I can spot in 90% of accounts is:

The investments in the account are various 'structured', packaged, or heavily processed 'things', some of which may have a connection to investments, but all of which have a connection to fees. Fees for the dealer or manufacturer who packaged the 'investment'. Investors today are being sold products which can have up to five (or more) fees built into them, sold by people who have no license and no business being in the 'advice' game. Eighty percent of the industry has become a broker/dealer game of harvesting investors, rather than the promised service of helping investors.

If a FINRA, (USA self regulator) or IIROC, (Canadian self regulator) registered broker, (aka "advisor") is dishonestly hiding their true license and agency duty from client view, how honest are they being with you at the outset of the relationship?

Firms are pushing clients into 'products' with fees and commissions and packaging fluff, instead of into the more nutritious, 'investment' based aisles of the investment supermarkets, and they are being literally 'herded' into these products by hundreds of thousands of false 'advisors'.

That is what I see in far too many of the accounts that I get to look at. Fees, fees, fees, advisor fees, product fees, management fees, derivatives, things that might look like an investment…who knows? Often these fees are buried in a 200 page prospectus which no retail investor can follow. Why should they, when they are assured that they have the financial equivalent of a "doctor' on their side to do this and 'advise' them?

There is a move afoot, to get retail investors to believe in the false-promise of a commission broker who hides their license and duty, and then uses this falsely earned 'trust' to take advantage of them with complicated, convoluted and diluted investment products. So far it is working perfectly.

Second is the move to push investors away from the most sound and value-related investments, and into house-brand and fee riddled products. Recall the OSC study that said up to 26 times more money can be made from those types of investments. For the dealer…not the client.

From my industry experience, I know that rules and regulations are mere 'paper and puppet' obstacles, which the industry manipulates <u>after</u> they have made their billions. Paying regulators' salaries means they can force the regulators to 're-write the rules' to suit...or else.

Governments, media and regulators are the 'paper and puppets' that need to be taken care of, and thus consumers have virtually no one protecting them.

Around the time of the 2008 crash consulting Analyst Diane Urquhart said to me, "do your investing only in areas that you perfectly well understand, your business, inventory, land, whatever, but watch out for the myriad of synthetic investments being created today". Too many are as real as...virtual reality.

Or, as Warren Buffet said about derivatives and other synthetic creations of the financial industry, they are "weapons of mass destruction".

One more observation; Due to market size and dominance of big dealers, it is becoming increasingly difficult to find investors who own these old-style investment accounts. Brokers today are under so much pressure to generate thousands of dollars of fees and commissions....every day....that the customers are being steered, like cattle into the 'fee based" chutes. It is like observing the entrance to the kill-floor in a meat processing plant, with millions of retail investors playing the role of the livestock.

===========

As quality investments disappear, the flakier ones take center stage. The Wall Street Journal's Jason Zweig gives good reason why.

Stock Picking Is Dying Because There Are No More Stocks to Pick
By Jason Zweig
Jun 23, 2017 9:17 am ET
In less than two decades, more than half of all publicly traded companies have disappeared. There were 7,355 U.S. stocks in November 1997, according to the Center for Research in Security Prices at the University of Chicago's Booth School of Business. Nowadays, there are fewer than 3,600.

Excerpt from:
https://blogs.wsj.com/moneybeat/2017/06/23/stockpicking-is-~,...
because-there-are-no-more-stocks-to-pick/

===========

Another financial defense suggestion: Inform any investment dealer, in writing, that you are relying upon them 100% for fair, honest and professional investment advice. For advice that is entirely in your interest and in the interests of none other…..in other-words, you are assuming that your financial relationship with the "advice giver" is one of a fiduciary level of care, as it is understood in law. Keep a copy of this letter. If you get a rejection of your account, keep a copy of their rejection and be grateful that you dodged a financial bullet.

Ask them to confirm receipt of this in writing to you and you will either have it in writing (major firms only, no fly-by-night, and on firm letterhead only), or the 'market dominant' position that they have in North America will cause them to simply fire you.

===========

Recall the Bev K (victim) quote from chapter 18:
"Everyone connected with the investment industry is looking for excuses NOT to protect seniors financial interests in the investment industry".

===========

Today's society has become so fake that the truth actually bothers people at times. Please forgive me if my writing bothers you. I am hoping to protect vulnerable people who deserve to not be abused.

In just one generation I have gone from entering the financial world as a young man, believing that the industry was honest, and any exception was criminal. To today, where financial abuse of customers is the rule, and honesty is the exception. Coming to realize this in the 1990's turned my world view upside down.

Down was not down but it was up. Sometimes, but not always. Wrong was not wrong, but right. Often, but again, not everytime. Bad was good and good was bad. Don't take my word for any of this. Ask someone experienced in it. Anyone over 50.

===========

"How tough is it to become a licensed advisor in Canada today?

"Two correspondence courses and a job offer. The courses are not even that hard," notes Jim Kershaw, senior vice president and regional manager, Ontario Main, with TD Wealth Private Investment Advice in Toronto.

My haircut last month took place in Las Vegas. The young lady there said her course requirements to be licensed to cut my hair was 1800 hours of training, if I recall. She mentioned that in Utah they needed 2200 hours. I hope I remembered the numbers correctly. The point is, that you can be pretending to be a financial advisor and selling mutual funds in 30 days, 90 days if you get licensed to sell (not advise on) the full investment product spectrum. A true fiduciary Adviser takes years and years, plus requires millions of dollars of money management experience. A license to sell investments is 1/20th as difficult as it is to be a licensed hairdresser.

===========

Fraud, misrepresentation, mis-information. All form some of the requirements for civil—and in many cases criminal—cases. However the financial industry, as we have seen, have layers upon layers, of self-regulation, and other protections, which keep their activities off the radar of police or prosecutors.

Layers of lawyers, also act as the perfect 'buffer' between industry criminality, and criminal code prosecution. 'Never the twain shall meet' in a system of truly well organized financial crime. (For millennials…Two things which are so different as to have no opportunity to unite)

If you have been victimized, it will likely be solely by your <u>own efforts</u> that you get any money back. In thirty years I have yet to meet an agency with the incentive or the backbone to take on the world's strongest financial institutions, plus the regulators, plus the self-regulators, plus the lawyers lined up to defend the above. There is no one willing to rock that boat, it is a career ender.

This is especially true when these institutions pay hundreds of millions in salaries to the regulatory systems. Just the top four Canadian regulators share $1/4 billion in salaries, and of course, those salaries are 100% funded by the people they are supposed to police. There are another roughly 100 financial "bodies" in Canada, mostly protecting their turf.

Until financial victims stand up and succeed in getting their money back—and also succeed in getting free of industry gag-orders, it will always be a battle of <u>one-victim at a time, against the world's strongest entities</u> or entire 'webs' of connected entities. Yes, it is unfair and it is dishonest, and it is just the way they designed it to be. In that regard it is the perfect system. For abuse.

My advice is to avoid industry-established complaint agencies, as they have a reputation for being set-up <u>by</u> the industry, <u>for</u> the industry. Victims I know of have wasted years of their lives going around in circles, hoping for justice, while never understanding that they were caught in a whirlpool. It is an intentional rigged design to exhaust victims and prevent them from getting real accountability from the industry. The industry establishes kangaroo-courts more to insulate and deflect justice away from their members, than to protect consumers or the public interest.

If you can afford it, get legal help and go straight to independent courts of justice and common law. Including the court of public opinion. Some systems, like FINRA-broker dealers are rigged so well, that this is not even possible. If you can imagine it, millions of American investors are forced into signing industry arbitration agreements before they can even do business or invest in many US accounts. This is the equivalent of <u>signing up for your own rigged treatment in advance</u>, signing away your constitutional rights to fairness, as well as your access to justice, and is perhaps the best example of an industry which has perfected the abuse of investors, using their positions of market dominance.

If you cannot afford it, or your case is too small to litigate with legal help, I still suggest staying away from industry complaint resolution until they are truly fair and objective—which is years away. At a 'harvest' in Canada, of easily one billion dollars per week, ($10 billion per week in the US) the industry is in no particular hurry to make things fair and honest.

Take your situation to small claims court, even without a lawyer, if you have to. Remember, right and wrong is still recognized in smaller courts, whether small claims or otherwise. Over the years I have met many feisty, informed, and aware Canadians who are taking their investment dealers to court—yes, even small claims court—and winning (or getting settlement offers when it becomes apparent their complaints are valid). (Judges in small claims court also seem to act more like Judges...than those in upper altitudes)

Sadly, the settlement offers usually come with confidentiality agreements, and thus the proceedings are prevented from being shared with the general public. Just imagine if other kinds of abusers were the world's richest people, and could silence their crimes with money? That is what our strongest financial predators do every day.

Silence (industry gag orders) allows investors to be abused or taken advantage of financially, in a secret and hidden way. It is an abuse of market dominance when billion dollar corporations can violate millions of investors one at a time, and rarely, will the public ever be informed.

Of course, we have our Competition Laws, and The Competition Bureau of Canada, and nobody in my experience is working harder, to <u>ignore</u> abuse of financial market dominance.

=========

Also of interest is that the official Canadian Ombudsman for Banking Services and Investments (OBSI) was 'neutered' in 2013:

"*OBSI's Terms of Reference were amended in December 2013 to remove OBSI's systemic issue investigative powers.*"

Just to be clear what "*remove OBSI's systemic issue investigative powers*" means to Canadian investors…it means that if the official Canadian Banking and Financial Services Ombudsman comes across a problem with Mrs. Jones investments, and it appears as if that same problem is popping up in similar accounts all across Canada, OBSI CAN NOT do more than investigate each victim's case, one at a time. While banks and dealers can abuse 1 million people at a keystroke…

Even if it turns out that one million investors are being cheated, gouged or shortchanged by banks or investment dealers, they cannot touch anything that appears systemic. That, in my view is a crime of hundreds of billions against Canadians, and a gift of hundreds of billions…to the banks.

https://www.obsi.ca/en/download/fm/528

===========

In 2011 TD Waterhouse, RBC Capital Markets Ltd., Investors Group Securities Inc., Macquarrie Group and Manulife Financial Corp. filed an application with to be exempt from using OBSI to resolve disputes with disgruntled customers.

Investment dealers are required by mandate to participate in OBSI but in recent years, a number of the bank-owned brokerages have been aggressively agitating to "opt out" because they want to use other complaint resolution providers. Privately hired guns. More 'complaint' guns.

"OBSI has already been irreparably damaged by the public disagreement," investor protection groups wrote in a letter to industry regulators. "Because of all the negative publicity and hostility, OBSI will never the same again."

Eventually RBC and TD took a hike, unilaterally opting out of the use of OBSI to resolve disputes (as was required of them), and they hired their own dispute resolution parties instead. Hire your very own referees? Just standard practice in an industry that can also hire it own regulators.

The next blow to OBSI as Canada's last independent line of consumer protection was to neuter this body from having <u>any</u> investigative powers over systemic matters. That means they can pick on one bad apple at a time, here and there, but they are <u>no longer</u> allowed to look into <u>anything of a systemic nature</u> (system corruption) in the industry that they oversee. "Let the looting increase!"

Here is the link to the document where that is put in place
https://www.obsi.ca/download/fm/149

"To align with regulatory requirements on the banking side of OBSI's mandate, and regulatory expectations on the investment side, OBSI will no longer investigate systemic issues." OBSI December 19, 2013 https://www.obsi.ca/download/fm/147

Police can investigate million-dollar bank robberies, but Canada's Banking Ombudsman is no longer allowed to investigate when banks rob or shortchange millions of Canadians…

===========

It is a dramatic abuse of market dominance when there are virtually no industry tribunals that are objective, un-conflicted, or not privately paid and run…

To read one case which went all the way, and thus found itself on public record instead of being gagged, see the case of "Mr. Markarian (the elderly victim) verses CIBC World Markets". (Google it)

It is so rare to find a bank-judgement that is not gagged that the government of Canada was called upon to translate this Quebec case into English, to ensure it could be seen by all. Here is one that reads like a thriller, and shows what some banks act like:

http://investorvoice.ca/Cases/Investor/Markarian/Markarian_index.htm

The judge in this case uses the word "fraud" 155 times to describe the actions of CIBC against an elderly client that it victimized.

The web site www.investoradvocates.ca has 44 topics, all from myself or other investment industry experts, about how to defend against financial predators One topic is titled "Get Your Money Back". It is full of industry tricks and tactics on how to beat you out of fair, honest and good faith treatment, and it provides free public information about how to counter those tricks. It is free for anyone to learn from, and it works. Just be warned that it is a web site with production values so low that it qualifies as antique. The good news is that cookies, ads and annoying web trackers are way above my technology level, so there are no such distractions.

I do forensic analysis of investment accounts, and after 20 years in the business I can spot commission sales tactics like an old cattle-checker can spot the weak members of the herd. It becomes very obvious once you have seen a few thousand examples, and worked about 30,000 hours inside the 'pens.'

I have tried to share what I have learned in videos, search Larry Elford on YouTube for my efforts. It's free!

www.investoradvocates.ca has had well over 1 million visitors and I hear from many people who it has helped. It's free!

You could also visit such sites as www.SIPA.ca and www.Canadianfundwatch.ca for great insights into the predatory and customer-abusive nature of the industry. There are years and years of reports, informed opinion, and analysis found there. It's free!

Social media is another source of Get Your Money Back help. Some of the worst investment abuses in the country have been solved, and compensation gained, by those who have rallied around a social media site and made enough noise to overcome the strength of financial players.

If you have a systemic investment abuse matter, you may find help at the following group for "Investment System Fraud" at Facebook. It is interested in and covers abuses from all over North America.

Or at the Facebook site for the Small Investor Protection Association of Canada:

https://www.facebook.com/groups/240100382792373/

===========

BE ROSA PARKS…Please.

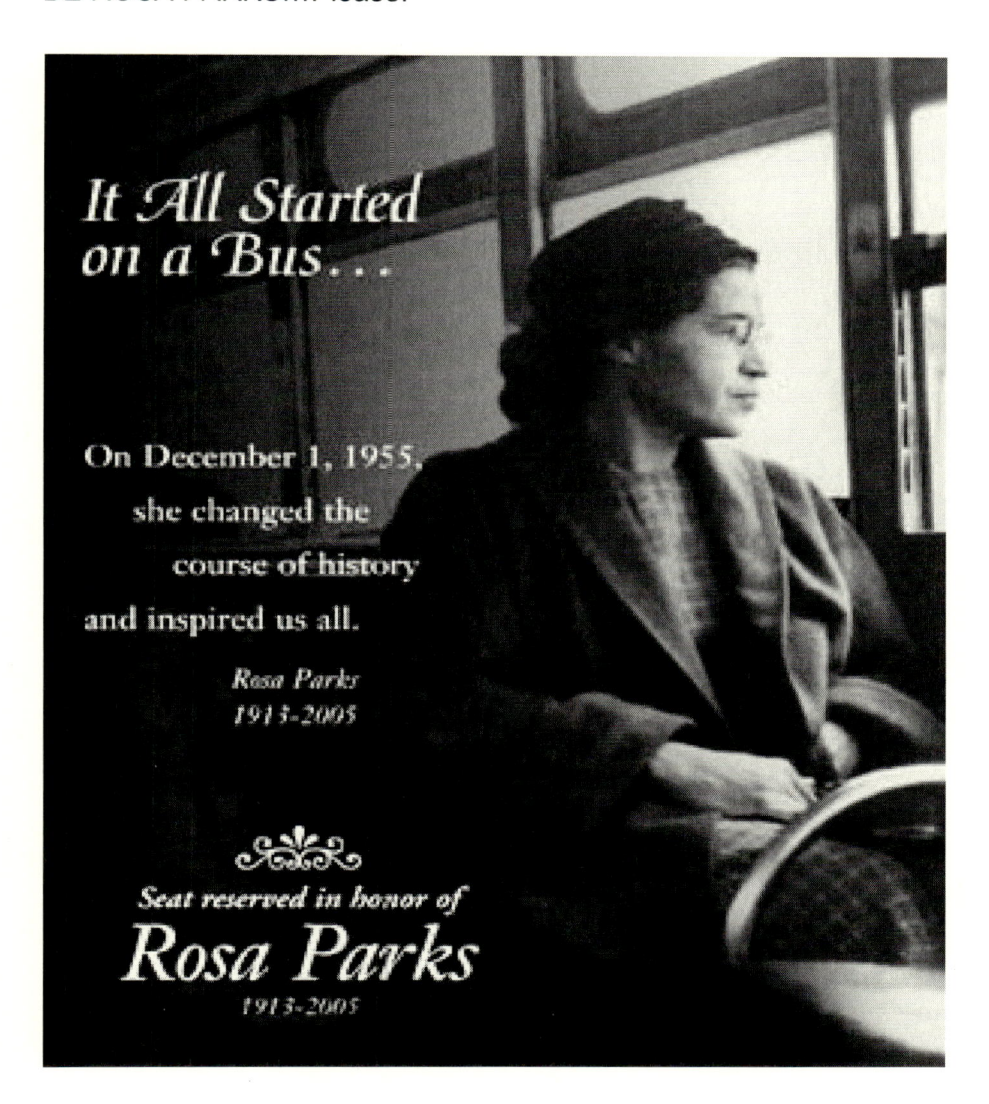

> *It All Started on a Bus…*
>
> On December 1, 1955, she changed the course of history and inspired us all.
>
> *Rosa Parks*
> *1913-2005*
>
> Seat reserved in honor of
> **Rosa Parks**
> *1913-2005*

Investor protection must no longer be left to the impulses of men and women paid for, and chosen by, the investment industry. The current regulatory regime is gaining a well earned reputation for being a 'facade' of regulation. A mere pretense of public interest protection.

"Foxes should not be trusted to guard the henhouse" is time honored wisdom, and we are ignoring completely it with nearly all top regulatory positions either picked or paid, by industry.

Systemic Problem:

> Self-regulation is often nothing more than gang rule, by gang members. It allows an honor system to be 'bestowed' upon certain industries, and it does not seem to work. Gang members cannot be trusted to be the policing agent of gang activity, no matter how expensive a suit of clothing they acquire.

Solutions:

1. There needs to be dedicated, investor protection bodies with a single mandate to protect the specific interests of consumers.

2. The criminal code, not self-regulated games (or gangs), must become an essential part of the process. Currently, the ability to "self" regulate, simply brings immunity from having criminal codes apply to one's activity, which is especially valuable…when they are acting criminally.

3. Special investigators and trained prosecutors must be given a mandate to go after the most harmful, systemic methods by which the investment industry can professionally 'extract' money from society.

I believe it will happen. I have no expectations of when it will happen. Part of the problem is that there may be two or three million people in my country, who are employed or connected to the financial industry. Many simply do not wish the system to be changed, since the broken parts suits them just fine.

I can tell you this, however: it will happen a decade faster when the first 'Rosa Parks' moment happens. When a clearly abused investment public stands up and says, "I refuse to be abused

When the first client takes not only the abuser to court, but also regulators who have been willfully blind in assisting the abuse. (update, May 2017, Canadian Provincial Regulators have had new Bill's passed, granting them immunity from civil liability for negligence…when done in good faith.

When a victim or group of victims files private criminal charges where criminal breaches are found.

When the man on the street stands up and shows the system how it is done—then it will begin to be done. Until that day, many will keep asking, "Why doesn't anyone do anything about this?"—never quite realizing that you must not ask…but act.

===========

Privately filed criminal charges

If police will not respond to systemic or large scale financial crimes against society:

What remains is the right of every person in the land to file their own 'information' (criminal charges) with the courts. It allows those who have been criminally violated, no matter by whom, to file this information and get a chance to stand before a judge with their case. This still does not guarantee your case will be heard, due to political interference possible in this process, but it is a beginning.

The proper response is not to fight in established kangaroo courts, but to get fraud moved to criminal courts, and to the court of public opinion. Fraud should be dealt with in the light of day, not the confined darkness of a self-regulatory body.

Get criminal 'breach of trust' by regulators taken into criminal courts. Get class actions certified to tackle the biggest man made economic disasters in the land. If we do not, we risk destroying North American society, that we were once handed in pretty decent shape.

It is possible that after ten, or ten thousand persons have filed criminal charges with the courts, the judicial view of financial abuse by high-status professionals may change.

Look at how the public mood has changed due to high status sexual abusers. Financial abusers are no different, just better "insulated" …at the moment.

===========

Proposed solutions for regulatory improvement, regulatory simplicity:

#1. If persons selling investments refer to themselves as "salespersons," then there is little need for fiduciary responsibility debate, as well as less risk of consumer misrepresentation. (the misrepresentation is when commission salespersons try to hide their sales role behind non-lawful titles)

#2. If persons selling investments refer to themselves as "advisors," "advisers," or any of the other similar terms or titles, then they should accept a fiduciary responsibility. (similar to the "do no harm" oath of medical professionals)

#3. Any titles, names or license categories must carry a simple warning/explanation of the legality, the agency duty, and the fiduciary (or non-fiduciary) duty owed to the customer.

This simplicity meets the standard of fair, honest, and good faith dealing promised by the industry. It also meets the "true, plain, and clear" disclosure requirements.

Words like 'registered representative' are meaningless jargon designed to misdirect and misinform the public. Would consumers allow the medical industry to dupe them by referring to their members in such a non-informative manner? Use of terms which are able to be twisted to mean many different things, should not be foisted upon an unsuspecting public.

Jargon is currently allowed to confuse the public and assist those who would mislead and misdirect for commission or fee purposes. Any industry claiming to deal in trust and honesty must demonstrate the maturity to move beyond sleight of hand.

Canada and the U.S. need to professionally 'grow up' if they are to halt the destruction of trust in the financial industry. This destruction also has a side effect of harming democracy and society in a myriad of ways.

Self defense: Do not invest with anyone who does not carry the adviser license (the one that requires them to owe you a fiduciary duty). That's adviser spelled with an "e" at the end, as is found in the law of the Securities Acts in both Canada and the USA.

Self defense: Do not invest with anyone who says any investment they sell you must be "suitable." (Suitable is a subjective term, much like "drinkable" or "edible," and if you will settle for their definition, you can (and probably will) end up with the poorest choice of investment…with the highest choice of fee or commission. (it is still suitable…:)

Consider the "Suitability" standard to be the "deception" standard, and you will be better informed.

Self defense: Go right now and check your broker or advice giver out at this site: "AreTheyRegistered" in Canada or "BrokerCheck" in USA.
http://www.securities-administrators.ca/nrs/nrsearch.aspx?id=850

Enter the name of your advisor and see if they hold an "adviser" license, or a broker or dealing rep license.

In the USA you can search https://brokercheck.finra.org, but keep in mind that FINRA is a 'self' regulatory body with $2 billion in assets (pg 29) and top ten execs earning about $1 mil each (pg 25). Source, 2016 Financial Report found here
http://www.finra.org/sites/default/files/2016_AFR.pdf   FINRA is the big bad wolf, dressed up as your granny…

Most in Canada (96%) will be licensed in a category (if you can even find it) titled "dealing representative". This is neither an adviser nor an advisor, whatever spelling trick might be employed, and if your person is representing him or herself in this manner they may be breaking the law (fraud), the securities act (misrepresentation), or simply using a title to mislead you. (deception) People who do this in other professions get a jail term. People who do this in finance get a new condo.

The title "dealing representative" replaced the category formerly known as "salesperson". It was altered in September 2009 by the Canadian Securities Administrators (CSA) to help cloud the waters a bit, in my opinion. This is what tainted regulators are truly paid to do.

Until then it was very clear to see who was a licensed adviser and who was a simple commission salesperson. Why? Because it said so on their license. No more clarity today. The CSA, in its wisdom, or to help out the industry that pays them, <u>carefully deleted every reference in the country to the word salesperson,</u> in 2009. Instant consumer disclosure-darkness, brought upon millions, merely by paying Canadian regulators.

"Dealing representative" means that they "represent the interests of the dealer". First and foremost, their loyalty is to the dealer like a salesperson in a car dealership.

No industry (outside of the tobacco industry of the 1960s) has done a more careful job of misrepresentation, while doing intentional harm to its customers. I have produced a video that is freely available on YouTube for those who would like to utilize the law and gain their money back from this kind of fraud. It is Titled, Investment Advisor Bait and Switch, GET YOUR MONEY BACK!

===========

Ordinary citizens, from non-finance occupations (and not married to finance persons), should make up, 60% to 80% of regulator positions. It is a matter of having a safe society. This might help prevent the "revolving career advancement door" where regulators cozy up to the industry, display their loyalty, and find their next career move as a payoff.

Solution: Ensure that the criminal code is applied and enforced for securities offenses and abuses. Today, a myriad of regulators, self-regulators, ombudsmen, offices, and agencies provide the perfect insulation and cover for criminal acts, and the perfect excuse for police and prosecutors to turn a blind eye.

They believe the industry has it covered, and this is usually true. The industry does have it covered, as in 'covered-up'—never to be referred to police; not to be prosecuted. To be handled under cover of darkness.

Solution: Establish special expertise in accepting customer complaints, investigations, prosecutions—even training for judges if need be—training for the special tricks available to the financial industry…including judge shopping.

If you will allow me to beat a dead horse for a moment, the financial industry brought the entire world to near economic collapse (2008), and yet prosecutions for doing so have been few and far between. We should not choose to live in a world where stealing hubcaps or a hundred dollars is very likely to get you a conviction, whereas stealing a hundred million is most likely to get you a yacht. Do we truly wish to live in a world where the greatest rewards go to the greatest criminals, because that world is called the Hunger Games…when you play the tape to the end?

That is not capitalism, that is lawless capitalism, which is nothing more than looting. That is what North America has become today, a constant, daily, monthly, yearly Los Angeles-type riot, when police were held back from entering the neighborhood. They were more worried about Brentwood, Beverly Hills and Bel Aire. (A fitting image for financial public protection efforts)

 It became 'winner take all' until order was restored. Today, North America is in 'winner take all' mode, with no police in sight, except cracking the heads of people holding up protest signs about the robbery.

Solution: Another solution I like is found at Democracy Watch. They have action and accountability campaigns for various industries which have gained enough strength to be 'above the law.' Or at least above needing to be fair or honest with their victi ... er, customers.
http://democracywatch.ca/campaigns/

Duff Conacher is an Ottawa based army for this effort, who cut his teeth at one time working under Ralph Nader.

The other plan they have is found here:
http://democracywatch.ca/campaigns/citizen-association-campaign/

Solution: Citizen Association Campaign (again from Democracy Watch) is a near self-funded proposal to force those industries which may be subject to claims of "abuse of market dominance," (banks, cell phones, cable, utilities, etc.) to inform its customers on how to join a consumer protection group. Mail-outs are included in the bank statement or utility bill giving consumers the choice to opt-in and join the consumer group. The end result could be a strong voice or protective watchdog group that supervises the actions of the industry, making sure citizens are treated fairly and honestly. Below is a quote from their website:

"Advocating the creation of citizen watchdog groups for all business and government sectors using an innovative pamphlet method that has given millions of people in the U.S. an easy way to join strong watchdog groups over big businesses."

It seems like a wonderful way to combat abuse of corporate market dominance, which has become North America's most common abuse.

Canada was built upon abuse of market dominance. It is the old British tradition, which the United States moved somewhat away from (revolution) while Canada stayed with the old British boys' clubs. I believe this forms a solid foundation on which to build a permanent "Canadian disadvantage" when compared to the better systems that other countries have in place.

What is a financial <u>disadvantage</u> to a nation, is a financial <u>advantage</u> to the nation's financial predators. In that area, Canada wins the abuse of market dominance gold metal.

Speaking of solutions and abuse of market dominance, another solution would be to have a Senate inquiry into the <u>Competition Bureau of Canada</u>, the "private" agency responsible for prosecution of abuse of market dominance. They have been silent when it comes to tackling Canada's largest and most powerful corporations.

If you wish to know why gas prices get full 'monopoly-multiplying' freedoms, as do banking giants, look no further than the 'private' organization that is well versed in ignoring our well written Competition Act. (yes, I too assumed that the Competition Bureau was a Government of Canada agency…but no such luck) The further I look, the deeper the private capture of so-called public bodies goes.

Nearly every communication I have had with them about investment banking misrepresentation has been treated as if radioactive. Refusal to respond in writing, requests for 'telephone conversations only', failure to engage, all have made me feel as if I were talking to a secret agency…in Russia…in the '80's.

In my travels to find a government public servant I have been rejected by all, from Justice to Finance to the RCMP. But none have acted in as strange and secretive a fashion, while ignoring billions of dollars in public harm, as the Competition Bureau of Canada.

<u>Public Action Step</u> you can take: Send a letter to the Competition Bureau asking them to investigate and prosecute the misleading representations whereby most investment salespeople incorrectly claim (or imply) that they have an advisor license and duty.

1. Misrepresentation is also found under the Competition Act, and

2. The Competition Bureau is simply taking the easy way out by ignoring this and buck passing. That is precisely how organized crime works.

Solution: Professionalize, publicize or ban outright, the practice of letting securities commissions have <u>discretion to give exemptions to our securities laws.</u> Exemptions to the law are nearly always to the benefit of financial corporations, and almost never of benefit to consumers. Many times they allow consumers to lose billions, which means they are helping financial players to skim billions.

Securities commissions do not seem to have a process, or even a care, in these damages to your money and to society. They have never been forthcoming with answers when asked. Giving financial players secret passes to be exempt from our laws, should be met with criminal code sanctions, for those who do it with little to no reasons, and who do it while it harvests billions from society. These (exemptions) are perhaps the greatest "intentionally man made financial disasters" I have seen....and yet they continue to enrich those who pay the commissions salaries.

Solution: Further to the Democracy Watch Citizen Association Campaign, I hope to see some form of consumer and/or industry required litigation support, so that corporate victims do not have to suffer costs of hundreds of thousands of dollars in legal fees, simply to have the same access to justice that the strongest financial institutions in the world can buy with victims money.

Thousands of industry members argue strongly against having to respect their customers' best interests when giving investment advice. They use the excuse that the concept already exists in common law. (In other words, we don't want it in our rules, we want to keep it out, and let clients sue us if they feel they have been wronged.)
http://www.osc.gov.on.ca/en/38075.htm

Quebec has far better requirements for investment advice to be in the best interests of the client (as if anything else is imagined by any client), and also has an investment compensation fund for victims of financial abusers. This is a necessary requirement elsewhere, which of course will be debated endlessly and opposed by all persons who have a salary or loyalty to the investment industry. Society would be safer if we could just be more like Quebec, as far as justice is concerned.

The time for lying, and harming investors must end. It is now time for new systems of protecting investors financial health. End the charade of store-bought regulators who do little except insulate the industry. That model works too much like the tobacco industry...of the 1960's.

============

Here is a wild one that I must throw into the soup:

How about a "statutory fiduciary duty" to be imposed upon any financial advice-giver, AS WELL AS any politician, regulator or public servant?

How would that go over in a world containing some of the sharpest organized criminals found anywhere? I do not care to debate, but since I get to write this, I may as well lay it out there, as one possible solution to rampant criminality against society.

============

These are some personal observations about the smartest people I have met:
1. They are the folks who do not go big. Big house, big car, big vacations, big show. Read The Millionaire Next Door: The Surprising Secrets of America's Wealthy, by Thomas Stanley and William Danko to learn more. My own #1 indicator of those who have financial freedom is people who have lived decades in a modest home. I predict you will find more full-bore financial millionaires in this category than in any other. The authors of the book, also point to those who drive a Ford F150 as one of the common features of the typical Millionaire Next Door. Hard working folks is what they are. The 'Rule of Larry' is, "if you want to be richer, just act poorer". The corollary is, "if you want to be poorer, just act richer".

2. One step better than #1 above is for a young person today to own a modest home with a separate rental suite in it. They can live in one part of their home and rent out the other part. This will pay many of the expenses and allow you to easily

gain ten years of financial freedom. I see more of this kind of thinking these days and it makes sense.

3. Stay away from all investment dealers, brokers, and middlemen. Either be an 'investment participant' or be none at all. Never be an investment 'spectator.' The only exception to this is if you can guarantee to yourself that you know and understand the difference between the title-only (faked) advisor and the true fiduciary professional adviser. Putting a 'genuine-phony' commission middleman between you and your investments will often cost half your future retirement. These people (dealers) are not in the game for your financial health, even if you found the honest salesperson. Even with the very best, behind them is a corporation to whom <u>the investments are not the product. The retail investor (mom and pop) is the product!</u>

4. Only three simple ingredients are required for investment success: 1.) Quality, 2.) Diversity, 3.) Time. Use these three, and you will slowly learn all about them without too many costly mistakes. You will become your own expert, and I promise you that will be the best investment you ever make.

==========

Ninety-nine percent of industry 'spin' concerning investment fraud is designed to tell you it (fraud) is a rare thing, with a few bad apples whom they are 'right on top of' with regulatory supervision. This is simply not true. In my experience inside Canada's largest bank owned dealers, the opposite is more true than the marketing pitch.

Fraud, by deception and other means, is the business model and the standard operational process of any giant financial institution in Canada which I have studied. It is not the exception, it is the unwritten rule.

I have also learned that the 'unwritten' rule is always the most strictly adhered to rule. The ones written down are for "show" only…like the special couches in your grandmother's front living room that no one could touch.

The harm done by single bad apples is mere pennies when compared to the systemic cheating done by the more cunning members of the industry. There is more money to be made in telling the public precisely the opposite, and that is how the very best Organized Financial Crime in the world works. (OFC)

I maintain that <u>investment dealers</u>, <u>lawyers</u> for the industry, lawyers who serve <u>regulators</u>, (who in turn serve the industry), and a few other handmaidens (<u>media</u>, accountants, <u>politicians</u>) allow an entire industry to cheat or shortchange the public out of billions upon billions of dollars.

An entire society can thus be defrauded by a half-dozen, or more system-agents, acting in concert. What was that RCMP definition of Organized Financial Crime again...?

The racket is so profitable as to be irresistible to otherwise honorable men. The 'organized crime' nature of the system is so strong that anyone who does not walk in lockstep with the industry is disposed of rather quickly.

I once visited the 'hottest' RBC salesperson in Medicine Hat, Alberta, at that firm when I worked with them. I asked him why he was selling tax shelters, movie deals, and MURBS (Multiple Unit Residential Buildings, which were also tax shelters). Almost 100% of these eventually flopped (as investments), but all we knew at the time was they looked rather iffy.

When I asked him what was prompting him to sell these to his clients, his answer was just three words: "Ten percent commission."

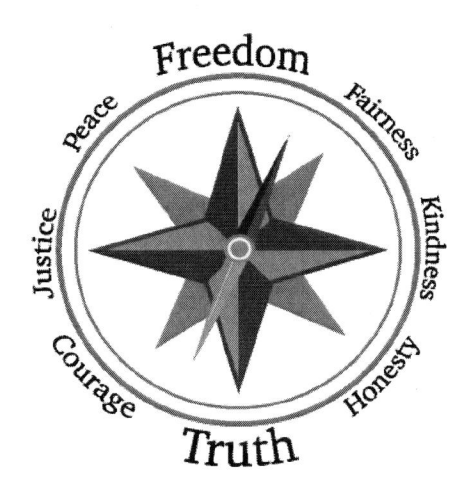

CHAPTER TWENTY FOUR

CLASSIC CARS AND PROCESSED FOOD

"This was a 640 billion dollar market and it turned out to lose 65 percent of its value, though these securities were sold as gold standard triple-a securities to pension funds local governments. Financial institutions all over the country. They were sold as rock-solid and safe but they lost 2/3 of their value.

That's like going to a grocery store you trust and you bring home some food and it turns out that two-thirds of it it's toxic.

That is an unprecedented kind of thing and these banks were able to use their size their influence and their complexity to deceive the public and deceive the investors about the qualities of the securities they were selling."

Marcus Stanley of Americans for Financial Reform at 14:00 to 16:00 min mark of the following video

293

Webinar and Panel Discussion on Glass-Steagall Mobilization
https://youtu.be/SbLjsv5mvg4

===========

I met with a 'classic' investor recently.....with a large account which her "advisor" wanted to put her into the latest investment dealer trend, a "Fee Based Account". This would have added 2% fees to the account and otherwise done little else, and would have added sixty thousand dollars in fees to this account. (broker needed a new speedboat...)

As client age, they become more vulnerable to salesperson induced complexity and salesperson pressure, and (non fiduciary) dealers find ways to squeeze greater and greater fees from their trusting elderly clients. The salespeople go along with the incentives, since they have no other viable choice, and of course, the double bind...

The trend toward fee-based accounts and products creates an "annuity" to the dealer, from the accounts of their clients and not always done for the best interests of the investor. It is sold as a non-conflicted way of avoiding ever paying another commission.....and it truly is just a way to pay an annual amount on your investments for _ever_ and _ever_...and _ever_ more.

This may be about the most harmful thing possible to your finances, unless you have fees (all in) of 1% or _less_ and unless you have a professional fiduciary money manager.

Tess was a sharp lady when she appeared in a discussion session held once each month. It was called "MoneyTalks" and it allowed people to come and have discussions about things investment, financial and economic.

By this time it was 2016 and it seemed to me like there were few media left who could be trusted to print what used to pass for news, or even the truth.

As part of the economic 'hollowing out' of North America, or financial 'looting' that I call it, barely a news media existed that could put out a stories that advertisers might find offensive. Seekers of economic truth had to find creative ways to find out what was truly going on in the world, and in finance.

Tess asked me if I would chat with her about her investments and I was happy to oblige.

It turns out she had taken the Securities Course in the late 1970's as a younger lady, and had held a lifelong interest in learning how to invest. No firm would hire her, since she was a woman, and back in that day, the world of brokers was thought of as a 'man's game'. She was only offered clerical jobs in finance, so she set out to work for herself and be her own investment guide.

Her accounts, when she showed them to me brought back memories of decades past, of real "Warren Buffet" style investments, and it starkly reminded me of just how much things have changed.

She held <u>only</u> real investment 'ingredients'. I am going to use two different analogies to try and compare this with, so bear with the workings of my mind. I will paint a picture that I hope readers will understand.

As I told her, after reviewing her investments, one of her accounts (in the millions) 'sparkled' to me like a perfectly untouched, mint condition 1955 Chev Bel Aire, a classic auto from back in the day. For those who are car enthusiasts, this image will conjure up thoughts of old classic collectors' items. Things which today are very rare, beautiful, durable, simple, useful, and which, if cared for, are able to last well beyond a person's lifetime. They are not often seen in today's throwaway society, outside of collectors and museums. This is the kind of investments this account held.

This account was with a broker (aka advisor) in Calgary at one of the big banks, and I told her that I rarely get the privilege of seeing such a fine example of classic investing. The account was in my view perfect. She told me she loved this account, because she knew each and every company in her portfolio, she knew what they did, most were household names with decades of history of doing what they do, doing it well, and paying dividends and growing over time. I told her that Warren Buffet would be proud to own this portfolio.

This was very important, because the world was changing so rapidly, that she was at times unsure of what to believe anymore. By comparison, account number two, was held by her broker in Lethbridge, had an entirely different feel, as if it was created by a different personality altogether. One account was Dr. Jekyll and the other was Mr. Hyde.

I asked her about that and it turned out that this was why she had come to me. Her Lethbridge broker had put her into the investment firm's 'own' mutual funds, something which are usually referred to as the 'house brand', or proprietary funds.

The interest in doing this for the broker/dealer, is fees on top of fees.

She was seeking an impartial opinion about these two different accounts, with two seemingly different styles. She just needed some verification, some 'sounding board' to talk things over with, now that her husband had passed. Someone who did not have a hidden agenda, or a hidden commission pushing their views.

Having worked at firm #2 for some time, and known her broker #2, it was fairly easy for me to visualize the hidden incentives/pitfalls that she could not see. I had attended daily sales meetings and annual sales conventions for 20 years, and had a fairly good grasp of why her first account looked like a classic, and her second account looked like, well, it looked like most investment portfolios I see today, filled with broker-invented "fee products", and not so much "investment products".

As my friend Joe is fond of saying in his work, "every investment agent leaves a distinct forensic 'fingerprint' upon your account". This fingerprint can be seen and understood by an experienced forensic investment expert.

Here I am shifting analogies from comparison of investment portfolios to classic cars, to comparing the 'makeup' of investment accounts to the makeup of processed food products. I feel that more people might understand a story about food ingredients than continuing the car story. Please pick whichever image works best for you.

Her 'classic' investment account, is beautiful, it is understandable (most importantly to her, and secondly, to anyone else who might observe it), it is timeless, it is solid. It gave her great pleasure and great confidence to hear this from me since she was being pushed and pulled by broker #2 to "buy more house brand funds".

No one needs sales pressure and broker #2 was doing her a disservice and being a slippery-salesman and not an advice giver at all. This was the key difference in the accounts. One broker was helping her, and the second was more interested in farming her. A sad sight that I see every day now.

The other problem with broker #2, was that it consisted not of pure investments, but of investment 'products'. Products being things which are 'made up' of other things in much the same manner than food 'products' can be made up from semi-food ingredients and fillers.

The bad news in the 'processed products' account, is that as everyone knows, food manufacturers add 'fill' ingredients when making their food 'products', to save money. They can add chemicals, preservatives, sawdust and God only knows what, in order to make the bulk, the color, texture or product smell just right. Remember the bright orange color-dye that made the Kraft Macaroni and Cheese product look so "cheesey"?

(April 2015, Kraft announced it is dropping the artificial dyes in response to customers' concerns. Faced with rival brands boasting "organic" and "all natural" labels, as well as greater public awareness about nutrition, the international food giant says it has been considering cutting out the artificial ingredients in its Mac & Cheese for some time.)

At some point certain food products, like some 'manufactured' investments, start to look like Frankenfoods, and the ingredient list reads like a who's who of a chemical cabinet.

The same thing is happening inside the investment accounts of millions of North Americans. Thank you for bearing with me long enough to get that point out. A poor investment portfolio, but a common one of today, will read like the ingredient list of a heavily processed box of microwave mush, or coffee whitener, or anything else made in a lab.

This is what partially bothered her. Her #2 broker was trying to force the company sawdust product on her.

I still recall investment analyst, Diane Urquhart, who said to me in about 2006, that a large number of investment products being sold today, "look more like something cooked up in a meth lab, than like real investments…"

I understood what she was talking about when she said it, but to see this classic example of two different accounts, one being as classic as apple pie and vintage Chevrolet's, while the other like something from an alchemist, gave me a stark reminder of just how far we have come from "quality" investments, to the world of intensive farming of investment customers.

I have witnessed this progression, from a day when few people invested in stocks, most kept their money in banks, to more and more baby boomers learning how to invest using mutual funds and other creations designed to save time and effort. Call it microwave investing if you like.

Almost anything today can be packaged and sold as an investment, and it can take someone like me twenty minutes of reading the fine print, to figure out what parts of it contain even a smidgen of investment-like ingredients, which is the 'filler' to make it look like something is in the box, and which parts hide fees upon fees,…upon fees.

Look up the words "structured products" if you wish to learn more about what this looks like. They are things that 'may' contain some 'investment-like' ingredients, in the same way that a can of coffee whitener, purchased at the Lucky Dollar 'may' contain something which is not a petroleum product...

The net effect is that highly processed foods <u>and highly processed investments</u> are now the norm, the standard, and the #2 thing to be most wary of. Some investments have been found to contain up to five or six fees, all hidden in fine print, and incomprehensible to the average investor. Most products sold today by non-fiduciary sales agents, are designed more to make money for the firm, than to serve the investor.

Stick with investments ingredients you would understand as easily as you understand produce from a farmers market or your own garden.

============

Another reason for 'filler' investment products is this: The number of corporations in North America that are available for people to invest in is declining.

This article by Pam Martens and Russ Martens explains it, similar to how Jason Zweig of the WS Journal blog did earlier in the book: August 23, 2017
http://wallstreetonparade.com/2017/08/three-critical-steps-to-making-america-great-again-are-not-on-trumps-agenda/

In 1996 the U.S. had 845 Initial Public Offerings. Last year, after twenty passing years of research and budding new technologies should have fueled growth in the IPO market, the U.S. had a paltry 98 IPOs.

According to a study by the law firm, Wilmer Cutler Pickering Hale and Dorr, gross proceeds from IPOs in 2016 were $18.54 billion while the "average annual gross proceeds for the 12-year period preceding 2016 were $35.73 billion — 93 percent higher than the corresponding figure for 2016."

Not only has the U.S. seriously lost ground in IPOs but the total number of publicly traded companies in the U.S. is down by almost half in the same 20 year span. Last September, Jim Clifton, the

Chairman and CEO of Gallup, the polling company, explained why he thinks this is happening.

Clifton wrote:

"The number of publicly listed companies trading on U.S. exchanges has been cut almost in half in the past 20 years — from about 7,300 to 3,700. Because firms can't grow organically — that is, build more business from new and existing customers — they give up and pay high prices to acquire their competitors, thus drastically shrinking the number of U.S. public companies. This seriously contributes to the massive loss of U.S. middle-class jobs."

===========

Investment firms are being forced to 'invent' new ways to make fees, and one of those ways is to design complicated, derivative-based, meth lab, hypothecated nonsense.

Real investments (the ones with 100% investment, and no internal fees and fillers):

a) need no sales and marketing staff,
b) cost investors no money to own, once purchased, and
c) are understandable to myself and any 85 year old….or 15 year old.

With investments, companies still exist, Warren Buffet still buys and invests in them, smart clients still own them, as do many grandma's and grandpa's out there. Just know that any person reading market info today, will be pushed so hard by marketers, editors and advertisers, towards meth lab investment creations, that todays youth may never see, never even know what it is to own a classic, much less a quality investment.

Tess was quite relieved to learn what she suspected all along. She just needed someone to talk it over with who was not going to take advantage of her. THAT is one of the rarest things in the financial world, and another reason for me to say the words "Fiduciary Professional…or nothing". 'Do-it-yourself' if you cannot find the right fiduciary to handle your money professionally. But please, please, help put an end to the legally-fraudulent fake advisor game…

It must be noted that the next time I met with her she gave me the news that she did the mature thing, and made an appointment to visit and sit down with the broker who wanted so desperately to sell her more of his house-brand funds.

She bravely (ask me sometime about the 'Svengali-like' hold that bold salesmen often hold over vulnerable investors) told him what she had decided, that she wanted to be rid of those funds, and to make a change away from the fees. He promptly told her that if she wished to be rid of those funds, that she would have to be rid of him. He fired her in a salesperson hissy fit. It was unexpected, yes, but another example of a "Classic". Classic sales-bullying upon a widow, and I am so glad that his bully made it so easy for her to leave his grasp. She moved her account away from that firm….Another gift!

In today's world, investors actually need a financial 'bodyguard', to protect them from investment firms which have become so predatory and so market dominant. It is stark reality for any retail (mom and pop) investor.

===========

A thought diversion here….momentarily…forgive me.

Lest anyone think I am an 'activist', or some other intentionally negative label, let it be known that the name for my chosen role, which is more accurate and far less incendiary, is "protector". I simply care enough about what true financial professionals do, and what services get provided to millions of North Americans, that it is worth my speaking up. That is what protectors do. They speak out about harm and abuse. Right?

You could also consider me a "Criminality Theorist", while a detractor would use the label conspiracy theorist. This is because the detractor is trying to smear.

Ask Prof George Lakoff about the "frame" game of using specific 'labels' to "frame' the argument in any manner desired. Opponents of this book will likely utilize any linguistic tactic, any name calling slurs to diminish my message. Please read up on any of Prof Lackaoff's work before you fall for the game. Public awareness/protection from financial predators is the intent.

The man is a neuro-linguistic (cognitive linguist) genius and he is studied by every wise person in America. As well as every political organization in the world. His most famous work is titled <u>Don't Think of an Elephant: Know Your Values and Frame the Debate.</u>

Another notable mention is "The Political Mind : Why You Can't Understand 21st-Century American Politics with an 18th-Century Brain."

He is a professor of linguistics at the University of California, Berkeley, where he has taught since 1972. Listen to the man...

===========

Working within the investment industry made me hypersensitive to those in the industry who mock rules and laws. They preyed upon investors and got away with it daily. I was offended and threatened to be potentially labeled as one of 'them'. I had no desire to be as rich as an organized criminal. Or to be labeled as one.

There also are clients known as 'rogue clients'. These are investors who may have willingly 'chased after' bigger returns, lost money, and then chosen to blame the broker for not protecting them...from themselves. This does not happen as often as clients are exploited by a fake advisor, but it still happens, and I am just as sensitive to this type of dangerous client. Why? Because the truth is the truth, and it is always far higher in value than my own interests.

Plus, I have seen a few of these types of clients in 3-plus decades, and they can do great harm to a good industry-person's reputation.

===========

Back to the Tess story after learning that her trusted 'advisor' fired her as a client, because she did not wish to hang onto his high-fee, house-brand fund.

Such is the Mesmerizing 'hold' on some people that investment and financial advice-givers have on millions of North Americans.

Some investment pros, have a hold on many of their clients of a svengalli-like nature. It can be a relationship where they (even the fake advisors) are respected, admired, trusted, listened to, and sometimes, in the very elderly, the financial 'advice' givers are the only people who will listen to them. Like a trusted hockey coach to a rising star, a flight instructor to an aspiring pilot, and perhaps a hundred other positions of trust and authority, some 'advice givers' become bullies, abusers and exploiters. It happens.

In especially occurs in those parts of the financial industry that are in the <u>relationship management game</u> to a far greater extent than in the <u>money management game.</u>

I get to watch it, write about it and do what I can to protect the public from it. Imagine if there were no more economic predators? No pretend-regulators who allow legalized-fraud? Then I imagine that an entire class of investors could be helped, instead of being farmed.

Here is a young man who will earn a billion dollars, inventing products for Wall Street to sell…

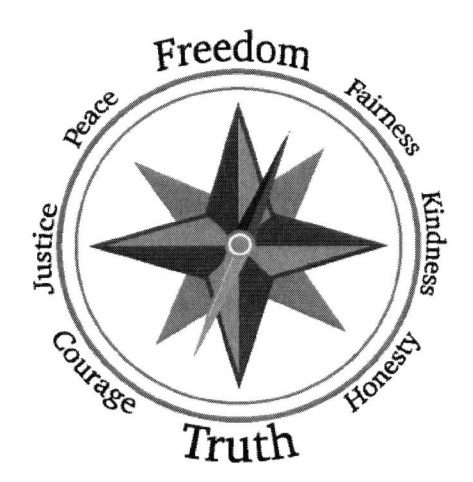

CHAPTER TWENTY FIVE

THE INDUSTRY OF ACCOUNTABILITY

I can envision an industry where peoples truth, peoples honesty and peoples voices will be valued, paid and rewarded, based upon the amount of benefit they bring to society.
-- Larry Elford

=========

Stanislav Petrov was never famous in Russia, just another forgotten pensioner, so the news of his death at 77 in Moscow on 19 May only recently reached other countries. He wasn't all that famous abroad either, but people in the know think he may have saved the world from nuclear war.

"The siren howled, but I just sat there for a few seconds, staring at the big back-lit red screen with the word 'Launch' on it," he told the BBC's Russian Service in a 2013 interview. "I had all the data

(suggesting that there was a US missile attack underway)....All I had to do was to reach for the phone to raise the direct line to our top commander – but I couldn't move.

It was only three weeks since a Soviet fighter had shot down a Korean Air Lines flight and killed all 269 people aboard, including a US Congressman. Six months previously US President Ronald Reagan had called the Soviet Union an "evil empire" and called for a roll-back strategy that would "write the final pages of the history of the Soviet Union."

Stanislav Petrov didn't report it. It was a new system, and it could be making a mistake. Besides, Petrov knew that you only get one chance at a surprise attack, so logic says you should launch all your missiles at once – more than a thousand of them, in the case of the United States. Launching just five would be beyond stupid. So he waited.

And waited, for 23 eternal minutes, to see if the Soviet Union's ground radars also picked up the incoming missiles as they descended towards their targets. They didn't. "I realized that nothing had happened. If there had been a real strike, then I would already know about it. It was such a relief."

No good deed goes unpunished, so Petrov was officially reprimanded for failing to describe the incident in his logbook. He was initially praised by his commanding officer for doing the right thing, but then it was realized that if he was rewarded, the senior people responsible for the system that produced the error would be punished. So he was sidelined, retired early, and subsequently had a nervous breakdown.

With gratitude to Gwynne Dyer for allowing some of his work to be shared under a Creative Commons Attribution-Share Alike 3.0 License

Gwynne Dyer has worked as a freelance journalist, columnist, broadcaster and lecturer on international affairs for more than 20 years, but he was originally trained as an historian. Born in Newfoundland, he received degrees from Canadian, American and British universities. His latest book, "Climate Wars: The Fight for

Survival as the World Overheats", was published in the United States by Oneworld.

===========

I believe than an "Industry Of Accountability" will be as important to the future of a safe society as the industry of environmental protection has become to our world.

After all, a fair and safe financial environment is second in importance to our society only to a livable physical environment.

I also believe that we are on the cusp, if you will, of realizing that a society built upon lawlessness by the strongest, or richest, is a society that comes to an end. Usually an unfortunate end.

Unaccountable power and control, in the hands of men who are above laws and above public accountability, is the most dangerous risk in North American society today. It (the risks) have proven to be real for the last 2000 years of history.

Instead of crashing society, let's consider an entirely new system of accountability, an entirely new economic-booster based upon all citizens being enabled to become everyday heroes?

The environmental protection industry has sprung from nothing in my lifetime, and its benefits spring from "doing well by doing good". This is a model that works. <u>Doing well by doing good</u>...contains no downside. Doing well by doing harm, on the other hand leads to destruction of society. Today we are letting those who do harm, profit from harm to others.

The industry of accountability will, in my estimation, reward, enable, and eventually employ people who could be doing good things for society. It is as essential to our social environment as clean air and water is to our physical environment.

But it will only do so, when we clearly figure out the difference between those who are guilty...versus those who are responsible. Power and money is often guilty....but we are the ones who are responsible to do something about it. Let's get this discussion started. Let's work to separate the guilty from their positions of power, responsibility and money. Your next "job" or role could be to work as your very own boss, as a person who helps build accountability into our society. If Rosa Parks, a part time seamstress, could change the world in 1955, without an iPhone, then we have no excuse…

From the FaceBook group titled "Industry of Accountability":

We seek those who believe that the greatest act we can do for each other is to demonstrate kindness, rather than selfishness or cruelty.

Knowing that the kindest act we can demonstrate at times is to stand up for the truth, no matter who tells it, or who may be opposed to it.

Realizing that to tell the truth in a world filled with lies, sometimes requires the greatest level of courage known to man.

Those who can find this level of courage, are those whose voices are free, and un-owned by another.

Will you join us in a search for the freedom, to have the courage, to tell the truth, to bring increased kindness and prosperity to all, rather to just ourselves?

The industry of accountability will "oversee" government, corporations and those in positions of power. It will investigate and report on all forms of institutional bullying or abuses.

Abuse such as employment abuse, financial abuse, corporate abuse, legal abuse, government abuse, environmental abuse. Any area where powerful people, systems or institutions do harm is of interest to the Industry of Accountability.

This is not intended as a replacement of the Justice system, as our laws etc are often referred to as, but rather a social recognition that our current systems of justice may no longer suffice to protect society from modern-day abuses of power. Or as my friend Joe says, modern day systems of power have been hijacked, often by the people running the systems who have learned how to gain personal advantage from those systems.

Whistleblowers, truth tellers, financial protection, justice, environmental protection, etc., all and more, will be welcome areas where unchecked power and accountability might benefit from having a million eyes of public oversight looking into them.

This is hoped and imagined to be a seed planted towards growth of the newest and potentially largest industry in the world. What can be possibly lost by assuming that our safe social environment is at risk, and that we can protect it with some changes in action and awareness.

What potential could exist when millions of dollars start to flow in the direction of awards or prizes, writers, investigators, and everyday accountability heroes? How about billions of dollar being pushed in the direction of cost savings, crime savings, corruption reduction and rewards for society benefitting work?

I think it is time to stop hiding behind our fears, as a society, and begin standing up to the greatest abusers among us. Whether it is an awakening to sexual predators, thanks to courageous men and women speaking against the Hollywood power abusers, or corporate employees, who become heroes by speaking out against corporations who are harming society.

We all have a shared interest in our society, and it is time we all took a bit of responsibility in ensuring that this society is not stolen and abused by the greatest human and corporate predators.

INDUSTRY OF ACCOUNTABILITY

One Recent Example of Accountability:
(Here is an encouraging sign of a justice system that still functions in the U.S., while I believe that Canadian justice systems would never ever permit the godfathers of Canadian finance to be similarly be held to account. Canada has a 'lock' ...somehow)

Texas Jury Finds JP Morgan Chase Violated Estate Administration Duties and Awards More Than $4 Billion in Punitive Damages

Dallas Widow and Step-children Awarded Millions in Actual Damages and Attorney Fees for Bank's Malicious Mismanagement of Estate of Deceased Airline Technology Innovator

NEWS PROVIDED BY

Loewinsohn Flegle Deary Simon LLP

Sep 26, 2017, 19:43 ET

http://www.prnewswire.com/news-releases/texas-jury-finds-jp-morgan-chase-violated-estate-administration-duties-and-awards-more-than-4-billion-in-punitive-damages-300526398.html

"Surviving stage 4 lymphoma cancer was easier than dealing with this bank and its estate administration," Mrs. Hopper added.

SOURCE Loewinsohn Flegle Deary Simon LLP

===========

Then, there is the "Industry of Non-Accountabiilty", which is well played by lawyers who make money ensuring that justice is not done, that fairness is avoided. It is its own hundred billion dollar sucking sound, which is draining the life out of North America each year…by making sure that honesty and fairness is bypassed by cleverness.

As so well stated in the book "No One Would Listen" by Harry Markopolos when he tried to interest SEC lawyers in the Bernie Madoff scam…for years and years. His book is worth reading to look back at how milk-maidish even the SEC lawyers and system can be. Some select quotes from his book:

"First, banish the lawyers from the land."

"Lawyers need to be removed from most positions of senior leadership…"

"The typical SEC attorney would have trouble finding fireworks on the 4 of July…"

His book should be re-read today as a warning of what industry milkmaids and handmaids are stealing from America…every day.

Join me in discussion, and let's raise awareness. Let's at least try to change the world of financial abuse, and fuel the new industry of accountability.

Twitter @RecoveredBroker
Facebook Group "Industry of Accountability"

One of my colleagues had a plaque on his desk which said, "He who dies with the most toys…wins."

That is miles in the opposite direction from the truth. For he who does with the most toys, dies a child. Toys are nice, don't get me wrong, but toys are not even close to the meaning of ones life.

In the end only kindness matters. I'm just now learning that. I am just growing up…a little late.

Thank you for sharing this book with someone whom it may help. What a Gift!! (OK…that one was marketing :)

I thank you for using your voice to **speak as if your voice is yours to use as freely as you wish**.

In a free country, your voice is not something that is owned by your job, your corporation, your particular double bind, or your government. What a concept. For some, the only measure of freedom is whether or not you can use your voice…freely.

If you are an employee of, or involved with a giant financial corporation, legal system, government, regulatory, or anything for that matter, and you find yourself forced into "double-bind" situations where you may be:

- forced to abuse the public interest, or else...
- forced to violate rules, laws, codes of conduct, or else
- forced to keep quiet and "be a team player", or else...
- forced to act in ways that do not reflect the organization, nor what the public is promised, or else...
- forced to do harm, or else...
- forced into silence, or else...

Know this. You do not have to submit yourself to this kind of abuse, victimization, simply so that your organization, agency or company can gain money and or power at the expense of the public interest.

Rather than obey, why not make them pay...that is part the industry of accountability as I imagine it. Turn criminal acts into criminal charges. Turn civil harms against society into $100 billion dollar class actions. Turn catching the most powerful abusers in the act of abuse, into a system of rewards, awards and whistleblower payments. Make abusers pay. Make their abuses as public as any other scandal of the day.

Remember that the secret power of powerful abusers is the ability to keep their abuses secret. Let's "cowboy-up" and change how we act around abusers.

Imagine a Nobel Peace Prize-type of award where everyday heroes in the military, government, banking, pharmaceutical, any industry are awarded $100,000 prizes for their "Everyday Hero" acts. Is that possible? I believe it is. Some might mock my go-fund-me goal of ten million dollars. I see this amount of money as pennies compared to the size and budgets of giant corporate and government programs. I also see it as a mechanism which could very well bring about a "tipping" point in how the public looks at power and wealth.

Today we fear great power and we worship great wealth. That is how we find ourselves trapped in double-binds, where we must remain silent, and sometimes become participants in abuse.

We have an opportunity to turn the tables, to spot the criminals, and yet act like honest men and women. Hollywood abusers were an industry fixture for nearly a century, or as long as that industry existed, until the last few months of 2017, when it changed...in about 30 days. Tipping point.

We will turn environmental destruction for profit, into public shame, and criminal and civil actionable matters. Seize entire corporations under civil forfeiture and proceeds of crime principles or laws. Cancel the articles of incorporation of the most dangerous abusers.

Let's move beyond becoming socially aware of protection of just our physical environment, and let's pay attention to one of the last bastions of the rich-old-white-guys-abuse, our financial, legal and political/power environments. The very environments that serve to hold together the fabric of our society. Without fairness and honesty here, we may have no society.

The Industry of Accountability hopes to become a valuable beacon of hope to those who otherwise must suffer in silence, be abused, be morally injured...or else.

This is no way to run a society, and it is hoped that people will learn to gain strength through public numbers, public voices, and public shaming of the subclinical psychopaths in the world who place our shared society at great risk.

Rather than allow the powerful entity to threaten and intimidate people, using financial, legal and any bully tactics to force them into acts which violate their moral standards, these people, if standing tall in numbers, speaking in voices which cannot be ignored, will turn pain into gold. That is right, they will take the worst circumstances possible, and turn that abuse around and put responsibility and accountability (and financial penalty) back upon the entity itself.

Whistleblowers, truth tellers, investigators, lawyers, saviors of the abused. All will find a new role and some new meaning in working towards turning upside down the imbalance of power and strength of today's powerful abusers. The strength in numbers of the public will outweigh any abuser, and has done so throughout history when that power is engaged.

Begin with the political process, then the judicial, the corporate, and so on, using public awareness and public pressure to make illegal acts actually illegal....when done by the rich, the influential and the powerful.

Imagine these groups being slowly 'outed' instead of 'aided' by their insiders, their employees, and so on. Imagine an industry where thousands of people earn a living auditing, researching, publishing, and revealing the societal harms of the world's biggest abusers.

A multi Trillion dollar industry could be created just to clear up and identify (and reward those who do so) any and all of our biggest public enemies.....those who now prey upon and abuse the public with impunity. With power.

Society saving heroes who teach us all how to use our voices for change, instead of hiding our truths in fear of repercussion by power. Just imagine a world where when any employee is placed into that corporate 'double-bind' where they tell you to "do this...or else", that employee has another choice...the choice of telling the truth in an environment made safer for truth-tellers. In an environment that rewards truth-tellers. Someday, a society where financial rewards are in the millions for those who protect society....instead of rewards in the millions for those who damage society. Just imagine.

Let's build an entire social movement on standing up to criminally abusive powers, any abusive powers. Let's rebalance the fairness structures of our society. Hell, lets actually try and save some of our society.

CROWDFUNDING HOPES

Look for me on GoFundMe.com, "INDUSTRY OF ACCOUNTABILITY". https://www.gofundme.com/industry-of-accountability

EVERYDAY HEROES AWARDS

I picture an annual awards banquet, where a dozen "everyday heroes" are granted $100k awards for doing everyday heroic things for society each year. Selfless things. Things which may have caused good men and women to become 'punished', even jailed in the past.

===========

My message is this:

It hurts me when unfairness, cheating, lying and stealing becomes the predominant business model for trusted servants in our society. Whether those servants be financial, judicial, political, whatever.

It hurts society a great deal more, and I hope we can start to open up to new ways of thinking, before we reach a tipping point in North America, from which we cannot return to the great society that we once held in our grasp.

For 20 years I was a child,
For 20 years I was a slave,
20 more it took to grow up,
For 20 years I now repay
-- Larry Elford

End of Book...Beginning of The Journey of Every Person's Voice

Some Action Steps

1. Pass this book along to someone you care for, to help them become more financially street smart. Tell them if and how much you feel it helped you, or might help them.

2. Better yet buy five books and make sure your five closest friends get a copy... (second self-interested sales pitch:)

3. Vote with your money and move away from anything that sniff's of self dealing, "alternative facts". Run away from non-fiduciary, investment dealers, brokers and wirehouses. (spellcheck almost changed that last word to 'whorehouses'...)

4. Street proof your money by learning how to look after it yourself. Even if you have to pay $500 or $1000 to sit with a coach, a fee-only planner, a financial bodyguard etc. Just avoid any that have a connection to a product or a dealer. There are good people out there willing to help you.

5. Tell your political representatives you are not voting for any member who protects corporate rape and pillage, over humans. Tell them you will rather support the call for a Fiduciary duty for any public servant, and robust criminal code enforcement against public servants who violate their oath to serve and protect the public.

6. Join the Facebook Group titled "Investment System Fraud" and together lets make the world a safer place.

7. Follow @RecoveredBroker on Twitter

8. Join the "Industry of Accountability" group on Facebook

9. Help to Crowdfund the Everyday Heroes project within the Industry of Accountability. Rewarding people who stand tall, and who stand up for others.
https://www.gofundme.com/industry-of-accountability

10. I am not looking for a salary, I am looking for a chance to serve, and to work towards a positive change for our world. If this book is about anything, it is about hope for positive change.

11. Will you help spread these concepts of investor protection by sharing a social media post and/or a review of this book

online? Use any method you prefer, social media, blog, web site etc., if you think it might help others.

12. Everyday Heroes awards, like a Nobel Peace Prize, awarded each year by the Industry of Accountability. Why not?

13. Better yet, get enough signatures and run for office as your own contribution to the movement, and the improvement of society.

14. Sections 122 and section 336 of the Canadian criminal code on "BREACH OF TRUST", involves taking advantage of a position of public trust for a personal benefit.

15. Citizen Public Inquiries should be encouraged and welcomed, to ensure that the public never places 100% trust and reliance upon power structures alone.

===========

"When lives or economic safety is at stake for millions of people, it is imperative that we use our voices." Silence to protect ourselves allows an entire society to be destroyed...Our society.
-- Larry Elford